Tribes of India
Realities and Representations

Tribes of India
Realities and Representations

Edited by
Ruby Bhardwaj
Charu Kala

Vitasta

Published by
Vitasta Publishing Pvt Ltd
C-29, Sector-7, Noida, Uttar Pradesh - 201301
info@vitastapublishing.com

ISBN 978-93-90961-92-4

First Edition 2022
First Reprint 2026

MRP ₹ 795

Editorial Advisor: Prof Swati Pal
JDMC Editorial Team: Ankan Dhar and Anuj Kumar
Vitasta Editorial Team: Dhanalakshmi Ayyer, Aishwarya Singh, Alisha Verma
Cover and layout: Somesh Kumar Mishra
Printed by Manipal Technologies Limited, Manipal

CONTENTS

CONTRIBUTORS

Adiba Faiyaz: Department of English, Aligarh Muslim University

Asmita Khalkho: Assistant Professor, Post Graduate Department of History, Magadh University

Durba Mandal: Junior Research Fellow, Center for English Studies, Jawaharlal Nehru University

Jisha Ponnachan: Department of English, Parvatibai Chowgule College of Arts and Science, Goa

Krishna Kumar Sharma: Research Scholar, Department of History, North-Eastern Hill University

Pouriangthanliu: Department of Sociology, Janki Devi memorial College, University of Delhi

Sanjukta Naskar: Department of English, Janki Devi Memorial College, University of Delhi

Shubhaangi Thakur: Assistant Professor, Department of English, Parvatibai Chowgule College of Arts and Science, Goa

Sneha Sawai: Department of English, Kalindi College, University of Delhi

Sneha Umarye: Department of English, Parvatibai, Chowgule College of Arts and Science, Goa

Srestha Bhattacharya: Independent Researcher, M Phil, University of Delhi

Vandana Madan: Department of Sociology, Janki Devi Memorial College, University of Delhi

Vinay Brandon: Department of Sociology, Delhi School of Economics, University of Delhi

ACKNOWLEDGEMENTS

We deeply acknowledge our gratitude to Prof. Swati Pal, Head of the Institution, Janki Devi Memorial College, University of Delhi, for conceptualising the book and reposing confidence in us to take the idea forward. We express our heartfelt thanks to Prof. Pal for not only being a source of inspiration and guidance, but also for penning the preface of the book. We are indebted to Padamshree Prof. Anvita Abbi for contributing the foreword to the book at a very short notice. Our sincere thanks to our collaborating institution, Mahatma Gandhi Govt. College, (Pondicherry University), Mayabunder under the *Vidya Vistaar* Scheme of the University of Delhi.

Without the support of Prof. B. Prabhuram, Principal MGGC, the National Seminar to which we owe the genesis of this book, would not have been feasible. Our gratitude is due to all the contributors and more importantly to the reviewers for their valuable feedback that enhanced the quality of the papers. We appreciate the support of Librarian, JDMC, Dr. Nivedita Sharma and her team along with the efforts of Ruchika Bhatia, Samiran Ghissing and Jaya Yadav from the Department of

English. The book would not have been possible without the constant hard work, insights and technical support provided by two invaluable members of our editorial team, Ankan Dhar and Anuj Kumar, from the English Department of our college.

Our heartfelt gratitude to Seema Namibiar for painstakingly going through the manuscript at such a short notice. Her dedicated and detailed reading has enhanced the quality of the manuscript.

FOREWORD

External forces are dispossessing traditional peoples of their lands, resources, and lifestyles; forcing them to subsist in highly degraded environments; crushing their cultural traditions or ability to maintain a balance between Nature and human life. Dislocation of a community from mother earth in the name of 'Development' dislocates languages and ultimately kills them. Over generations, tribes have accumulated a wealth of wisdom about their environments and their functions, management, and sustainable use. Traditional ecological knowledge and practices often make indigenous people, minorities, and local communities highly skilled and respectful of the ecosystems. Indigenous tribes carry unique philosophies, histories, cultural artifacts, ceremonies, and irreplaceable environmental knowledge of biodiversity accumulated over millennia through their tales and stories. The folklore of the tribal world always connects the integrated worldview of man with nature. Their nature includes the entire cosmos as well as the environment they live in. Tribes live with nature and are solely integrated into it, so much so that the two entities, the 'self' and the 'world of nature' they live in is ONE. If this intimate and inextricable relationship between the tribe and the indigenous land is broken, a tsunami of despair and loss of language, culture, knowledge, religious beliefs, myths, and self-confidence will sweep the community.

Rampant urbanisation and disturbing expansion of cities are rendering indigenous occupations and livelihoods under threat that generate alienation, asymmetry as well as social and environmental toxicity. All these issues and many more were addressed in the conference 'Learning and Unlearning Tribal Culture' held on December 9-10, 2021.

I am happy to see the various presentations of this conference in a published form for posterity and wider dissemination of unusual and unique features of tribal culture of the country. I congratulate the team members of Janki Devi Memorial College, New Delhi, especially their principal Dr Swati Pal, and the team of Mahatma Gandhi Govt. College at Mayabunder, Andaman and Nicobar, to sensitise issues regarding tribal life, their problems, and pains in an ever-changing world of greed and commerce through this mammoth conference held in a bilingual mode. It was overwhelming to witness the vast spectrum of topics this conference covered from historical, anthropological, cultural, literary, sociological, linguistic, and ethnographic dimensions, both in the colonial and post-colonial period. This joint endeavour deserves accolade as it is not every day that one comes across a discussion of multidisciplinary research papers on varied tribes from the Himalayas to the Andaman and Nicobar under the same roof.

Prof Anvita Abbi

(Padma Shree)

February 10, 2022

N.J. USA

PREFACE

While definitions of 'tribe' abound across disciplinary studies and even in common parlance, the one trait that is most significant is, solidarity. Whether the tribe is one that is formed due to a common interest or occupation, cohabitation in a region, a specific social identity or political ideology, it is clearly discernible that every individual in a tribe has a tremendous sense of belonging and of connectivity, with the spirit of the tribe. In a world that is constantly fractured by conflict, where mud, barbed wire and the sound of ammunition seem to be the only 'talk' one can hear despite aspirations of engaging in 'dialogue', it is the concord that exists in a tribe that in itself makes it compelling for study. Of course, nothing is ideal and tribes too have their share of discord that ruptures the fabric of their society.

How do tribes build the sense of community of a collective? And, how do we form certain perceptions of a tribe?

The tendency to romanticise the tribal way of life in India springs largely due to folk literature, but mainly due to folk songs. A fine example can be seen in West Bengal where those of the 41 scheduled tribes, like the Lepchas or the Totos who have not fallen prey either to Hindi film songs or other influences, and lead a more isolated li.e. have folk songs related to practically every aspect of living. So, they have songs related to agriculture, war, love, lament, humour, ceremony, and so on. These songs are melodious, thus, creating a sense of harmony when sung by the tribals in their farms as they till the field. Tribal communities like the Totos are averse to sharing the exact version of the songs. They obviously see the songs as distinctive of their culture and are possessive about safeguarding that culture. This lends an element of mystique to the tribal way of life.

That living beings are prone to 'tribalise' can be seen in every domain and educational institutions are not free from this propensity. One of the first signs of the donning of 'tribal' culture can be seen in the songs and even the slogans you hear most on university campuses. In the late nineties, as a young University student of Jawaharlal Nehru University, New Delhi, I came across many such songs and slogans of the then predominantly Communist student community. In fact one of my first encounters with Ho Chi Minh was through the loud cry of 'Ho Ho Ho Chi Minh; we shall fight, we shall win' which could often be heard as students walked the campus in protest. Undoubtedly while most knew who Ho Chi Minh was and what he stood for, many adopted the slogan because that was a ritual aspect of belonging to the collective. Some of the other 'badges' that are worn within the academic institution are names of clubs and societies/political leaders/colours that students wear on their clothes to indicate the particular tribe they belong to. The saffron that is so visible in contemporary India on campuses and outside is yet another example of allegiance to a political ideology and is symptomatic of the same innate desire to be a part of and be identified with a tribe. This adoption of the paraphernalia or trappings of a particular tribe stems very obviously from the need to identify with something bigger than the self which gives a certain sense of purpose as also provides the psychological and physical benefits that we as humans crave for.

All of these, songs, slogans, colours, clothing, etc. are best seen in stadia. Anyone who is a sports addict can talk about the fetishised aspects of a sport which are almost manically and ritually flaunted be those who support the sport. Most visible on soccer and cricket fields, it is undoubtedly a moving experience when an entire audience breaks into the same anthem (of the team being supported), and the team colours that are striking and definitely motivating for the players. Material things, including mascots, go a long way in creating a certain climate for the performance on the sports field even though the final victory is of course of the team that proves its mettle, with or without the strident display of team spirit or as one could put it, tribal loyalty. Sports tribes, in a certain sense are really quite powerful and are ready to fight for their tribe. The aggression during India-Pakistan cricket matches on either side of the border is only one example of such tribal cohesiveness of otherwise peace loving peoples.

Which brings one to an important question, are nations akin to tribes? Anyone who has been to the borders of the country, be it at the Wagah or at Tripura, and seen the overt display of masculinity in the change of guards ceremonies (partially, of course, because of the tourist value of it), would perhaps think that nations, in their military overtures at least, are tribal. If we erase the original, rather pejorative use of the word 'tribe' by the imperial powers, and view the term in a more generalised way, then perhaps the terms could be almost interchangeable.

However, the writers who have contributed to this book, which arose from a national seminar held by Janki Devi Memorial College, University of Delhi in collaboration with Mahatma Gandhi Government College, Andamans, have carefully examined the many layers that encapsulate the term 'tribes'. A relevant contribution to the existing body of knowledge on tribes, the book hopes to awaken interest in lesser known tribes and perhaps, validate them and conserve them. For, it is a known fact that many tribal specifities especially languages are becoming extinct. It is really important for the academia to take note of such a dangerous possibility and engage with the tribal not just in the notional sense but more empirically.

Swati Pal
Principal, Janki Devi Memorial College
Delhi University

REFERENCES:

Folk songs of Tribal West Bengal by Dr Manik Kumar Raha, https://snarepository.nvli.in/bitstream/123456789/2872/1/JSNA%2831%2920-49.pdf

The importance of finding your tribe. Story by Kelli Wells, https://www.uow.edu.au/the-stand/2017/the-importance-of-finding-your-tribe.php

Mascots: Performance and Fetishism in Sports Culture by Mary C Daily, https://intranet.royalholloway.ac.uk/dramaandtheatre/documents/pdf/platform/031/mascots.pdf

INTRODUCTION

The term 'tribe/tribal' is at the heart of several contentious issues of contemporary Indian society. An examination of these issues becomes a valuable resource in comprehending the complexity of Indian life and reality. Some of the major questions that this examination brings forward are related to the contemporary political and social concerns of the country: forest rights, acquisition of agricultural land, loss of tribal identity, language, and culture.

Janki Devi Memorial College, University of Delhi, in collaboration with Mahatma Gandhi Government College, Pondicherry University, Mayabunder, Andaman and Nicobar Islands, under the Vidya Vistar Scheme of the University of Delhi organised a two-day National Seminar *Tribes: Learning and Unlearning Tribal Culture* on 9-10 December 2021. The seminar received a tremendous response and participants from across the country presented papers on the multiple themes related to tribal life and culture, and their representation in mainstream literature, cinema and arts.

To contribute to the academic resources available on the

subject, Janki Devi Memorial College proposed the publication of some of these papers in the form of a book. Thirteen papers were finally selected after a rigorous blind-peer review process. The keynote speaker of the seminar, Padmashree Prof Anvita Abbi, kindly agreed to pen the Foreword of this volume. The preface has been written by Prof Swati Pal, the Principal of Janki Devi Memorial College. The papers are reflective of several inter-related themes and concerns, which give a comprehensive view of tribal society and its transformation in the contemporary era.

This volume presents myriad perspectives to the understanding of tribes. The mutli-disciplinary approaches and methodologies enhance the understanding of tribal cultures and existential concerns. The book is divided into two sections. The section *Tribal Realities: Historical and Ethnographic* brings together six articles that premise their discussion on historical and ethnographic findings. These include the study of cultural assimilation of tribes, both in the past and present times, through repressive apparatuses like the colonial regi.e. and also ideological systems like pan-Indian Hinduism. The challenges posed by modernisation and globalisation on linguistic realities and its effect on tribal identity and culture is also examined. The difference between material cultures of tribal and non-tribal communities, through the study of currency is also addressed in this section. The papers have also engaged in evaluating the contribution of anthropological and demographic studies in India, which have, in their attempt to create data and documentation of tribes, provided a repository of nuanced and insightful information related to tribal life.

The section *Tribal Representations: Textual, Oral and Visual,* is a collection of seven papers adopting novel perspectives and methodologies. These include the representations of tribes in the works of noted writers like Mamang Dai, Mahashweta Devi and Hansada Sowvendra Shekhar. Popular thrillers are also studied for tribal representations. Feminist readings of the tribal version of the epics provide insights into female agency among the Bheels and Adiyas. Novel methodologies such as the phenomenological analysis of autobiographical narratives in the blogs written by persons of tribal origin, and visual anthropology enriches the cognising of tribal realities.

The scholarly works that form part of this volume provide glimpses of issues relating to a wide range of tribes. These include the Adis and Membas from Arunachal Pradesh, Bheels of Madhya Pradesh, Asurs, Santhals, Bhumijis, Mundas and Oraons from the Bengal and Bihar belt, Jarawas from the Andamans, Kunbis, Gawdas and Velips from Goa and the Adiyas from Kerala. Some of the recurring themes associated with realities and representations of the tribal life can be identified from concerns explored in the 13 chapters. These themes sensitise the reader to the polyphonous nature of tribal life and the multiple perspectives of engagement with them. The essence of tribal realities captured in the themes presented below permeate through the two sections.

Othering of the Tribal Communities

Othering results from asymmetrical power relations between the in-group, or the 'us' and the out-group, or the 'others'. Otherness in India is made complex by historical, geopolitical, social, linguistic and cultural factors, that are also instrumental in creating a chasm between the tribal and non-tribal populations.

Based on the geographical position, othering is experienced by both tribal and non-tribal groups. The tribe faces othering in areas where non-tribal population is predominant and vice versa. Identity politics is central to othering identity threat and discrimination are the outcomes of othering.

Conflict of identity, as a result of otherisation, as experienced by the Goan tribals and expressed in their narratives, is examined by Sneha Umarye. She discusses, how from a post-colonial perspecti.e. one can discern the way the Goan tribes have been othered through the process of Portuguese colonisation.

Shubhaangi Thakur in her examination of Hansda Sowvendra Shekhar's short stories, studies the various ways othering is faced by tribal subjects as they migrate from tribal areas to metropolitan Indian cities. In two stories, food and eating habits serve as a conduit for the upper caste to assert their Brahmanical hegemony through vegetarian food. The consumption of non-vegetarian food by the tribals relegates them to an impure status.

Durba Mandal studies the Bengali popular genre of horror-thriller, and the representation of tribals by the bourgeoisie Bengali authors. The thriller romances produce othering of tribal communities through a dialectical representation of Hindu rituals and rites as Sanskritised, as opposed to tribal rituals being primitive and non-Sanskritic in nature. Exoticisation is another method through which the tribals are othered and stereotyped by non-tribal populations. Plot constructions of such narratives also create psychological othering, where the non-tribal and modern protagonist must rescue/conquer the tribal from a world replete with superstition and backwardness.

Othering has been an integral part of fieldwork tradition.

Fieldwork represents a space of possibilities and yet can be constraining in nature. It serves as a medium for discovering the difference of the 'other', which at times can also be a means of stressing the uniqueness of the culture of the anthropologist. Malinowski's seminal contribution of participant observation as research methodology accentuated the need for anthropological naturalism. Does this mean that the object of study was presumed to be in a pristine condition whose purity could be discovered through field work? Does this affirmation of otherness also lead to an affirmation of the superiority of the western culture?

The field of anthropology and that of the anthropologist are politically and epistemologically interlinked. Fieldwork is not merely a research technique, but also serves as constituting an experience of both the anthropologist and the related anthropological knowledge. Vandana Madan discusses how the anthropological knowledge is accrued from the presence and experience of the anthropologist. The reflexivity of the anthropologist, has a bearing on the nature of knowledge produced. Apart from describing the emergence of anthropology as a discipli.e. she also discusses, in the context of tribal studies in India, the pioneering work of Verrier Elwin and Christoph Von Furer Haimendorf. Both wanted to understand and preserve the tribal mode of life and have been accused by their critics of being too 'inquisitive' and 'involved' with their tribal subjects. Hence, the methodological monism reflected in their work, distinguishes it from that of methodological dualism which is characteristic of conventional research.

Sanjukta Naskar focuses on the ethnographic study of Indian tribes and castes from the European perspective.

H. H. Risley while studying the tribes of Bengal emphasised the need for emergent documentation in the Indian society. This documentation was essential for discovering and preserving the richness of tribal culture. The census data usage revealed the gradual vanishing of aboriginal tradition and practices along with their assimilation into the mainstream Hindu society. Tribal tales and folklore emergent as predominant themes in the work of both fiction as well as nonfiction genres of literature. Folklore also represented a homogenised view of the tribal society as perceived by the non-tribal population. It was British administration which paved the way for discovering and documenting tribal folklore and culture. The administrator-turned-ethnographer, along with several missionaries and travellers, collected a valuable repository of information related to tribal life.

Encroachment, Disruption and Marginalisation

For centuries the tribal communities have been subjected to domination and control by the outsiders and have been victims of cultural genocide. As a result, their relationship with forests has been violated, their lifestyle that epitomised harmony with Nature, stands denigrated causing colossal disruption of the everyday practices.

Tribal communities in India share an emotional bond with Nature and forests. This emotional bond finds expression in their music, dance, paintings, and other forms of art. Not only are the forests integral for survival and livelihood, but Nature, ecology and habitat are inextricably linked to the cultural practices of the community. These communities have retained the distinctiveness of their culture due to their geographical isolation from the larger Indian society. The physical and social seclusion of the tribes from the rest of the society facilitated political and economic autonomy. Most tribes lived in self-governed communes with complete control over their land and forests. Land was communally owned and families had the benefit of usufruct rights. *Jhum* or slash and burn agriculture was most commonly practised.

Colonial interest in the forests triggered by commercial and mercenary imperatives radically altered the tribal community's relationship with its land. Early years of the colonial rule were marked by the efforts at the expansion of agriculture with the intention to redouble revenue. Encroachment into the tribal areas was the most viable option. The expansion of the railways was a further blow to the integrity of the forests. In 1864, the Forest Department was created after it was reported by a government mandated commission that the Indian forests were jeopardised on account of their mismanagement at the hands of the local people. This set the tone for forest management premised upon the assertion of state monopoly and the exclusion of forest communities from their habitat. The first Forest Act was passed in 1865 followed by a more repressive Indian Forests Act of 1878. The Act curtailed the usufruct rights denying access to forest and pasture usufruct. Its main objective was to establish the state's property right over forests while simultaneously severing customary rights.

As a consequence of the forest policy the tribes lost control over their habitat. Furthermore, they were deprived of the autonomy over economic decisions and self-governance. The tribes along with the rest of India came to be governed by uniform political and administrative authority. This resulted in the erosion of control and access over resources. Seventy five years after independence, most tribal areas are marked by alienation of their inhabitants due to disruption of emotional bond with nature and ecology. Furthermore, physical displacement on account of encroachments on tribal land by large scale irrigation projects, dams, hydel plants, factories, mining projects, highways, and other development related projects resulted in displacement of the tribal population from their home and habitat. Most such projects are undertaken in hilly and forested areas that are home to tribal population. Displacement is violative of human rights. It raises issues of equity, justice and fairness since the real beneficiaries of these projects are the urban eli.e. for whom tribal communities suffer loss of homes, habitat, livelihood and dignity. Displacement causes psychological distress, trauma, stigma and marginalisation.

Three papers in this volume approach the issue of disruption of tribal communities. Asmita Khalko's article adopts a historical perspective to trace the marginalisation of the Santhals, Bhumijis, Mundas and Oraons who lived at the fringes of the civilization in the Jungle Mahals of Bihar and Bengal. Jungle Mahals remained practically independent during the Mughal times, though they remained within the ambit of the Mughal empire. Their travails with subjugation and encroachments began with the decision of the East India Company to extend its domination over region for economic gain political gains. They resorted to tact, enticements, coercion and military to establish control over the Jungle Mahals.

The chapter by Sneha Sawai presents the 'voices from the margins' of Adi tribe of Arunachal Pradesh as expressed in the poems of Mamang Dai, a celebrated writer from the North-Eastern part of India who belonged to the Adi tribe. Her phenomenological writings capture the spirit of the marginalised tribal community- their anxiety, hopelessness and dispossession. In order to promote its commercial interests, the colonial government promoted large scale deforestation in the North eastern regions of India resulting in loss of biodiversity, polluted environment and other ecological disturbances. Among the Adis, nature is perceived as knowledge and power that guides in everyday practices. The bond between humans and nature imparted a sense of unity and identity to the Adis. Hence, the denigration of nature and ecology was perceived as disruptive of the identity of the Adis. Dai's ecocritical writings celebrate the human-nature bond.

Shubhaangi Thakur's article is a reflection of the plight of the Santhals of Jharkhand at their systematic marginalisation due to encroachment and usurption of their land for mining and stone quarrying. Not only have they been dispossessed of their land, but their music and art forms have been reduced to mere formal performances for the entertainment of the rich. Her analysis is based on the interpretation of the stories of a noted Santhal writer Hansda Sowvendra Shekhar. One such story shows the harsh reality of a tribal village whose inhabitants are displaced by the decision to set up of a thermal plant and sadly the villagers are expected to put up a dance show at the inauguration of the thermal plant. The advent of external elements has resulted in the exploitation and commodification of Santhali women. Autobiographical writings of the Goans, in the form of blogs, are explored by Sneha Umarye to discover the voices of pain, poverty, discrimination and mistreatment.

Tribal Culture and Assimilation

Although the history of differentiation and stereotypical representation of tribals dates back to the pre-colonial times, the term 'tribal' itself emerges with the colonial encounter, classifying the *adivasi*s of peninsular and central India, and the communities living in the remote hills of the north-eastern region under a singular canopy. The narrative of tribal identity as marked by its insular, natural, and exotic location; its simplicity of life as demonstrated by costumes, food, lack of script and writing; animistic religious beliefs and practices has created a hierarchy within social categorisation, and the notion that the tribal is inferior to the mainstream Indian.

Examination of cultural formations like mythologies, customs, traditions, and language help in critiquing and reversing the homogenised and essentialised representation of tribals.

Myths have been regulated by the upper caste and have been congruent with the patrilineal ideology of the Indian society. The tribal interpretation of epics reflects divergent views of the marginalised groups. Jisha Ponnachan examines the tribal elucidation of the *Ramayana* and the *Mahabharata*, as perceived by the Adiya tribe of Wayanad and the Bhil tribes. These radical versions challenge the Brahmanical hegemony by portraying female characters as strong and liberated, in contrast to the stereotypical and passive representation of women in the Sanskrit texts. Women are also considered synonymous with nature. These tribal mythical representations reveal a close affinity of nature with culture.

The post liberalisation period witnessed another major socio-economic transformation within tribal communities as reflected in literature. The most important aspect of change is the emergence of writers from within the tribal communities. This new wave of writing resists earlier representation of tribals and the non-tribal, eschewing the tribal 'subject' as either primitive or a victim. In fact, the protagonist would earlier be always an outsider, who would be the messiah for the oppressed tribal groups. Sneha Sawai studies the poetry of Mamang Dai, who as member of the Adi tribe of Arunachal Pradesh documents the changes in her culture and eco-system, brought about by modernisation and assimilation into non-tribal culture. Through the poetic medium, tribal writers are able to both articulate the pain of losing one's cultural identity and at the same time express the problems of the tribal subjects in adjusting to a constantly changing world.

Post-colonial ethnography has highlighted the close distinction between tribes and non-tribal culture. Tribal societies have not been perceived as being in a static, isolated state, but as communities undergoing transformation. In fact, the change has been conceptualised in the tribe as ultimately becoming a caste. The latter represents a divergent mode of behavioural pattern and lifestyle, whereas the tribe is associated with homogeneity. Does the process of subjugation and assimilation imply a complete disintegration of tribal practices and tradition? Does the imitation of the mode of life and ritual practices of the upper caste appear as a means of elevating the tribal status as well as the identity of its members?

Sneha Umarye's chapter touches upon the discrimination faced by the Goan tribal communities. Many of them have discontinued the use of traditional language, ritual practices and donning of traditional garments. Hence, by becoming

Sanskritised, they strive to attain higher status, acquisition of land and material success in life. The same issue of Sanskritisation is addressed by Adiba Faiyaz in her chapter where according to her, the Asur language is not able to face the challenge of dominant language and consequently is on the verge of disappearing.

Sanjukta Naskar also examines the process of assimilation and Hinduisation of tribal groups. This can be illustrated in the example of the Bhumij of Western Bengal where adoption of Hindu practices without renouncing tribal status is discernible. The indigenous language has been lost. They speak Bengali and their worship of Hindu gods complements the worship of the tribal gods. She mentions a very interesting example of loss and subsequent creation of a new caste identity, thereby asserting the commensality operating as a defining feature of the caste system. In Orissa, a new caste called Chattar-khai was formed, comprising of people who lost their caste in 1866, as they had committed the sin of eating in relief kitchens.

Language and identity are essential aspects of the tribal world. Language not only facilitates communication, but also epitomises emotions, solidarity, and cultural unity of the tribal communities. What happens when the indigenous language faces threat from the outside world? Does it succumb to the pressure and becomes extinct? Is there a possibility of resisting the challenge and the revival of the disintegrating language?

As discussed earlier, Adiba Faiyaz's chapter deals with some of these issues related to the language of the Asur tribe located in the Gumla, Lohardaga, Palamu and Latehar districts of Jharkhand. The associated Asur language is struggling for survival and efforts are being made to revive it. The role of technology, government and government policies have made significant contribution in this direction. She stresses the importance of spoken language, as mere documentation does not ensure its survival.

Krishna Kumar Sharma by drawing on both primary and secondary sources of information, discusses the history and culture of the Memba tribe. Their language also faces threat of survival. The community follows the Nyingmapa School of Tibetan Buddhism. Yet, similarity with North-Indian Hindu mortuary, marriage and ritual practices can be discerned. They are endogamous and patriarchal groups having more than 20 clans. Sneha Umarye also discusses the ethnocentric bias in the attitude towards tribal languages, which have constantly faced the threat from dominant languages.

Tribal culture is associated with a particular mode of li.e. tradition, norms and practices and a worldview, which relies heavily, for their perpetuation, on oral culture. Is there a way of capturing a glimpse of the exotic culture through a visual lens of time? Visual ethnography has made a significant foray into the everyday world of the non-western culture. The exotic, elusive and at times mythical reality is transformed into something which is tangible and empirical, and rendered visible to the outside world.

Pouriangthanliu discusses the photographic collection of Milada Ganguli, a Czechoslovakian citizen whose centre of interest were the Naga Hills, then a district of Assam. This collection facilitates a comprehensive understanding of the political structure, material culture and everyday life of the community. The photographs capture the essence of the material culture of the Nagas, by highlighting their use of bright colours, decorative thread, weaving patterns, beadwork, and embroidery.

Vinay Brandon's chapter focuses on a very important aspect of material culture viz currency. Traditionally, primitive money has been viewed in terms of the sacred-profane dichotomy, forming an essential aspect of exchange. It was also used for negotiating status boundaries or hierarchies of the tribal system, but by and large remained operational in the domestic domain. It has also been differentiated from the rational, state-controlled market exchange system, characteristic of the non-tribal communities.

Resistance and Reclamation

Tribal societies are dynamic and resilient. Though they have faced the challenges of disruption, displacement, onslaught on their indigenous institutions, yet it is not as though that they have mutely accepted their fate. They offered stiff resistance, protested and rebelled against the atrocities. Tribals have incessantly protected their habitat and resources and resisted their exploitation by the colonial state, money-lenders, and commercially driven interests of the corporate sector.

History bears testimony to the endurance, grit and tenacity with which some of the tribal communities have retaliated against the oppressive taxation and rent policies of the colonial government, land alienation, and incursions on their little republics. Some of these rebellions like the Santhal Insurgency and the Munda Rebellion date back to the 19th century. In recent times, demands for statehood have culminated in formation of Chhatisgarh and Jharkhand. Identity politics that mark the agitations for Bodoland in Assam, and Gorkhaland in

West Bengal which depicts the fervour with tribal communities assert their demand to reclaim identity.

The chapters in this book explore myriad forms of resistance and endeavours to reclaim the language, culture and identity.

Asmita Khalko's chapter provides ample illustrations of the attempts of the rajas at resisting and circumventing the dictates of the colonial rule. The *rajas* of Jhargarm and Ghatsila Jungle Mahals resisted to coloniser's subjugation in order to preserve their autonomy. The British demand for onerous revenue and their policy of dispossession and confinement on failure to pay it, forced the *zamindars* and *rajas* of the Jungle Mahals to adopt a novel form of resistance. The disgruntled *zamindars* and *rajas* of Bishnupur and Burdwan rallied with the bandits to sustain themselves.

The zamindar in whose jurisdiction robber was committed, could then seek exemption from the payment of revenue, while the spoils of the dacoity were then shared between the bandits and the *zamindars.*

'Writing Back' is another interesting form of resistance. Shubhaangi Thakur's chapter discusses Hansada Sowvendra Shekhar's literary works (short stories) as a form of 'writing back' to the empire. He narrates the atrocities and mistreatment meted out to the tribal women with the deliberate use of raw and abusive language to recreate a sense of brutal and crass behaviour of molesters.

Similarly, Sneha Umarye explores another form of 'writing back' through the blogs of tribals of Goa. These autobiographical writings are replete with lived experiences of discrimination and the resultant low self-esteem and othering among the Goan tribal groups.

Shrestha Bhattacharya delves into the narrations in Mahashewta Devi's novels, to explore how the cultural performances and the rituals of the Mundas reflect the socio-political ramifications of their marginalised existence. She perceives the song and dance performances of the Mundas as a form of asserting political resilience that challenges state-sponsored violence against their marginalised tribal identity. Birsa Munda, a revolutionary tribal mytho-historical tribal leader asserted the identity of the tribals from the Chhota Nagpur regions by singing, dancing and playing musical instruments. The songs that are part of musical performances are songs of revolution with lyrics arousing the Mundas to overthrow the oppressors. It is only through the cultural labour of performances that the Mundas can reclaim their identity and overcome their marginality. Mahashweta Devi imparts agency to the tribals characters to forge their unique mode of resistance that not only questions the dominant regi.e. but also re-creates their own identity and re-establish their bonds with nature.

The book sensitises the reader to a nuanced understanding of tribal issues. The chapters present a plethora of differential realities of tribal life that necessitates an empathetic approach of the scholars and readers. While the tribal communities have been the victim of oppression and exploitation, it is not as though they have passively accepted the high handedness of the perpetrators of excesses against them. On the contrary, recent times tribal have witnessed history of resistance and protests that have culminated in the reclamation of lost identities. As part of being exposed to the larger world, educational and employment facilities are now accessible to all. Education is a new tool to assert identity through the written word – both textual and virtual media that has set in motion the replacement of oral traditions. Modernisation and Sankritisation, though often considered diametrically opposite forces of social change, have worked in tandem to the construction of the new order of the tribal world. The understanding of this diachronic tribal world necessitates intensive research through the adoption myriad methods and perspectives.

Ruby Bhardwaj
Charu Kala
Associate Professors, Department of Sociology,
Janki Devi Memorial College, University of Delhi

SECTION I

TRIBAL REALITIES
HISTORICAL AND ETHNOGRAPHIC

CHAPTER 1

Indigenising Virtual Currencies

Vinay Brandon

In this conceptual review, I take exception to the naive high-modernist view of the tribal economy, especially with relation to the 'invention' of 'abstract' or 'virtual' money in the quotidian organisation of tribal economic life. Conventionally, this view has been associated with the ken of the discipline of Economics where 'modern money' seamlessly fulfils multiple functions – *medium of exchange, store of value, means of unilateral payment (settlement),* and *measure of value (i.e. as a unit of account)* – to bind local issues of exchangeability ('moneyness') with state-sanctioned realisation of value (the 'money of account'). The latter has been referred to as money's 'despotic power' (Mann, 1986 in Ingham, 2004, p.4), i.e. the measure of enforceability that makes money a political claim on the social product. There is a strident debate across disciplinary registers, whether to privilege the exchange function or a nominalist accounting framework in reconciling the primacy of means through which money may meld (im)personal social trust with legitimacy for a transactional community. Insofar as money 'enables the calculation of actual and potential costs and benefits, profits and losses, debts, prices' (Ingham, 2004, p.4), i.e. allowing a measure of value to spontaneously emerge from exchange, it needs to be bound in a common ledger of social accounting which allows it to perform other roles.

In essence, if 'money is [really] the basis for the progressive rationalisation of social life' (Ingham, 2004, p.4) then it is this accounting convention which determines and drives consensus in measuring and according value, subsuming within it, the sociability of exchange, i.e. the 'moneyness' function. This has been evident since the earliest historical record, going back to pre-agrarian egalitarian tribes and clan formations in the fertile crescent (Henry, 2004 in Wray, 2004, pp.79-98). Thus, 'the very idea of money, which is to say, of abstract accounting for value, *is logically anterior and historically prior to market exchange*' (Ingham 2004, p.25).

Within this episteme, however, it becomes *a category error* to confuse 'money-stuff with money' (Ingham, 2004, p.34) since money is at its heart, its very existential basis, 'a generalised social relation of credit and debt denominated in a money of account' (Ingham, 2004, p.12). The 'Money of Account' function, thus, assumes a logical primacy, becoming *the* founding conceptual fiction that subsumes and subverts myriad forms of local exchange (gifting or barter or commodity money or local currency), within a higher level of accounting abstraction – the source of an innate hierarchy *in* money. It was this 'invention' of a more 'abstract', 'depersonalised' and 'virtual' form of money (a general-purpose credit relation) which attested to the prevailing dogmas of 'economic rationality' in the social sciences.

Thus, in order to generalise social relations of credit and

debt across human societies separated in historical space-ti.e. the *neochartalist position*[1] ended up creating an ontological myth of 'progressive abstraction' (Ingham, 2004, p.90) to arrive at an axiomatic definition of Money – 'Money is socially constructed abstracted value, measured by its own scale of value' (Ingham, 2007, p.268). This has virtualised the very existence of money, which may only exist as an indexical record in some abstract ledger pooling together various frameworks of accounting conventions and technologies – modern, primitive and archaic, to establish social trust.

A Short History of Social Debt

In his magnum opus *Debt: The first 5000 Years*, David Graeber (2011) has succinctly brought out the tensions between the social alchemy and institutional hierarchalisation of money in vivid ethno-historical detail. In a seminal work of historical anthropology, Graeber (2011) takes to task the origin myths of money while offering a sweeping historical-anthropological analysis problematising the teleological understanding of the 'progressive abstraction' (and de-materialisation) of money. He shows how the expansion of state form (agrarian, feudal, imperial, colonial, democratic) affected and interacted with local debt-systems to create ever new forms of transactional communities.

1 The logical nominalism, or nominalist ontology of the 'money of account' is central to the 'neochartalist consensus', i.e the theoretical position taken as a point of departure for tribal money in this chapter. It has steadily emerged as the dominant position in the social theorising of money assigning a constitutive role to the social accounting function as a logical a priori upon which to predicate all other functions – the store of value function (the commodity view), the fiat function (for amalgamating social trust through inviolable tax debts), and most consequentially for social payments – the 'moneyness' function, through exchange and sociability. (For a critical debate within heterodox economics, Ingham, 2021; Sgambati, 2020, 2021).

Graeber (2011) showed how the bundling together of several 'primordial debts' across cultures – spot trade, penal tallies, sacrifices, gifts, tributes, peonage and taxes – became institutionalised through distinct periods of history, creating yet more complex debt-systems. Thus, standardised accounting frameworks of higher abstraction were always overdetermined by local modes of circulating obligations. Detailed pricing systems, first arising when legal codes interfered with local village laws, merged asynchronously with primordial debts requiring the adjustment of local relational costs and benefits through different social scrips and money forms. Multiple channel of 'social payments' to square tallies or lay a creative social claim to credit have thus always been the norm. Through the march of history, these warring accounting conventions were mutualised by the hegemony of expansive state-structures to settle political claims of enforceability, coercion, and standardisation in a '**debt dirigisme**'. The journey of this social and political institutionalisation of 'primordial debt' has led to an entanglement of multiple debt systems, across ever-widening sociopolitical collectivities, shaping the dialectics of money as an oscillation between commodity equivalence (paper/token currency issuance through a gold standard) and credit issuance (as a politically secured promissory relation) across four epochs[2] of world history.

2 Following the 'Axial Age' (800 BC – 600 AD) where coinage first emerged to scale, he showed how this dynamics continued with 'The Middle Ages' (600 A.D to 1450), with the commodity form becoming dominant again during the Age of the Great Capitalist Empires (1450-1971). He characterises the contemporary age (1971 -) marked by the dissolution of the gold standard and the rise of flexible exchange rates as 'the beginning of something', a sign of the contradictory currents driving new money formation in the contemporary neoliberal era.

Thus, Graeber showed *how* the political dominance of the 'money of account' function came to historically jostle for legitimacy with the regime of the commodity, depending on what could circulate faster to maintain control and power through credit creation,[3] new claims to mutual obligation.

By piecing together ethnographic evidence of this oscillatory dialectics in a single social history of debt he spelled out the fundamental analytical tension between the primacy of exchange and the accounting function, which has played out across different social sciences, creating a pantheon of contending western monetary folk theories. Crucially, this historical analysis of social debt shows how different sub-systems monetise or commoditise is both a local and historical question and cannot be subjected to transcultural comparison. Thus, there is no clear progression at a world-historical level in how reciprocal obligations would produce 'equal exchanges' through some intervening media of local-money, gifts or barter – an ethnographic problem shaping much comparative work on primitive and indigenous money.

Within any territorially bound local configuration—primitive valuables, gifts, obligations, loans, debt peonage, barter, etc. all inter-operated across various levels of trust, amalgamating at higher orders of monetary communitas to

3 When one surveys decades of anthropological literature on credit and debt, an astonishing consistency shines through much of the ethnographic data. Seemingly, everywhere that credit and debt are discussed, we find many informants who enunciate a moral stance that credit is considered beneficial and liberating for the creditor whereas indebtedness is more likely to be seen as burdensome and imprisoning for the debtor. (Peebles, 2010, p. 226)

facilitate inter-group exchange (Gregory, 2012) . Thus, old money and new were always 'thrown together' in a historical dialectics of production/ownership and obligation/transfer. Reciprocal norms of obligation that Mauss (1925/1990) asserted as constituting a social totality were in fact generated at the inter-personal level of 'primordial debts', created locally to keep tabs of who owes what to whom, eventually becoming bound within a common social register of memory through rituals, myths and ceremonies as an ethnographic record. I document this pattern for Yapese stone money later.

Graeber also challenges the origin myth of state-theories of money, that 'taxation arose as state appropriation of debts to god' (Graeber, 2011, p.63) by showing through concrete historical evidence how gift cycles interact cross-culturally by opposing out-group value systems of commodity (materiality) and credit (obligations) in a dizzying variety of cultural patterns. Throughout history, 'gifts to gods' and 'gifts to men' became inter-operative across various scales of accounting for fiscal penalties, debt peonage, community fines, moral rents and commercial interest, within different tribal, peasant and national formations, conditioning behaviours of both economic thriftiness (well documented for Melanesia), opportunism and downright usury.

Gregory (1980) has elsewhere shown how the destructive-principle in a competitive 'gifts-to-God' exchange system like the North-American *Kwakiutl* Potlatch can paradoxically reveal the epigenesis of calculati.e. commercial interests, unlike the competitive gifts-to-men systems (thriftiness associated with debt-avoidance catalogued across various tribal contexts).

Graeber (2011) shows how this inter-operability of

quantitative scaling of debt may have worked locally through different myths and clan-religions across pre-agrarian societies of Mesopotamia, and various peasant communities in Indochina and Africa.

Thus, creditory promises, calculative agencies and commercial interests could arise in indigenous contexts existing together with stable bonds of collective or moral sentiment. Thus, 'economic calculation is not [simply] an anthropological fiction' (Callon and Muniesa, 2005). It has shaped how alternate systems of value have collided and interacted across historical space-time to bind communities in highly textured and intricate forms of mutual obligation. At the level of profane commodity exchange, in general, the transaction of goods arose more like an intertemporal spot trade among known neighbours than the often quoted 'myth of barter' (Graeber, 2011, pp. 22-41).

This has been tackled elsewhere by Humphrey (1985, 1997) as a feature of cultural or communicative breakdown in collectively addressing local shortages, which gave way to bartering among strangers, enemies or essentially with non-group members whom one cannot trust. Thus, the economistic 'myth of barter' should be associated more as the primordial basis for 'international trade' rather than some standard of 'equivalent exchange' occurring in an imaginary village or tribal settlement—a 'special-purpose-money', becoming historically realisable as a pre-market commodity form .

In summary, a means to exchange value as quantifiable social debt across various scales of value, first emerged in tribal and pastoral contexts. As Ingham (2004, pp. 105–106) puts in no uncertain terms, 'All evidence points to the historical origins of money as a means of calculating obligations and debts in pre-market tribal and clan society. The first money calculating societies for which records exist are the agrarian command economies of the ancient Near East.' Thus, the progression of 'monetary abstraction', from barter to commodity to credit relations has been pieced backwards, being a product of obdurate modernist presentism.

All archaeological evidence (Ferguson, 2009, pp 28-30) points to the origins of money through an accounting logic of credit and debt. The first piece of recorded writing on a Mesopotamian clay tablet (2nd century, BCE) is in fact a promise to pay the bearer 330 measures of barley at harvest time (Ferguson, 2009, p 29). Primordially, the invention of money was first to account and transact debt as future promises, a kind of a social IOU borne of an interactional spot trade among kin or neighbours. Thus, money has always been, materially and literally, 'trust inscribed' (Ferguson, 2009, p 31).

While successfully establishing archival evidence for the primacy of the accounting function in the creation and circulation of social debt across historical time, there remains a conceptual difficulty in reconciling contrarian evidence found in the detailed ethnographic descriptions of the social and symbolic elements contained within tribal monetary exotica. It seems that debunking the myth of the progressive abstraction of money would not at once remedy the dematerialisation myth. The problem is compounded if we think of indigenous money as operating within a distinct sphere of moral, sentimental or symbolic exchange where the material agency in creating money objects is very much at stake.

Separate Spheres of Tribal and Modern Money

Through the patronising gaze of modernity, tribal money has been largely approached as being 'static', 'primitive', 'elementary' or 'domesticated', involving reconfigurations of 'cultural' elements that inform a diverse range of exotic phenomena. These have been analysed using several theoretical frameworks of different disciplinary schools, variously emphasising;

i) a satisfaction of individual biological needs adaptive to the whole social system (functionalism);
ii) a material or indexical ground for differentiating social relations of rank and prestige (trends in American Cultural and European Structural Anthropology);
iii) (re) balancing of status boundaries through public symbols, social meanings or liminal transformations (symbolic anthropology);
iv) the putative emergence of the material commodity form (primitive communism) through the local dynamics of gifting exchange or barter (the Political Economy turn in Economic Anthropology).

Ironically, this tendency of studying the tribal economy as an 'instituted process' has rendered the actual social design of tribal money systems as epiphenomenal, and their calculative rationality as being reflective of a 'primitive mentality' (Levy Bruhl, 1922).

This becomes problematic in locating the existence of a historically prevalent social calculus of debt that underlies the abstract accounting framework of modern money.

In most early anthropological accounts, the common worldview tied to primitive money was associated with a normative urge to criticise a disciplinary straw man – the *Homo Economicus* of market rationality (Hann & Hart, 2011, p 43). This produced unintended consequences effectively demoting tribal money in a double sense, either as a facile instrument (non-money) serving a specific 'cultural' purpose through non-commercial exchange, or, as a 'fetish', which would derive its analytical value in a separate sphere of affects, morality or inscrutable native sentiment. This 'provincialisation', through early colonial and mid-century disciplinary anthropology, stemmed mainly from a disavowal with modern money's 'depersonalising abstractions', the pedagogic story at the heart of Polanyi's *The Great Transformation* (Maurer, 2006, pp 17-22). This has been taken to task by recent studies in Economic Anthropology that look at how quantification and number can produce subjecti.e. moral, ambiguous, ineffable, and adjectively marked monies that can even 'resacralise', transubstantiate, integrate, and interoperate across different scales of value (for a detailed review Maurer, 2006, pp. 22-24). In this vein, some commentators have even emphasised the rational dimensions of non-commercial social payments or calculative dimensions of gift societies (Appadurai, 1986).

However, in the main, the 'separate sphere' of tribal exchange has been viewed as being supra-or-para rational – providing cultural 'peculiarities', associated empirically with the domain of 'special-purpose-money (SPM[4])' (Bohannan, 1959), restricting

4 A term utilised variously in the canon, it was made analytically salient by Bohannan (1959), who was influenced by substantivist ideas that the 'real' economy is grounded in actual social relations of community and morality, as opposed to the 'fictitious' economy of commensurating calculative abstraction. Essentially, it refers to a media of exchange or monetary form, which performs only one or two functions of money in the 'formal' economic sense.

the rationalising processes of quantification, abstraction and commensuration associated in a nominalist and unqualified sense with modern money proper – Ingham's (2004) virtual container of all 'moneyness' – the *abstract money of account* that emerges as a *means* of politically settling claims of credit and debt. Where this was supposed to be realised in full measure, it was the domain of society-wi.e. state-sanctioned, 'general purpose money (GPM)' – the universal 'general equivalent' of Western Monetary Folk Theory (Maurer, 2006, p.19).

These separating tendencies[5] were incorporated within the emerging subfield of Economic Anthropology during the heyday of the formalist-substantivist debate (Hann & Hart, 2012, pp.55-70) where anthropologists intensely debated the immediate methodological consequences of Karl Polanyi's (1944/2001) seminal critique of economic formalism. The separate sphere of the formal 'economy' was seen as 'disembedding' means-ends calculations associated with market behaviour, from an organic division of labour that was to be instituted by a pattern of socially conditioned transactions

5 A hand-me-down of Polanyian thinking, the concept of SPM still provides a useful analytical touchstone to evaluate the social content of a process or media of exchange, within a 'separate sphere' of exchange (Bohannan, 1959). While anthropologists have continued to investigate the structural relationships between spheres of market and non-market exchange in novel ways, western folk theories of money have succeeded in repurposing a false binary with modern, capitalist money by insisting on rationality as a feature of uniscalar valuation and universal commodification associated with GPM. As Appadurai (1986), Granovetter (1985), Guyer (2004), Parry & Bloch (1989), and Zelizer (1996, 2017) have variously argued 'One can simply lift off the boundedness of the model [of spheres of exchange] and connect each sphere to its regional trading networks,' (Guyer, 2004, p. 28). One then sees 'not barriers [between spheres] but institutions that facilitated asymmetrical exchanges across value registers' (Guyer, 2004, p.28). In this chapter, I utilise this methodology to compare virtual currencies past and present.

in provisioning exchange, reciprocity and redistribution[6] concerning the general provisioning of material wants in society. This analytical separation led to the long lineage of considering abstract calculation as being disembodied from the Domestic Moral Economy (DME), where, to use Polanyi's famous formulation, the tribal economy was 'housed' in kinship and other social relations (Gregory, 2012, p. 380), and following Bohannan (1959), constituted a 'separate sphere' from the National Political Economy (NPE) – the domain of consequential abstractions, contradictions and contestations between world markets and national currencies. This has been reinforced by a tendency to separate the moral (thought in terms of 'collective sentiment' and relational hierarchy) and the commercial sphere (thought in terms of maximising individual behaviour in market exchange) in documenting local accounts of primitive exchange (gifts, goods, commodities and precious valuables) and settlement of reciprocal obligations (primordial debts), a tendency reaching a crescendo with the formalist-substantivist debate. Thus, the separate spheres idea unwittingly promoted an analytical separation of functional (material exchange) and fictional (accounting convention) encounters between 'tribal SPM' with 'world GPM'.

6 According to Polanyi (1944), these together constitute institutionally embedded processes which substantively moulded the division of labour in pre-industrial societies. These assume the form of socially conditioned transactional patterns which shape and coordinate all production and distribution activity in the socially embedded economy. 'Reciprocity' refers to socially or politically mandated obligations that define one's functional duties and income privilege. 'Redistribution' refers to collection of goods at a centre for periodic function and ceremonial dispersal. 'Exchange' refers to transactions involving the swapping of goods that are supposed to be of equivalent value.

It is in the sphere of the NPE or GPM that historically prior stages of clan societies, agrarian empires, feudalism, mercantile trade and capitalist domination were brought together under a uniform accounting framework through the coercive abstraction of state and credit theories of money (Graeber, 2011, pp. 46-52). Through the historical course of the 'debt dirigisme', maturation of state power and institutional domination became central to the interactive encounters between the separate spheres of 'world GPM' & 'tribal SPM', a process which Polanyi (1944/2001) has characterised as 'double movement'.

This constant crossing-over between tribal SPM and world GPM became a source of both hegemony and domination. When world money (national currencies, international remittances, digital money forms) circulates alongside tribal money forms new dynamics ensue within primitive circuits of exchange. Gifts frequently become commodities (Gregory, 1989) to adjust to emergent scarcities in customary exchange; merchant relations emerge as opportunistic economic intermediaries to balance hierarchy in traditional kinship networks; bride-price emerges due to tribal SPM being crowded out by state GPM shortage. As we have shown in our review of the social history of debt, this monetary mutation is not merely one way. If a sovereign currency devalues or faces inflationary pressure, precious metals or primitive valuables regain prominence as gifts, modes of debt repayment and stores of value. Everywhere, there is confusion, adjustment and frequent obfuscation in established exchange practices. Debt becomes situationally realised as a 'generalised drama of relational-accounting and the 'Great transformation' (Polanyi (1944/2001)) becomes a runaway process.

Thus, money's founding functions (the 'big four') and fictions themselves became contested field-sites in the historic march of a discipline seeking to inscribe the intrusi.e. homogenising and depersonalising effects of its 'great transformation' (Maurer, 2006, especially, pp 17 -22). However, in laying the ethnographic groundwork for comparative generalisation, disciplinary anthropology unwittingly ended up furthering the schism between primitive and modern money.

Methodological Issues in Approaching 'Tribal Money'

The methodological tensions central to anthropological theory, between form and content, local and global, particular and universal, idiographic and nomothetic, etic and emic, all inflect the study of 'tribal money', by extension. As we have discussed in the previous section, marking away separate epistemic and cultural spheres for primitive and modern monetary forms, functions and meanings has had serious methodological consequences for economic-anthropology. This has produced conceptual tensions that have played out throughout the archive at three distinct levels:

i) At the level of comparative analysis : How to approach and qualify the 'moneyness' of exchange in tribal societies? This constitutes a Manichean reappearance of the philosophical problem of induction, which was meant to be exonerated by the integrity of ethnographic fieldwork or recourse to methodological holism in comparative generalisation. An important illustration will take us back to the very foundations of the discipline. In the Argonauts of the Western Pacific (1922), Malinowski lists seven types of transactions, from pure gift to trade (1922: 177-91), while emphasising throughout the distinction between *kula* (ceremonial gift exchange carrying social prestige) and *gimwali* (profanised individual barter that usually accompanied Kula). While the former became the ideal-typical primitive valuable associated with the altruistic ethos of tribals, the latter was described as a form of selfish haggling, which Adam Smith had naturalised two centuries ago as the innate human propensity 'to truck and barter', offering to western folk theory *the* origin myth of money. Despite the catalogue, Malinowski (1922) desisted from comparing the circulation of these primitive tokens with modern money as state-issued 'currency'. According to him, these did not function as a medium of exchange and standard of value. Mauss (1925/1990) took Malinowski to task for reproducing the bourgeois opposition between commercial self-interest and the free gift (Hann & Hart, 2011, 52) insisting that primitive valuables are like money precisely because they confer the holder with 'purchasing power', which has a 'figure set on it' that cycles its way throughout a social totality (Mauss (1925/1990)).

ii) At the level of ethics and ontology: Can forms of primitive exchange and tribal money objects be considered as monetary systems in their own right? This question requires us to take an ethical issue in aligning subalternate or qualitative systems (Gregory, 1997) of value transfer (tribal SPM) with superalternate or quantitative systems (GPM) as they inflect local customs of exchange and idioms of value transfer – whether gifts, money, debts or tributary payments.

This is especially significant in the Indian context since most of the literature on tribal monies in India subordinates their value as special-purpose-money (SPM), or considers their monetary practices as epiphenomenal. In this reading, tribal customs involving money are merely ritual enactments satisfying the requirements of a superordinate value system – that of pollution or purity. These include examples of cooperative gifts-to-men (via gifts-to-God) exchange systems involving the transfer of morally obligatory debts ('*dan*') for which no reciprocity accrues and which 'should be endlessly handed on' (Parry, 1986, p. 462). These do not contribute to quantitative value creation or transfer, and hence, may be considered as 'social transfers' in a strictly iterative sense. They are useful only as conceptual sign vehicles to observe social facts of *parochialisation* or *universalisation* (Marriott, 1955) or the 'levels' in Hinduism (Dumont & Pocock, 1959). Such rituals are denied coevality and validity as mechanisms of social payment under GPM, considered as merely functional to maintain order within the cosmology of a 'little tradition' (Redfield 1956) or as a cultural osmosis between 'a great and little tradition' (Marriott, 1955, pp. 197-200). This typification of indigenous money in India is reflective of the continual hegemony of the methodological philosophy of holism – where underlying reciprocal obligations or circulations of debt are eschewed to reproduce myths of a stratified, synchronic, time-less, 'traditional' rural society. This has a lot to do with studying the village rather than studying in the village – and the problematic assumptions that tribal cultures constitute pre-commercial islands where the calculative ethic was subsumed within the 'moral economy' embedding individuals within the mechanical solidarity of kinship networks. It was 'as if' tribal lifeworlds were static and devoid of money and commerce, a virtuous, virtual world of timeless, stable bonds, left unsullied by the mathematics of modern monetary commensuration. This may be because money, in the emergent disciplinary context of Indian social anthropology, was traditionally thought of 'as the coloniser's dominant symbol [which would] pay best for the coloniser's needs, knowledge, trades and values' (Zickgraf, 2017, pp 73-74).

iii) At the level of theoretical abstraction: How can we generalise across a range of similar or disparate empirical phenomena within a discipline that privileges the integrity of the ethnographic record? What distinguishes gifts-systems with debt or commodity-systems of circulation and how do we approach their peculiar local entanglement with modern money, given their myriad internal classification?

The vast literature in Economic Anthropology has variously approached these tensions between conceptual generalisability, ontological ethics and concrete specificity through questions of qualification (Are primitive valuables money?), realisation (How do they meld exchange into a promissory social payment or obligation), and valorisation (at what scales and to what effects do they inter-operate with modern state-money to achieve a contiguous standard of value?), For Mauss, it lay in the ubiquity of 'the Gift' (Mauss, 1925) as a form of primeval exchange, which contains the essential obligatory character which fuses social payment with a mutualised dimension akin to money (a 'total social fact' bringing into play the whole of society and its various institutions – legal, economic, religious, affinal and aesthetic); for Polanyi, it was realised through the disembedding of fictional commodities – land, labour and money – from the real economy of household ties and ethnic solidarities; for Sahlins, it was established in the outward expansion of 'circles of reciprocity' (Sahlins (1972/2017) allowing gifts to transgress their immediate social ties to become part of a wider social totality of primitive exchange; for Gregory (1982, 1997) it involved the transformation of gifts to goods or commodity-debts (money), emerging as a feature of interaction of subalternate and superalternate value systems across territorially bound circuits of pre-capitalist commodity exchange (Gregory, 1997, ch.4 & 5).

I use **'tribal money'** as a historico-anthropological ideal-type that bundles together the material, numerai.e. symbolic, personal and moral dimensions of indigenous money systems as a heuristical device and humanistic category, becoming analytically important to reconcile 'rival cognitions' and 'unresolvable antagonisms' (the quotations and spirit of the argument is borrowed from Gregory, 1997, p.6). In what follows, I argue that tribal money is eminently comparable with contemporary 'virtual currencies (VCs)' despite seeming to be cultural-categories drawn from separate epistemic registers, 'world's apart' in their level of sophistication or abstraction.

Indigenising Virtual Currencies

By 'Virtual Currency', I mean a chain of deferred promises circulating within a community of transactors who agree to share such promissory value as a quantifiable, iterative and transferable property of a money media, which can be realised as a 'social payment'.

Virtual currencies, thus, become a channel to realise promissory value solidified by the political productivity of an 'imagined [transactional] community' (Anderson, 1983), It is this community aspect of their moneyness which gives 'virtual money' its specific character as a 'currency'; it can pass from person to person as a claim to 'futurity' that a social relation will generate a claim to be exchanged as money.

This view is consistent with the neochartalist position on money, which was shown to be the essential monetary fiction that has allowed the exchange function, the 'moneyness' of a material object and the sociability of carrying out the transaction, to be subsumed into a virtual account.

I propose to utilise the above definition as an ideal-type to compare 'tribal money' (a historico-anthropological archetype that has ubiquitously occurred as a social payment through a relational calculus of social debt) with contemporary virtual currencies. To do this, I first unpack each of the underlined qualifications for a money media to become a virtual currency. VCs have to be iterable, i.e should be passable through a direct peer to peer exchange which would generate and validate a social network.

They have to be transferable as 'debt' since what matters is the sharing of a promise to be redeemed or performed as a social payment, i.e., a private exchange between individuals should be indexical with a transaction that would hold as promissory value for the whole social network. Thus, for a virtual currency to qualify as a social payment, the value consensus between individuals should hold good for the entire transactional community bound together by some form of mutual expectation, i.e., an agreement over what constitutes a 'promise to pay'.

For State-Money this comes through enforcing a political logic. For 'tribal money', Sahlins' (1972/2017) generalised, balanced and negative *circles of reciprocity*[7] are typical of primordial scales of circulating promissory obligations in this sense of the term.

The quantification of a promise requires some clarification. We have seen through the snapshot history of social debt how gifts, debts, alliances and tributes can have a calculati.e. yet personal dimension to them. They can even be inter-operated across 'different scales (numerical, personal and ontological) of value' (Guyer, 2004). To show how social payments become quantifiable across different scales of value, the relational earmarking of a money media can be inextricably tied to a social payment (Zelizer, 1996, 2017). In essence, for a social IOU to become quantifiable as a virtual currency, agents needs to do some relational work (communicati.e. symbolic, inter-personal, or performative) to carry out a social payment.

Zelizer (2012, p.145) defines relational work in social accounting as the process of differentiating meaningful social relations through specific media-of-exchange, i.e., money forms (objects or customs). 'For each distinct category of social relations, people erect a boundary, mark the boundary by means of names and practices, establish a set of distinctive understandings that operate within that boundary, designate certain sorts of economic transactions as appropriate for the relation, bar other transactions as inappropriate, and adopt certain media for reckoning and facilitating economic

---

7 Generalised reciprocity involves giving without the expectation of return, and is associated with the family. Balanced reciprocity involves exchanges of equal value between people, and is associated with the community. Negative reciprocity involves economic activities in which people seek to gain at the expense of others (e.g. barter, theft), and is associated with dealings with strangers or people outside the community.

transactions within the relation' (Zelizer, 2012). Bandelj (2020, p.253) in her genealogical review of the concept issues an important clarification in how relational work is different from sociality (through the existential requirement of four relational packages[8]), spelling out a methodological distinction with the concept of embeddedness (Granovetter, 1985). Essentially, the difference between the two perspectives is that relational work investigates relations and relationships from an emic (insider's) perspecti.e. while the embeddedness approach investigates them from an etic (outsider's) perspective. As we have seen in the preceding discussion on social debt and tribal money, it is this quantifiability of a promise which is accounted very differently across different tribal cultures. Thus, relational work always involves a creative interplay of social meanings, which get refracted across different inter-personal relationships varying widely across money medias and social networks.

Satisfying all these claims, make VCs indexical operators of social trust. The networks of relationships embed social trust through their very existence. Modern state-money does this through a coercive monopoly over validating a legal status of a currency – according to the sovereignty principle, which is backed by the political regulation of fractional reserve banking, territorial integrity and conventions in constitutional and international law. This is a centralised system where the transactional community settles claims through a political

8 Relational packages consist of combinations among (a) distinctive interpersonal ties, (b) economic transactions, (c) media [of exchange], and (d) negotiated meanings (Zelizer 2012, p. 151). Actors seek to find viable matches across these four components while categories of social relations strongly inform this process, deriving their meanings from broader and historically variable cultural, institutional, and legal frames (Bandelj, 2020, pp.253)

accountability to the state that issues general-purpose-money. Any community or special-purpose-money gets automatically embedded through the logic of taxation and by a political relationship between citizen and sovereign.

For digital virtual currencies, this is a matter of technical design, where a payment channel created by a trusted third party or a community maintained transactional infrastructure is supposed to replace actual social relationships to securiti.e. validate and authenticate any peer-to-peer transaction across the network, without needing to mutualise consent at any single 'node' of transaction. 'Trust is thus distributed through the network' and promissory valued is shared through digital transactions.

For 'tribal money' such a promise was shown to be underwritten historically by particular local ties and norms, which bound the community together by securing transactional faith through settling mutual obligations through the creation of new debt-monies by utilising precious objects, ceremonies, and rituals or, in certain cases of crises of shortage, penury or debt-repayment, evolving myths and customs to find a credit-line to each other's wealth (may be balanced or negative reciprocity) through common-property claims. Below, I lay out two cases across historical space-time through which this was done.

Distributing Trust across the Social Network

Sibel Kusimba's (2016, 2018, 2020, 2021) oeuvre has utilised the concept of '*wealth-in-people*' to explain how distributed networks of mobile-money technology – users, transactors, retail agents and network providers – transpose community trust onto digital networks through the transfer of virtual remittances.

She has shown how the sudden adoption of digital money (at a nation-wide scale) was a 'leap *backward* (Kusimba, 2021, p.51), by inaugurating a gift cycle which strengthened and extended tribal kinship solidarity through the evolution of a new fintech infrastructure for social payment. Peer-to-peer transfers enabled by mobile-money technologies allowed individuals (especially women) in Luhya, Bukaso, Naitiri and other rural tribal communities of Western Kenya to see themselves as part of wider transactional groups of collectivities – savings groups, cross-cousin kinship networks or extended families, thereby strengthening their age-old bonds of 'uterine kinship' (Kusimba, 2018).

For Luhya women losing their financial autonomy within a patrilineal household, inter-scalar transfers of cash, airtime money and ease of circulation of e-gifts and small-savings loans leant to an emergence of 'hearthholds of mobile money' (Kusimba, 2018). Matrilineal transfers to cousins were often secret, not disturbing the patrilineal solidarity or household autonomy of a family, while rendering support to promote 'the diverse economic strategies, domestic money needs, and mobility of hearthholds'. (Kusimba, 2021)

The multiple forms of mobile money and digital finance ushered in Kenya represent a plural monetary repertoire which has strengthened kinship networks by mobilising them together into 'a monetary public sphere.' Over 40 per cent of all transactions in Kenya (as of 2015) took place exclusively through mobile money (inferior to digital wallets), which is simply an sms transfer of a virtual currency requiring a third party retail agent to convert it back to cash. This socio-technological network has promoted employment, financial savings and targeted microfinance without the creation of new banking infrastructure.

As a concept, wealth-in-people has had a long genealogical journey in the study of pan-african kinship systems and multiple monetary repertoires. It has been utilised within anthropology to justify various phenomena of embodiment of trust in the common-property-resources of the network (Guyer, 2004 and Kusimba, 2020). Characteristic of 'tribal money', 'it is associated with institutions frequently described in sub-Saharan Africa, such as gerontocracy, patron-client relations in East-African pastoralism, especially characterising the high-status of 'big man' who publicly distributes wealth' (Kusimba, 2021, p.51). Wealth-in-people offers a culturally-grounded theory of relational accounting that matches the 'rights-in-things' to the 'rights-in-people' allowing for a new conceptualisation of embodied value where the community is transformed into an interpersonal, organic 'social network'. Such a trust network endows participants with the ability to do things with, for, and through other people, especially when trust networks pool together to create an idea of a new common property.

For the mobile money networks among matrilineal tribes in Kenya, it thus becomes a source of 'material agency' with which to distribute promises and circulate debts through small-scale money transfers (as mobile credit). Kusimba (2021, p. 51-52) further clarifies the utility of the concept in the context of 'mobile hearthholds' (Kusimba, 2016, 2018)

'I use it in a more focused sense to describe a world in which rights in people are the main basis of presti.e. power, and access to resources. Consequently, people seek, claim, and call upon rights in others—to their labour, support, reproductive capacity, or property. In so doing they use things, whether goats, currency, or digital money to…influence and mobilise others, and draw on their labor, knowledge and skill, loyalty, affection, and material resources..[that] shape ties of obligation, debt, and alliance with others.'

Wealth-in-people thus becomes a mode through which virtual currencies are mobilised to perform new social payments while tapping onto the embodied value of the social network. It is a site to see how different quantitative and qualitative scales of value may inter-operate as social trust through a creative and personalised interplay of new and old money media

Thus, in different contexts of tribal money it emerges as a VC in two different ways:

i) an emotively enforceable store-of-value (embodied social ledger), particularly in the context of ritual payments and the subtle balancing of ties with matching communicative (in)action;
ii) a collective resource (property, knowledge or wealth) for settling internal conflicts (Bahre, 2007, 2020), and for negotiating hierarchies and inequalities (Kusimba, 2021, pp. 50-52).

While the contemporary 'hearthholds of mobile money' among the *Luhya* and *Bukasa* women of Western Kenya (Kusimba, 2016, 2018) offers an instance of the former, the development of a decentralised distributed ledger to transfer ownership through the 'Rai' stone-money in Yapese society offers an instance of the latter.

An Ancient Analog to the Bitcoin Blockchain

To look at an indigenous virtual currency which is a genuine progenitor of a hypermodern digital cryptocurrency network like Bitcoin, I present the case of the Yapese stone money called 'Rai' – a stone slab which is 'mined', in the first instance, with great difficulty from the Palauan archipelago (a neighbouring island in Micronesia). All the design features which power decentralised cryptocurrencies – scarcity, difficulty in mining (resource-intensive), community verification in transferring title of ownership, proof-of-work mechanism to reward stone miners, and the idea of a community owned public ledger to transfer value, are found in the case of Rai, albeit with material and technological differences.

Like the apocryphal and illusive creation myth of an anonymous cryptographer like Satoshi Nakamoto, the Yap have an analogous myth of heroism, exploration and bravery where an ancient navigator Anagumang (Fitzpatrick & Mckeon, 2019, p.5) went to great lengths to address local currency shortages (before European contact, i.e., 1783, as put forward by the authors) by first discovering limestone sites in the Palauan archipelago. A rich collection of oral tradition (as contrasted with cypherpunk subcultures of cryptographers solving problems of security in peer-to-peer or disintermediated value transfer) is at the heart of tracking ownership through a public ledger which takes both:

i) material – through carvings upon Rai (to mark ownership) prior to public display (bitcoin ownership is contained in a unique cryptographic key).

ii) symbolic forms – through the public performance of elaborate rituals to ceremonialise a transference of ownership, sustained in public memory through an elaborate oral tradition of myth and fable regarding the ownership of each Rai (in bitcoin, this happens through the distributed consensus algorithm where the system copies ownership transfer across all nodes through the process of community-verification, i.e., Bitcoin mining).

The information is immutably stored through an eminently auditable and universal record on the decentralised ledger of the public blockchain). The fact that both bitcoin and Rai are difficult to mine (resource intensive) and materiali.e. i.e., 'bring to life' (through distributed consensus) also fed to a prestige and demand among Yapese chieftains to own and display in front of their house, much like the current Bitcoin goldrush.

Without going into the micro-details, the most striking similarities in production, record and exchange between Rai and Bitcoin have been reviewed by Fitzpatrick and Mckeon (2019, p. 8) along the following dimensions: (a) scarcity; (b) new units generated solely through the contribution of work; (c) resource intensity; (d) transfer via public announcement; (e) distributed, transparent ledger of ownership; (f) physical possession not required for ownership; and (g) scaling challenges.

For our purposes, the Rai offers a salutary case of demonstrating the imaginative potential and ingenuity of tribal communities in resolving the problem of centralised trust by making community trust indexical in the inherent material-value of Rai (compare Bitcoin's 'digital metallism', Maurer et al, 2013).

REFERENCES

Aglietta, M., & Broder, D. (2020). *Money: 5,000 years of debt and power.* Verso Books.

Anderson, B. (1983). Imagined Communities: Reflections on the Origin and Spread of Nationalism. Verso.

Appadurai, A. (1997). Modernity at Large: Cultural Dimensions in Globalization. University of Minnesota Press.

Appadurai, A. (1986). *The Social Life of Things.* Cambridge University Press.

Bähre, E. (2020). Wealth-in-people and practical rationality: Aspirations and decisions about money in South Africa. *Economic Anthropology, 7(2),* 267–278.

Bandelj, N. (2020). Relational Work in the Economy. Annual Review of Sociology, July 30, 2020. *doi:10.1146/annurev-soc-121919-054719.*

Bohannan, P. (1959). The impact of money on an African subsistence economy. *Journal of Economic History, 19,* 491-503.

Carrier, J. G. (2012). *Gifts and Commodities: Exchange and Western Capitalism since 1700.* Routledge.

Carrier, J. G. (2012). *A Handbook of Economic Anthropology* (2nd ed.). Edward Elgar Publishing Ltd.

Callon, M. (2020). What does it mean to say that economics is performative?. In D. MacKenzie, F. Muniesa & L. Siu (Eds.), *Do Economists make markets?* (pp. 311-357). Princeton University Press.

Callon, M., & Fabian, M. (2005). Peripheral Vision: Economic Markets as Calculative Collective Devices. *Organization Studies, 26(3),* 1229 – 1250.

Clifford, J., & Marcus, G. E. (Eds.). (1962). *Writing Culture: The Poetics and Politics of Ethnography.* University of California Press.

Desan, C. (2014). *Making money: Coin, Currency, and the Coming of Capitalism.* Oxford University Press.

Dodd, N. (2014). *The Social Life of Money.* Princeton University Press.

Dumont, L. & Pocock, D. (1959). On the different aspects or Levels in Hinduism. *Contributions to Indian Sociology,* 3(1), 40-54.

Fabian, J. (2014). *Time and the Other.* Columbia university press. (Original work published in 1983).

Ferguson, N. (2009). *The Ascent of Money: A Financial History of the World.* Penguin Books.

Fitzpatrick, S.M. & McKeon, S. (2020). Banking on Stone Money: Ancient Antecedents to Bitcoin. *Economic Anthropology, 7(1),* 7–21.

Fox, D., & Green, S. (Eds.). (2019). *Cryptocurrencies in Public and Private* (pp. 281-306). Oxford University Press.

Geertz, C. (1973). *The Interpretation of Cultures.* Basic Books.

Gilbert, E. (2005). Common cents: situating money in time and place. *Economy & Society, 34(3),* 357-88.

Graeber, D. (2011). *Debt: The First 5000 Years.* Penguin Books.

Graeber, D. (2002). *Toward an anthropological theory of value: The false coin of our own dreams.* Springer.

Granovetter, M. (1985). Economic Action and Social Structure: The Problem of Embeddedness. *American Journal of Sociology, 91(3),* 481-510.

Gregory, C. A. (2012). On Money Debt and Morality: Some Reflections on the contribution of economic anthropology. *Social Anthropology,* 20(4), 380-396.

Gregory, C. A. (1997). *Savage Money: The Anthropology and Politics of Commodity Exchange.* Harwood Academic Publishers.

Gregory, C. A. (1996). Cowries and Conquest: Towards a Subalternate Quality Theory of Money. *Comparative studies in Society and History, 38(2),* 195-217.

Gregory, C. A. (1982). Gifts and Commodities. *The Cambridge Journal of Anthropology, 8(3),* 95-98.

Gregory, C. A. (1980). Gifts to Men and Gifts to God: Gift Exchange and Capital Accumulation in Contemporary Papua. *MAN, 15*(4), 626–652.

Guyer, J. (2016). *Legacies, logics, logistics: Essays in the anthropology of platform economy.* The University of Chicago Press.

Guyer, J. (2012). Soft currencies, cash economies, new monies: Past and present. *Proceedings of the National Academy of Sciences, 109(7),* 2214–2221. https://doi.org/10.1073/pnas.1118397109

Guyer, J. (2004). *Marginal Gains. Monetary Transactions in Atlantic Africa.* University of Chicago Press.

Guyer, J. & EnoBelinga, S.M. (1995). Wealth in People as Wealth in Knowledge: Accumulation and Composition in Equatorial Africa. *Journal of African History, 36,* 91-120.

Hann, C. & Hart, K. (2011). *Market and Society: The Great Transformation Today.* Cambridge University Press.

Hann, C. & Hart, K. (2014). *Economic Anthropology: History, Ethnography, Critique.* Polity Press.

Harari, Y. N. (2018). *Money.* Vintage Digital.

Hart, K. (2019). *Money in a Human Economy.* Berghahn Books.

Hart, K. & Sharp, J. (2016). *People, Money and Power in the Economic Crisis Perspectives from the Global South.* Berghahn Books.

Hart, K. & Ortiz, H. (2014). The Anthropology of Money and Finance: Between Ethnography and World History. *Annual Review of Anthropology, 43,* 465-482.

Hart, K., Laville, J.L,. & Cattani, A.D. (2013). *The Human Economy: A Citizens Guide.* Polity Press.

Hart, K. (2001). *Money in an Unequal World: Keith Hart and His Memory Bank.* Texere Publishing Ltd.

Hart, K. (1986). Heads or Tails? Two Sides of the Coin. *MAN, 21(4),* 637-56.

Heider, K. G. (1988). The Rashomon Effect: When Ethnographers Disagree. *American Anthropologist, 90(1)*, 73-81.

Helleiner, E. (1999). Historicizing Territorial Currencies: Monetary Space and the nation-state in

North America. *Political Geography, 18,* 309-39.

Henry, J. F. (2004). The Social Origins of Money: The Case of Egypt. In: L. R. Wray (Ed.*), Credit and State Theories of Money* (pp. 79-98). Edward Elgar Publishing.

Humphrey, C., & Hugh-Jones, S. (1997). *Barter, exchange and value: An anthropological approach*. Cambridge University Press.

Humphrey, C. (1985). Barter and Economic Disintegration. *MAN*, *20*(1), 48–72.

Ingham, G. (2021). In Defence of the Nominalist Ontology of Money. *Journal of Post Keynesian Economics, 44(3).*

Ingham, G. (2007). The specificity of money. *European Journal of Sociology/Archives Européennes de Sociologie*, *48*(2), 265-272.

Ingham, G. (2005). *The Nature of Money*. Polity Press.

Kusimba, S. (2021). *Reimagining Money: Kenya in the digital finance revolution.* Stanford University Press.

Kusimba, S. (2020). Embodied Value: Wealth-in-People. *Economic Anthropology 7(2)*, 1–10.

Kusimba, S. (2018). It Is Easy for Women to Ask!: Gender and Digital Finance in Kenya. *Economic Anthropology, 5 (2),* 247–60.

Kusimba, S. (2018). Money, Mobile Money, and Rituals in Western Kenya: The Contingency

Fund and the Thirteenth Cow. *African Studies Review, 61(2),* 158–82.

Kusimba, S. (2016). Hearthholds of Mobile Money in Western Kenya. *Economic Anthropology, 3(2),* 266–79.

Mann, M. (1986). *The Sources of Social Power.* Cambridge University Press.

Marriott, M. (1955). Little Communities in an Indigenous Civilization. *Village India: Studies in the Little Community*. University of Chicago Press

Maurer, B. (2015). *How Would You like to Pay? : How Technology Is Changing the Future of Money*.

Duke University Press.

Maurer, B. (2012). Payment: Forms and Functions of Value Transfer in Contemporary Society. *The Cambridge Journal of Anthropology, 30(2),* 15-35

Maurer, B. (2007). Incalculable Payments: Money, Scale, and the South African offshore Grey Money Amnesty. *African Studies Review, 50(2),* 125-138.

Maurer, B. (2006). The Anthropology of Money. *Annual Review of Anthropology, 35,* 15-36.

Maurer, B. Musaraj, S., & Small, I. V. (2018). *Money at the Margins: Global Perspectives on Technology, Financial Inclusion, and Design.* Berghahn Books.

Mauss, M. (2001). *The Gift: The Form and Reason for Exchange in Archaic Societies* (W.D Halls, Trans.). Routledge.

Parry, J. (1986). The Gift, the Indian Gift and the 'Indian Gift'. *MAN, 21(3),* 453-473.

Parry, J. & Bloch, M. (1989). *Money and the Morality of Exchange.* Cambridge University Press.

Polanyi, K. (2001). The Great Transformation: The Political and Economic Origins of

our Time. Beacon Press. (Original work published in 1944).

Polanyi, K. (1957). The Economy as an Instituted Process. K. Polanyi, C.M. Arensberg, & H.W. Pearson (Eds.). In *Trade and Market in the Early Empires: Economy in History and Theory.* The Free Press.

Sahlins, M. (2017). *Stone-Age Economics.* Aldine. (Original work published in 1972).

Sgambati, S. (2021). Historicizing the Money of Account—a Rejoinder. *Journal of Post Keynesian Economics.* DOI: 10.1080/01603477.2021.1993071

Sgambati, S. (2020). Historicizing the money of account: a critique of the nominalist ontology of money. *Journal of Post Keynesian Economics, 43(3).*

Singh, S. & Slegers, C. (1997). *Trust and Electronic Money.* Circit.

Singh, S. (2013). *Globalization and Money: A Global South Perspective.* Rowman & Littlefield.

Swartz, L. (2020). *New Money: How Payment Became Social Media.* Yale University Press.

Walker-Said, C. & Seligman, A.F. (2015). Wealth in Pluralities: Intersections of Money, Gender, and Multiple Values across African Societies. *The International Journal of African Historical Studies, 48(3),* 387-92.

Weatherford, J. (1998). The History of Money. Crown Business.

Weiner, A. B. (1988). *The Trobrianders of Papua New Guinea.* Holt, Rinehart and Winston.

Wright, W. K. (19223). [Review of the book *La mentalité primitive,* by Lucien Lévy-Bruhl]. *The Philosophical Review, 32(4),* 419 – 421.

Zelizer, V.A. (1996). Payments and Social Ties. *Sociological Forum, 11(3),* 481-95.

Zelizer, V. A. (2017). *The Social Meaning of Money.* Princeton University Press.

Zickgraf, J.M. (2017). Becoming like money: proximity and the social aesthetics of 'moneyness'. *HAU: Journal of Ethnographic Theory, 7 (1),* 303–326.

Zickgraf, J.M. (2020, May 16). Moneyness: The property we share by the name of value. *Money is what we share by the name of value!*

https://moneyness.info/moneyness-the-property-we-share-in-the-name-of-value/

CHAPTER 2

The Asur Tribe and its Role in Language Revival

Adiba Faiyaz

'A definition of language is always, implicitly and explicitly, a definition of human beings in the World.' (Williams, 1989, p 21) Raymond Williams brings this idea in the second chapter of *Marxism and Literature* (1989) where he conveys that language not only includes linguistic forms, but also social aspects such as culture, gender, religion and nation-state. The total number of languages and dialects vary by source and counting method, and many Indians speak more than one language. Though the language debates have been formulated in the education sector yet linguistic rights of every linguistic community are yet to be restored. Some scholars like DP Pattanayak are of the opinion that the education system has to strengthen the grass roots multilingualism of our society. Philosopher Ivan Illich also suggests in the same work that we need to make every possible effort to empower the languages of the underprivileged. To quote Pattanayak (1981), 'if participatory democracy has to survi.e. we need to give a voice to the language of every child.'

Importance of Language

Language is significant to identity as it speaks volumes about its culture and place. We often see the overpowering nature of the dominant language in suppressing the minor or endangered languages. Anthropologists label this view of 'other language' as ethnocentricism. People often think of their own language and customs as superior and that of others as inferior. All dominant languages and groups have an inevitable habit of enforcing their customs and practices over the 'others'.

Languages shape our sentiments, emotions and cultural ties. Kenneth Hale, a well known linguist, in an interview said, 'When you lose a language, you lose culture, intellect, wealth, a work of art. It is like dropping a bomb on a museum.' (Elaine Woo, 2001) So language is one of the best known representation of its culture, intellect and its art form. For social justice and social inclusion, all indigenous and minority languages deserve to be reclaimed. Language loss is an inevitable loss. This mode of communication comes to an end forever. Language loss immediately affects the sovereignty of the natives. The hegemony of dominant language gets exerted over these indigenous languages very smoothly. It is only imperative to maintain and sustain the diverse variety of languages spoken by people other than us. To exemplify this on a macro level, let us consider the case of Hindi as a dominant language in the Indian context with respect to other Indian languages of our time. Salman Rushdie brings this aspect more clearly in his critical piece 'Commonwealth Literature Does Not Exist'. Here he elaborates on how writers like Suresh Joshi compulsorily write in Gujarati because they believe it is under serious threat of Hindi. For such people, it is not English or the West, but

Hindi which is the real problem. So, 'the greatest area of friction in India has nothing to do with English Literature, but with the effects of the hegemony of Hindi on the literatures of other Indian languages particularly other North Indian languages.' (Rushdie, 1991, p.69).

Why Revive a Dying Language?

According to our present day linguists, out of the 7000 languages spoken in the world, half of them no longer exist and some are on the verge of getting extinct. (Austin, 2011). Throughout the centuries many languages have been replaced by other languages. This privilege given to one language over other also prioritises one culture, history and beliefs over the others. David Crystal in *Language Death* (2000) writes:

> A language is said to be dead when no one speaks it any more. It may continue to have existence in a recorded form, of course – traditionally in writing, more recently as part of a sound or video archive (and it does in a sense 'live on' in this way) – but unless it has fluent speakers one would not talk of it as a 'living language'. And as speakers cannot demonstrate their fluency if they have no one to talk to, a language is effectively dead when there is only one speaker left, with no member of the younger generation interested in learning it. But what do we say if there are two speakers left, or 20, or 200? How many speakers guarantee life for a language? It is surprisingly difficult to answer this question. One thing is plain: an absolute population total makes no sense. The analysis of individual cultural situations has shown that population figures without context are useless. In some circumstances, such as an isolated rural setting, 500

> speakers could permit a reasonably optimistic prediction; in others, such as a minority community scattered about the fringes of a rapidly growing city, the chances of 500 people keeping their ethnic language alive are minimal. In many Pacific island territories, a community of 500 would be considered quite large and stable; in most parts of Europe, 500 would be minuscule. Speaker figures should never be seen in isolation, but always viewed in relation to the community to which they relate. (Crystal, 2000, p.11-12)

Crystal makes a pertinent point when he asks when should one be alarmed regarding the death of a language. He does not depend on the number of speakers of that language. So the revival of language should focus on the community which speaks that language. The situation becomes even more critical if it is a tribal language and especially when it is not documented. The marginalisation of such language gets multiplied and these suffer from the risk of getting endangered and extinct.

Keeping David Crystal in mind, one can immediately suggest that translations of such vulnerable languages into the dominant ones could be an easy way out to help us reach the language and literature of the former. Also, it must be noted that translation indeed has been very successful in its attempt to revive endangered languages. However, there are other dynamics of translation as well. David Katan in *Translating Cultures* puts it, '...the translator is a bilingual mediating agent between monolingual communication participants in two different language communities' (Katan, 1999, p. 16) which brings us to the fact that translators not only serve as mediators between different languages, but also tend to be 'intercultural mediators.'

Thus, translation performs a crucial role in our understanding of the cultural 'other'. Nevertheless, in our context of Asur tribes, their take on reviving their language does not depend on other languages. It does not matter that the development is not as fast as it could be, yet a steady progress can be noticed because of their intense dedication towards revival of the Asur language.

Understanding the Asur Tribe

As elucidated by UNESCO, the Asur language figures in the list of 'definitely endangered languages' and is among the 119 Indian languages belonging to 'vulnerable', 'severely endangered' and 'critically endangered' categories. The Asur tribe is a very small ethnic group of around 30k population (2011 census) living in Gumla, Lohardaga, Palamu and Latehar districts of Jharkhand and comprises of only 0.13 per cent of the total population of Jharkahnd. The total number of speakers varies by sources and counting methods. A small population of the Asur tribe can also be found in Bihar and West Bengal and few other states. This very miniscule population is fighting tooth and nail to keep their language alive. The language spoken by this tribe are mostly Asur and Birja among others. The Asur tribe is one of the nine PVTs which does not have access to better roads or transportation facility. With their limited resources, they have not stayed away from working towards the revival of the dying Asur language. The merit of this revival of their dying language is certainly not short-lived. This revival is not just significant for the present generation, it is more valuable for the future generations who otherwise might remain unknown to its worth. Thus, one of the preliminary consequence of revitalisation of a decaying language is to save it from language loss and also from cultural disaster.

There is no denying the fact that indigenous languages such as Asur are reduced to a handful of people. Out of the 32 different tribes of Jharkhand, only a few such as Santhali, Ho and Kuruk have documented languages.

The Asur adivasis' efforts to revive their language and historical identity in collaboration with local civil societies is a noteworthy step. Rohit Kumar of Bikash Bharti, a non-profit organisation, works with the adivasi communities in Jharkhand. Asuri exists only as a spoken language and lacks written script. The social system of the Asur tribe is divided into three types, namely, Brij Asur, Birajiya Asur and Agaria Asur who are basically iron smelters by profession. Being one of the minority groups of Jharkhand, the Asur tribe at present, is dominated by the local dialects and other languages.

A study of Asur folklores and dance forms reveals how they are imbedded with lofty morals and preachings. Their own cultural beliefs, their own faith, their own deities, their historical past, their festivals and festivities, their dress and habitat, their life stories—all find expression in these cultural forms. Their folk songs are for each festival and season. Thus, they have a separate song for each occasion and the songs are loaded with meaning apart from being morally charged.

One of the reasons why the language of Asur tribe could not survive on its own is poor academic support. This is a major factor behind the death of any indigenous language. Since these languages have no institutional support, they lose their speaking audience and hence, decay. Also, its orality has also contributed to its ephemeral nature. Asur, as a tribe of Jharkhand also became a part of the politics of exclusion that Jharkhand as a state has been a victim of. The hierarchy of language and culture of states, where one state and its culture is prioritised over others, has always been in practice.

Role of Technology in its Revival

Eisenlohr in *Language Revitilization and New Technologies: Cultures of Electronic Mediation and Refiguring of Communities*, (2004) writes:

> Studies of language loss and revitalization frequently stress the important role electronic mediation of discourse can play in situations of language shift. In particular radio and television broadcasting in dominant languages has been described as contributing to language shift away from lesser-used or minority languages, making the task of reestablishing the latter as a routine medium of everyday interaction... (Eisenlohr, 2004, p.23)

Eisenlohr categorically identifies the role of electronic media in language revival. Such methods can provide a large platform to the language speaking community. Also, such platforms can be made available to the speakers anywhere anytime. So, the use of radio, television in promoting any lesser known language works effectively. He further writes:

> Such recordings of sound and image can provide richer and more multidimensional records especially in the fields of phonology and prosody, as well as in performative and interactional contexts of use as compared to print media. These records are then available for future reconstruction of linguistic practices in the lesser-used language at a time when no proficient speakers are living, providing material for the relearning of the linguistic variety in question. Another area

> for the use of computer technology is the teaching of lesser-used or minority languages, in particular the search for easier and less costly ways of creating and disseminating teaching materials in endangered languages, such as books, sound recordings, and digital material combining text, sound, and graphics components. (ibid,p. 24)

Such kind of methodology is not just cost friendly but also provides reading material for multiple use. The recording in the form of audio or video appeals to more than one of our senses and has a deeper impact on the viewers/listeners. Also, teaching the same language from a book and from an audio clip is never the same. Reading any language from the book requires its literacy whereas the audio-visual medium encourages us to imbibe the language in our day to day activity first. That gives an advantage to such dying indigenous languages as it will get incorporated in their lives first than in their academics.

Methods Adopted for Reviving the Language

One of the methods by which the Asur tribe has tried to revive their dying language is the printing of calendars in the Asur language. Both the pictures have been captured by Abhijit Mohanty in his article 'Asuri: Holding on to a vanishing language' in *India Together*. The picture inside the calendar is that of Sarhul festival celebrated by them. A calendar can be easily found in our household and is still an important medium of marking dates and appointments. Even though smart phones and smart watches have replaced calendars for many of us, yet the printing and selling of calendars still exist. So, printing calendars in Asur language is definitely going to impact the speakers of the language in getting further acquainted with it.

Asur tribal right activists are continuously coming forward to preserve their language. The recording of Asur songs is being encouraged. Most radio programmes are being aired in the Asuri language. Slowly, attempts are also being made to impart primary education to the tribal kids in their own language. These are some encouraging developments in the field of revival of decaying language.

In *India Together*, Abhijeet Mohanty's report on the 9 August 2021, pays tribute to the day for being globally celebrated as International Day of World's Indigenous People. He quotes Tijjan Muhammad-Bande, President of the UN General Assembly, Department of Economics and Social Affairs, 'Every fortnight at least one indigenous language vanishes from the Earth.' So revival of indigenous languages is the pressing need of our times.

Asur Tribe as a Community

Papia Sengupta in *Language as Identity in Colonial India* (2018) points out as to how language identity has always been at the centrestage of any politics. It has and will always remain critical to the debates of 'citizenship, belongingness and upward mobility in society.' Hence, Asuri language certainly works as an identity marker not only at the individual level but also at the community level. Non-recognition of any linguistic identity, therefore, is a source of discrimination and exclusion. In this direction, a Conservation-cum-Development (CCD) plan has been framed by the government as well. As far as the policies of the government are concerned, the Ministry of Tribal Affairs has already implemented the scheme of Development of

Particularly Vulnerable Tribal Groups (PVTGs) exclusively for their upliftment. Annual plans are to be prepared for the PVTGs based on their need assessment report. The ministry too has strong intentions to conserve and develop the Asuri language.

The steps taken by the Asur tribe also speak volumes about their own self as a community. A close observation of their celebration of festivals shows their will for community living. The dance that they perform on any festive occasion such as *Sarhul* shows them holding hand, matching lyrics and dance steps with one another. That the tribe is coming forward to save its dying language through various practical means reveals that they are not just silent spectators. They did not wait for an invocation to drive them to take this initiative ahead. The entire practice so far has been personal and collective. The Asur tribes have laid the foundation of how one can save a dying language as a community. They are actually a source of inspiration for all the language lovers.

When David Crystal notes down the reasons for formation of a 'global language', he is not concerned with the number of speakers of that language. Rather it depends on who those speakers are. The Asur language is still struggling to find a solid base. The younger generation of the tribe has started to take recourse to speaking the state language. This only contributes to what Amartya Sen calls 'compounded disadvantage' of those who are already disadvantaged. We cannot, at least for now, afford to dismiss the politics of dismissal in which language plays such an important role. To quote Mahesh Dattani, 'All of us want to be a part of a society, of mainstream but we must acknowledge that it is a forced harmony.' (Dattani, 2010, p. 7) The Asur tribe's history is revealed through its long lost traditions. Except for the measures taken by some tribal activists, this endangered language was on the verge of dying and losing its identity.

The community's unique way of promoting its history, legend and other cultural aspects through oral mediums like folklore and dance forms, is a welcome step in its revival. It is equally true that fluent speakers of this heritage language are hard to find. However, expecting a drastic change at the very outset would be an impractical approach. The state language is certainly responsible for preventing it to flourish.

The younger generation prefers to speak the dominant language. For every such small tribe when it comes to language, survival is their main concern. This tendency has certainly made the task difficult for those who are working on this language and trying to document it. More than just the documentation, the revitalisation of such endangered languages should happen on a large scale. Joshua Fishman in *Stabilizing Indigenous Languages* (1996) says, '... an intergenerational mother-tongue transmission which helps in community building, and that is what is essentially required, in and through the beloved language.' (Fishman, 1996, p 72)

REFERENCES

Alsehri, A A (2016). Language Revival: Significance, strategies, Methods and Issues. *European Journal of English Language and Literature Studies.* 4(6),53-65.

Austin, Peter K, and Sallabank , Julia (2011). *The Cambridge Handbook of Endangered Languages.* Cambridge University Press.

Crystal, David. (2000). *Language Death.* Cambridge University Press.

English as a Global Language. Cambridge University press

Dattani, Mahesh. (2010). *Final Solutions.* Surjeet Publications

Eisenlohr, Patrick. (2004). Language Revitilization and New Technologies: Cultures of Electronic Mediation and the Refiguring of Communities. *Annual Review Anthropology* . 33, 21-45

Fishman, Joshua. (1996). *Maintaining Languages: What Works and What Doesn't, Stabilizing Indigenous Languages.* Flagstaff, Northern Arizona University Press.

Elaine Woo. (2001) Kenneth Hale, 67; Legendary Linguist. *Los Angeles Times.* https://www.latimes.com/archives/la-xpm-2001-oct-24-me-61058-story.html

Katan, David. (1999). *Translating Cultures: An Introduction for Translators, Interpretors and Mediators.* Routledge.

Mohanty, Abhijit. (2021, August 9). Asuri: Holding on to a vanishing language. *India Together.* https://indiatogether.org/asur-language-society

...*An Asur Calendar,* published by the Asur Adivasi Wisdom Akhra in Gumla District [Photograph]. *India Together.* https://indiatogether.org/asur-language-society

....Manita Asur and Sushma Asur Recording Songs [Photograph]. *India Together.* https://indiatogether.org/asur-language-society

Pattanayak, D.P & Ivan Illich. (1981). *Multilingualism and Mother-tongue Education.* Oxford University Press.

Sengupta, Papia. (2018). *Language as Identity in Colonial India.* Palgrave Macmillan.

Rushdie, Salman. (1991).Commonwealth Literature Does Not Exist. *Imaginary Homelands.* Granta Books.

Williams, Raymond. (1989). *Marxism and Literature.* Routledge.

CHAPTER 3

Subjugation of the Uncivilised A Case Study of Jungle Mahals

Asmita Khalkho

In 1765, the English East India Company (EIC) acquired the Diwani rights over Bengal and Bihar which included the strategic forest and mountainous buffer zone that demarcated the British possessions from that of the Marathas. Initially, for administrative convenience, the company officials divided this region into two divisions: the Jungle Tarai and the Jungle Mahals. Subsequently, in 1780, the Jungle Tarai division was dissolved and many of its constituents were merged with the Jungle Mahals. In general, it consisted of the districts from both, the Bengal and the Bihar provinces. The Bengal portion comprised the 'British possessions and some dependent chiefdoms lying between Birbhum, Bankura, Midnapore and the hilly country of Chota Nágpur'.[1] The Bihar portion on the other hand comprised the Chotanagpur estate and its dependent parganas and other forest areas. Geographically, Jungle Mahals formed a transition zone between the semi- acquatic rice plain of

1 https://cdn.s3waas.gov.in/s38e82ab7243b7c66d768f1b8ce1c967eb/uploads/2020/11/2020110321.pdf

the Gangetic delta and the rolling uplands of the Chotanagpur plateau. The soil here was highly infertile and cultivation was mostly confined to hollows containing soil suitable for culture. The frequent occurrence of flood and drought along with the dry climate made subsistence quite precarious in these parts. Most of the districts produced only two crops a year, while some districts like Ramgarh produced only one crop. Subsistence here was therefore characterised by a close integration between settled cultivation, pasture and forest.

Background

By the middle of the 18th century, Jungle Mahals sort of stood like an outpost of Hindu civilisation inhabited by the "tribals', the adivasis or first settlers, most of whom had not been assimilated into the Hindu or Muslim society'.[2] The main occupants of the western jungles of Bengal were the *Santhals* and *Bhumijs*. Further west, towards Chotanagpur, the population consisted primarily of the *Mundas* and *Oraons*. Initially, these tribes inhabited a small area which was nothing more than a forest clearing. With ti.e. their habitation developed into villages, which expanded their territorial base. Socially and administratively, these villages were closely associated with each other.[3] Years of living in close proximity with the plains, however, brought about certain institutional changes in these villages. The frequent incursions from the neighbouring plains,

2 Marshall, P.J., Bengal: The British Bridgehead Eastern India 1740-1828, Cambridge, 1987, p. 42.

3 Chaudhari, B.B., 'Tribal Society in Transition: Eastern India 1757-1920' in Munshirul Hasan and Narayani Gupta (ed), India's Colonial Encounter, Manohar, Delhi, 2004, p. 105.

compelled them to establish contact with the different villages of their own tribe scattered throughout the region, to organise a common defence. This led to the establishment of specific institutions like the *Manki* and *Parha* systems.[4]

State formation in this forest zone can also be attributed to their association with the plain countries. By the time EIC came into the picture, the region already consisted of various dynasties ruling over their forest kingdoms. Their emergence, however, cannot be ascribed to a single process. While some of these principalities were founded by the migrant groups through invasion or conquest like the Chero kingdom of Palamu,[5] others like the Barabhum Raj resulted from a 'constructive coagulation of traditional socio-political units of the Bhumijs'.[6] With regard to the Chotanagpur Raj and Mallabhum, there are theories of internal evolution as well as external factors which led to their establishment.[7] Apart from

4 Munda villages by batches generally of 12 came to be grouped together as a patti with the strongest and most influential amongst the headmen as the Manki or the patti chief. (Sarat Chandra Roy, The Mundas and their Country, Asia Publishing House, 1968, p.73) Similarly, in Oraon villages, Parha was a federation of seven, 12, 21 or 22 villages, over which there was a raaja who was the headman of one of the villages. (Sarat Chandra Roy, The Oraons of Chota Nagpur, Ranchi, 1915, p. 30)

5 Virottam Balmukund, *The Nagbanshis and the Cheros*, Munshiram Manoharlal, New Delhi, 1972, pp.23-24.

6 Sinha, Surajit, 'State Formation And Rajput Myth In Tribal Central India' *in Man in India*, vol. 42, No. 1, 1962, pp 41-42.

7 According to tribal traditions, the founder of Chotanagpur Raj was a son of a Munda Chief, whereas according to Brhamnical traditions he was a son of a certain Pundarika Nag who took the shape of a Brahman. According to K.S. Singh, Chotanagpur Raj was founded by one of the scions of Dravida Kawardha Nagbanshis (Chattisgarh-Vidarbha Region) when they were ousted by the Gonds in the 14th century. (K.S. Singh, 'The Chhotanagpur Raj, Mythology, Structure and Ramification' in Surajit Sinha (ed) *Tribal Polities And State Systems In Pre-Colonial and North Eastern India*, Calcutta, 1987, p. 62.

the tribes, certain groups from the plains also successfully carved out an area of influence in these forests like the *Sadgops.*[8] They were mostly concentrated in the forest tracts of Birbhum, Burdwan, Bankura and Midnapur where they became the largest agricultural castes and later founded the Midnapur Raj. Although by this ti.e. the rulers of these forest kingdoms claimed *kshatriya* status and were known as *Rajas, Thakurs* or *Tikaits*; the possibility of their tribal origin or lower caste origin in case of the *Sadgops*, cannot be ruled out.[9]

The establishment of these forest kingdoms was also accompanied by certain changes in their administrative mechanism. For example, in Barabhum, the principality was divided into *tarafs* under *tarafdars,* which was further subdivided into numerous tracts under subordinate chiefs called *sadiyals*. Under the *ssadiyals* were the *ghatwals* or village headmen. Within the village were the *paiks* who operated as foot soldiers under the guidance of the *ghatwals, sadiyals* and *tarafdars*. Although these kingdoms appeared to be quite similar to their plain counterparts, they were more like military administrative units[10] and still contained certain vestiges of the tribal institutions.

---

8 They were originally the dissident gops who belonged to a ritually unclean pastoral caste. (Hitesranjan Sanyal, *Social Mobility In Bengal,* Calcutta 1981, p.82.)

9 For example, while the brahmanical tradition of Mallabhum projects projects the first Malla raja as the son of a Rajput Kshatriya raja from the north; the Bagdis (semi-aboriginal group) regard him as one of their own. (Hitesranjan Sanyal, 'Mallabhum', in Surajait Sinha (ed) *Tribal Polities and State Systems in Pre-Colonial Eastern and North Eastern India,* Calcutta, 1987, p.77) Similarly, in the case of the Nagbanshis, the tribal traditions project the first king as the son of the daughter of a Munda Chief while the brahmanical tradition portray him as the son of a certain Pundarik Nag who took the shape of a Brahman. The process of hinduisation among the tribes simultaneously resulted in their departure from their tribal roots in their genealogy.

10 Sinha, *Op. Cit.*, p. 73.

For instance, *tarafdars, sadiyals* and *ghatwals* were considerably tempered by the existence of territorial councils of elders at all levels, where people met in an egalitarian atmosphere.[11]

Amidst all these changes, there were certain sections of tribes who never became a part of these forest kingdoms like the *Santals.* They organised reclamation of forest lands and cultivation under their autonomous chiefs called *Majhis.* Similarly, according to SC Roy, the establishment of the Chotanagpur estate also could not suppress the democratic instincts of the *Mundas* for long and some of them marched southwards and established a village named Khunti. Some went east and occupied the the Panch Parganas consisting of Silli, Branda, Rahr, Bundu and Tamar. Further east, they occupied the Parganas of Jhalda, Bygonkudar, Bagmari and Patkum.[12] These groups paid a certain nominal contribution to the Maharaja beyond which they had very little interaction with the forest principalities.

Prior to the British entry into this region, Jungle Mahals occupied a significant place under the Mughals due to its strategic placement. Although the jungle principalities were a threat to the Mughal state, they were also the natural defence against the Marathas. The Mughals, therefore, tried to maintain a delicate balance between subjugation and concession with the jungle chiefs. While it sent military expeditions to defeat the rajas, it allowed them to retain control over their territory. The Mughal state in fact developed a peculiar structure to

11 *ibid*, p. 44-46.

12 Roy, *The Mundas*, p.88

accommodate these forest kingdoms within the administrative apparatus as a vassal principality which paid a fixed tribute. Hereafter, the rajas were referred to as *zamindars* and were issued title deeds, which granted them the right to possess territories by virtue of office rather than hereditary rights. Initially the rajas were designated as *peshakash* paying *ghair amli zamindars,* but were later converted to revenue paying *amli zamindars.*[13] They were also conferred with the status of *Killajat zamindars,* which allowed them to build forts.[14] However, the most important measure employed by the state to assert its authority over these principalities was, the imposition of fixed annual tribute. Despite all these measures, the Jungle Mahals remained practically independent during the Mughal times and represented an inner frontier that was within the ambit, but beyond the effective governance of a large centralised state.

British Strategy in the Period of Transition

Unlike the Mughals, the EIC from the very beginning was keen to bring this region under its immediate control for various reasons. Firstly, to protect the nearby plain areas from the jungle chiefs and their subjects who often attacked and pillaged the agricultural produce, which caused financial loss to the company. Secondly, the region had a strategic value because it extended upto the borders of Bengal, Bihar and Orissa and contained routes that led to the Deccan. The possession of this region was, therefore, necessary for

13 Sanyal, *Op. Cit.*, pp.86- 87. *Ghair amli zamindars* were the *zamindars* who by imperial decree enjoyed the right of ruling their territory hereditarily as autonomous landlords paying a fixed amount of money by way of tribute.

14 Ibid, p.81.

the authorities to make it a buffer state against Maratha aggression. Thirdly, it had certain economic value because it contained forests with valuable trees like sal etc. Fourthly, the Indian merchants transported salt clandestinely through this region; so the authorities wanted to make arrangements to check illicit trade by establishing check posts. Thus, the company realised that it was necessary to bring this frontier within the effective administrative control of the government.

The company began its forays into the Jungle Mahals by sending an expedition under the command of Mr. Fergusson in 1767 to reduce the *zamindars* to the west of Midnapur. He was instructed to settle revenue with the *zamindars* individually and accept their subordination. Those who refused were to be expelled.[15] While some of the *zamindars* like those of Kalianpore and Phulkusuma agreed to make the settlement; others like those of Jhargarm and Ghatsila put up a resistance to preserve their autonomy. It was the attitude of the latter, which provided the company with a dual opportunity to display the superiority of their arms and also set an example of 'lenity and moderation, with a view of engaging others to a cheerful submission and allegiance' to the government.[16] In case of the Jhargram *zamindar*, Fergusson gave him 24 hours to surrender; and occupied his largest stronghold at Radhanagar, thereby, compelling the zamindar to surrender.[17] The advance

15 Firminger, W.K., (ed.), *Bengal District Records Midnapur (BDRM)*, vol. 1, Calcutta 1914, no. 109,p. 82.

16 Pri.e. J.C., *Notes on the History of Midnapur*, Calcutta, 1876, p. 37.

17 *Ibid.*, p. 41.

of the troops and the news of their tyranny caused much terror among the zamindars and brought many to submission.[18] The *zamindar* of Ghatsila, however, proved to be the most obstinate and refractory of all the jungle *zamindars.* He tried all means, from breaking the roads to barricading all narrow passes by felling the trees and even offering a bribe of Rs 5000 to safeguard his autonomy. After much struggle, however, Fergusson took possession of the fort of Ghatsila and apprehended him. His nephew Jagannath Dhal was proclaimed the new *zamindar* of Ghatsila and an annual settlement was concluded with him.[19]

The officials soon realised the futility and impracticality of pursuing every *zamindar* separately. They, therefore, adopted another method and stationed a force in central place in order to keep the inhabitants in awe of its military strength. The method bore fruit and Fergusson successfully made settlements with many jungle *zamindars.* The measure also brought about the voluntary submission of *zamindaris* like those of Patkum and Singhbhum who were subjected to regular oppression by their neighbours. It was in fact the first time that these *zamindaris* were brought under subjugation as they had never been reduced under the Mughals. The same method was applied again in 1774 by Captain Crawford who was assigned to protect the provinces of Bribhum, Burdwan, Bishnupur and Pachet. He fixed his camp at Jhalda, which was most centrally located and crushed the growing opposition from the *zamindars* of Jeypor, Jhalda and Bygonkudar. Captain Crawford also introduced another tactful method of inviting the

18 Firminger (ed), *BDRM*, L.N. 109, pp. 36-37.

19 Pri.e. *Op. Cit.*, p. 51.

rajas to attend his camp and performed a ceremony to install other *zamindars* in place of those who were obstinate. The measure provided the obstinate *zamindars* with a channel to make their submission. In order to deter the *zamindars* from taking recourse to violence in future, Crawford banished the *zamindar* of Jhalda by way of example. He was, however, granted a small village from his *zamindari* to prevent his being compelled through necessity to plunder. This deterred the *zamindars* who thought that anarchy could restore the country into their hands and assured them that they could expect no benefit from an open opposition.[20]

Patkum provided another interesting example of how the British officers employed tact and diplomacy to suppress the opposition in the Jungle Mahals. By the time Crawford marched, he understood that 'In Mountaneous [sic.] Conquests where there principal resource is Concealment, It is only possible to Compel the Chiefs to submit by making the Inhabitants who may fall into their Possession Prisoners & resting their being released on the submission of their Chiefs … as these are relations to the People Confined.'[21] He therefore collected nearly three hundred prisoners before the chiefs of Patkum came in. In order to prevent the *zamindars* of Jhalda, Jeypore, Bygonkudar and Bagmari from breaking into a revolt in his absence, Crawford carried their chiefs and soldiers along with him. However, to conceal his intention of taking them hostage, he organised them into a corps under the leadership of their chiefs and a daily allowance agreeable

20 West Bengal State Archives (WBSA), *Provincial Council of Revenue at Burdwan (PCRB),* vol. 8, letter dated 10 June 1775, p. 189.

21 WBSA, *PCRB,* vol. 8, letter dated 10 June 1775, p. 189.

to their ranks. They were dismissed only when the situation was under control.[22] Crawford also conferred material benefits on the subjects of Patkum for their support and obedience as he believed that people there had no 'conception of those finer and more gentler bonds by which more civilised people were attached to the state. It was [therefore] requisite to work on their minds by the grossed Power of immediate Interest.'[23] In districts where the *zamindars* were influential, he distributed numerous gifts among the leading men, which ensured the subjection of the entire community. However, in districts where the community had assumed unlimited independence, he used the chiefs to bring them within the bounds. He also engaged in extraordinary indulgence while confirming the chiefs in their lands and even took hostages from them until he was convinced of their loyalty after the troops were withdrawn from their quarter.[24]

The presence of unconquered districts in the vicinity of the subdued districts also created much anxiety among the officials. For example, even though peace was restored in Patkum, Crawford was apprehensive that 'the adjoining Independent Countries of Tamar and Singboom will in Resentment for the submission of that Country commit such violence on it as will add considerably to the other difficulties attending the collections by compelling the Inhabitants to ply to their Retreat amongst the Hills and prevent the Cultivation…'[25] He,

22 Ibid.
23 *Ibid.*
24 *Ibid.*
25 WBSA, *PCRB*, vol. 13, letter dated 4 March 1776, p. 84.

therefore, took hostages from several chiefs till they fulfilled their economic obligation. The Resident of Jhalda expressed similar concern and stated, 'The nearer each Zamindary is situated to an unconquered District the greater the Chance of Disturbances occurring in such zamindars.'[26] In order to preserve peace, he subjected those districts to a lighter assessment that lay close to Tamar, Barabhum and Singhbhum. In an attempt to prevent the depredations from these districts, he proposed the zamindars to enter into a league of offensive and defensive for 'Each zamindar singly would be vulnerable to the constant invasions of a superior force while collectively they will not only be able to repulse but severely Punish any of the neighbouring independent Inhabitants, who may commence Hostilities ...'[27] government, however, understood that these were only temporary solutions and therefore, sent expeditions to establish control over those independent districts as well. In Barabhum, for instance, Capt Briscoe destroyed 'immense quantities of gram, and Several villages' to 'distress all the poor inhabitants' in order to compel the raja to surrender.[28] The raja, however, continued with his refractory behaviour and was finally dispossessed of his *zamindari*. Similarly, Major Crawford marched into Tamar and launched an offensive. The inhabitants, unable to resist his progress were finally compelled to surrender, but, on the condition that they would not be delivered to the criminal court for trial of their past

26 WBSA, *PCRB*, vol. 22, L.N. 302, dated 22 November 1777, p. 113.

27 WBSA, *PCRB*, vol. 27, L.N. 314, dated 17 December 1778, p. 201.

28 WBAS, *PCRB*, vol. 5, letter dated 14 December 1774, p. 4.

depredations. Crawford consented to their terms as the object of the government was only to ensure the tranquility of Tamar. He also directed the people of Tamar to demolish the numerous strongholds which they had built and to return the plunder which they had captured from the adjoining territories.[29]

The company tried to keep the jungle *zamindars* under check by concluding a revenue settlement with them as payment of tribute, and rent also formed an important substance of submission. Surveys were conducted and collectors were instructed to make enquiries about the state of cultivation, actual amount collected, expenses occurred in collection, etc. to fix a reasonable revenue. The company from the beginning asserted that the main motive behind fixing the revenue was to 'Establish a peaceable and regular government over the inhabitants of that Country, not to burthen them with heavy taxes for the Sak [sic.] of increasing the Public Revenue.'[30] Several experiments were conducted in the sphere of revenue settlement like farming settlement, annual settlement, etc. to collect revenue. In 1790, the Jungle Mahals were settled completely for 10 years. However, as Hunter later stated, it in vain to expect the ancient rajas, encumbered with all the costly paraphernalia of their petty courts and military retainers to suddenly transform themselves into punctual tax-collectors.[31] Thus, whenever an opportunity arose these jungle rajas withheld their revenue. In order to keep these tendencies under check, the government stationed *sepoys*

29 WBSA, *Governor General Council (GGC)*, vol. 172, letter from Mathew Leslie, Collector of Rampur, dated 14th July 1789, p. 2166.

30 WBSA, *GGC*, vol. 20, L.N. 259, p. 463.

31 Hunter, W.W., *Bengal MS Records*, Vol. 1, 1782-1793, London 1894, p. 100.

and constructed police stations in several districts to keep the chiefs in awe of the Company. The measure was deemed not only necessary for the purpose of preserving the peace but also for the protection of the Collector.[32] In certain districts, the Company appointed their own representatives like *tahsildars* to collect revenue and maintain peace. Although these *tahsildars* were local people and were mostly maintained by the *zamindars* themselves, they were always regarded as the Company's servants.

The Effect of British Strategies

It is evident from the above descriptions that the EIC deployed numerous techniques to establish their authority over this region. Despite their efforts, the Jungle Mahals could not be brought under complete subjugation during the 18th century and there are several reasons for this; first and foremost being the environment. The thick forests and the climate posed the greatest challenge to the British troops. The government had resolved to send an expedition to Midnapur in 1766, but it was only in 1767 that the expedition took effect due to the onset of rains. The climate thus, played an important role in slowing down the pace of British advance. Colonial records contain numerous complaints regarding climate from the officers posted in different areas. For example, Charles Morgan posted at a camp in Haldipukur described it as the 'shockingest weather' that he ever saw in his life. He further wrote that his spies fell sick continually and that he was obliged to turn doctor himself and gave 'Furlington's drops' for all kinds of

32 WBSA, *Committee of Revenue (CR)*, vol. 52, letter dated 3 March 1785, p. 50.

disorders.[33] Similar opinion was shared by the Collector of Ramgur who found its climate 'very unfavorable'.[34]

The unfamiliarity of the troops with the jungle proved to be their major drawback and was exploited by their opponents to harass them. Despite having superior technology and knowledge at their disposal, British troops appeared helpless before their enemies and it took them some time to learn the tactics of jungle warfare. They were baffled and amazed at the same time by the new mode of combat.[35] Often the inhabitants resorted to methods like felling trees and burning villages to obstruct troops.[36] The villages and the surrounding areas were burnt to starve the enemy by depriving them of all possible means of food supply.[37] The military detachments were, thus, always under the necessity to carry a large supply of provisions when they entered a hostile country. All these limitations finally compelled the Company to look for other methods to restore order in the Jungle Mahals. It was hoped that lenient conduct on the part of the government towards the zamindars in general would be the means of bringing back 'the most violent amongst them to

33 Firminger (ed.), *BDRM*, vol. 2, Calcutta, 1915, L.N. 379, p. 96.

34 WBSA, GGC, vol. 96, letter dated 10 March 1986, p. 216, L.N. 180.

35 Firminger (ed.), *BDRM*, vol 2, No. 359, p. 78. Captain Charles Morgan, In charge of the Jungle Mahals in 1768 described his experience in the following words '...they have not the least idea if fighting; they are like a parcel of wasps: they endeavour to sting you with their arrows and fly off. It is impossible almost to kill any of them, as they always keep at a great distance and fling their arrows at you, which, you may suppose, seldom or ever to any execution. As the thing is to frighten these fellows as much as possible, I wish you would send one of the one-pounders with a pair of the new wheels as soon as possible. It will be necessary to keep that gun... which I believe will be of more service than an extraordinary company of sepoys.'

36 Firminger, *BDRM*, vol. 1, Calcutta, 1914, No. 127, p. 97.

37 Pri.e. *Op. Cit.*, p. 43.

a proper Sence [sic.] of their duty as well as retaining others, from throwing off their allegiance.'[38] Gradually, therefore, the government began to apply force as the last resort. For example, in 1780 when the recalcitrant chiefs raised disturbances in Palamu, Captain Crawford did not not resort to military action immediately. Instead, he wrote to the chief 'representing the folly and ingratitude of his conduct in the strongest colours' and 'assuring him of entire forgiveness should he return to his duty'.[39] The recalcitrant chiefs later returned and matters were settled without violence. Although in some cases it appeared to be too lenient a punishment, yet it guaranteed an effectual stop to anymore excesses. In case of the Tamar insurrection in 1789, the collector ordered an advertisement to be pasted where the recalcitrant *majhis* resided, ordering them to come in immediately and represent their grievances, or troops would be sent to punish them. When the *majhis* refused, the collectors prepared to launch an offensi.e. but before that, he deputed an officer to investigate into the cause of the disturbance and to 'assure the People who have joined the Mankees of a Strict and Speedy redress of any Grievances provided they will return quickly to their respective villages'.[40] In some cases the government even announced rewards to apprehend the criminals.[41] The conciliatory efforts of the government gradually bore fruits and led to the submission of many people who had actively participated in the rebellions and disturbances. After some ti.e. the inhabitants also became exhausted of the constant

38 WBSA, *GGC*, vol. 57, L.N. 493.

39 *Ibid.*, vol. 56, L.N. 433.

40 *Ibid.*, vol. 172, letter dated 14 July 1789, p. 2163.

41 *Ibid.*, vol. 200, L.N.3, P. 39.

state of unrest and participated actively in apprehending the rebels.

Another significant challenge that the company faced during this time were the growing incidents of banditry. Banditry served as an important means of procuring subsistence in this region as the precarious environment rendered subsistence difficult. Besides, it also played an important role in establishing the authority of the rajas for when the available cultivable land was insufficient for grants, the rajas embarked upon predatory warfare for securing honour, fame, booty and new lands over which they could rule, and which they could then grant to the supporters.[42] Thus, banditry became an important means for procuring economic resources and consolidating economic power. Politically, banditry acquired a different role under the Company whereby, it was used more as a means to regain autonomy that the jungle rajas enjoyed prior to British intervention. Banditry during this period was characterised by mass participation. The British demand for increased revenue and their policy of dispossession and confinement on failure to pay revenue left little hope for the *zamindars* to sustain themselves. To maximise their profit, the company embarked upon the policy to reduce the number of intermediate landholding like those of the *ghatwals* and *paiks*.[43] The measure thus ejected a class of *raiyat* out of the existing economy by depriving them of their means of subsistence.

42 Dirks,Nicholas B., 'From Little Kings to Landlord: Property, Law and the Gifts under the Madras Permanent Settlement', in *Comparative Studies in Society and History*, CUP, vol 28, No. 2 (April 1986), p. 312.

43 WBSA, CR, vol. 32, letter dated 20 September 1783, p. 264.

Against the backdrop of economic erosion, thus, emerged a kind of social coalescence erupting violently in search of social means of living.[44] For example, in 1776 when the *zamindar* of Bogri was deposed for arrears of revenue, he along with his *paiks* committed depredations on the neighbouring rajas of Raipur and Simlapal.[45]

An interesting feature that emerged during this period was the coalition between the people and the bandits. According to Marshall, it was the resistance to alien rule and the hardship and dislocation which seems to have acted as a unifying force between them.[46] This brought about a change in the character of these depredations in terms of leadership whereby apart from the disgruntled subjects, now even the dacoits looked upto the *rajas* for guidance. The dacoits mustered substantial followers and rallied around *zamindars*, small and big, like Jagannath Dhal of Ghatsila, *rajas* of Bishnupur and Burdwan, some of whom were given the derogatory title of 'Robber-Chief'. The *zamindars* derived dual benefits out of this coalition, first, those who sponsored the robbers enriched themselves with spoil of the plunder, and second, those *zamindars* in whose jurisdiction robbery was committed could claim exemption from the payment of the stipulated revenue.[47] The coalition created a broad spectrum of inter-district liaison, which the robbers could not have built unless supported by the *zamindars* or by the society at large. An interesting picture of this inter-district

---

44 Sen, Social Banditry, p. 24.

45 Das, Civil Rebellion, pp. 66-68.

46 Marshall, Bridgehead, p. 97.

47 Sen, Ranjit, *Social Banditry in Bengal: A Study in Primary Resistance 1757-1793*, Ratna Prakashan, Calcutta, 1988, pp. 32-46.

alliance of bandits is, however, represented by a section of people called the *chuars*. *Chuars* inhabited the region between Ghatsila and Barabhum and were originally *bhumijs* from the Jungle Mahals of Midnapur and other adjoining tracts of the *pargana*. They comprised the local militia of the *zamindars* and tilled their *paikan* lands in peaceful times. A letter from the collector of Midnapur described the *chuars* as inhabitants who 'are bred up as much for pillaging as cultivating, and pay a quit rent from the profits of both occupations …'[48] the British officials used the term *chuar* as an expression for the *zamindar's* men who practiced robbery in other districts and not their own. The *thanedar* of Bulrampore even went to the extent of equating them to *'Dekoits'*.[49] The Company records contain numerous references to the disturbances committed by the *chuars* throughout this period. Thus, Banditry became an important means in this period to defy British authority.

The company tried various methods to control the situation and their most effective strategy was the enrollment of disgruntled *paiks* in the Indian regiment. The Company raised a *paik* militia from the bewildered *paiks* to quell the disturbance in this region. *Paiks,* who were regarded as the most dreaded foe by the British authorities were thus transformed into loyal and efficient army of the Company. Several *thanas* were also established in the interior to keep the trouble at bay. However, all these measures still proved to be inadequate. Often the *paiks* along with the Company troops became indisciplined and committed excesses on the subjects, much to the dismay of the

48 Pri.e. *Op. Cit.*, p. 67.

49 WBSA, *CR*, vol. 33, dated 3 October 1783, p. 249.

authorities. Even the number of *thanas* were insufficient and undermanned to keep an effective watch over the area.[50] The frequent transfer of the battalions further added to the woes. According to the Collector of Ramgur, 'relieving the Battalion every year,... prevents the Commanding Officers from getting a Sufficient knowledge of the People and Country to enable them to act with proper effect, and takes off that dread that people would naturally have of an officer by whom they had once been worsted.'[51] The presence of independent districts within this region and Marathas in the border, further defied the British attempt to maintain peace, as it provided the malcontents with a safe retreat when pursued by the forces. The division of the country into various administrative divisions proved to be yet another hurdle. For instance, in Bogri, the disobedient *chuars* eluded the pursuit by taking refuge in the neighbouring districts of Midnapur and Bishnupur where the officer's couldn't follow them without special orders.[52] These situations rendered the police helpless even if it knew where the enemy had taken refuge. As a result resistance in various forms continued to raise its head during the entire period under study.

Another faction that strengthened the opposition of the jungle inhabitants against the Company were the Marathas. Their inroads into the British territory were a matter of great concern for the government. The officers stationed in the jungle districts had a dual task of driving them out and preventing the *zamindars* and other malcontents from collaborating with them. In 1772, when they attacked Chotanagpur, the

50 Sen, *Op. Cit.*, p. 102.

51 WBSA, *GGC*, vol. 162, letter dated 20 June 1789.

52 Firminger (ed.), *BDRM*, L.N. 532.

Company immediately deployed a military force to chase them out. However, some of the local rajas like those of Tori and Burwa assisted them. In fact, Raja Mukund Singh of Ramgur was very much in league with them and it was believed that the Marathas probably came at his invitation.[53] Although the government wanted to prevent such events from recurring, it was also aware of the fact that it was almost impossible to expect unwavering loyalty from its subjects, and that it was important to formulate other means to prevent this fatal alliance. It, therefore, devised a policy to reduce the power of the refractory border chiefs like those of Bundu, Tamar and Burwa and reduced the number of vassals they maintained to deter them from providing assistance to the Marathas.

The attempt of the Company to assert its dominance through revenue collection was also restricted by certain circumstances. The lack of exact evaluation of the districts greatly impaired the Company's ability to extract proper revenue. According to an official posted at Jhalda, 'The land in these Parts never having been measured it cannot be ascertained with any exactness what quantity of cultivated or waste ground is in each District this entirely prevents the Revenue being levied by the Bega or any fixed modes adapted in the Low Countries...'[54] Therefore, they became highly dependent on the revenue papers maintained by the local revenue officials which were soon discovered to be highly falsified. Desertions and migrations caused by natural calamities and rebellions also plagued the collections. Withholding the revenue infact became the most common method to express dissent. As early as 1768,

---

53 Virottam, *Op. Cit.,* pp. 136-138.

54 WBSA, *PCRB*, vol. 24, letter dated 28 March 1778.

Ghatsila was in arrears.[55] In 1779, there were complaints that the Chotanagpur raja had withheld the payment of revenue and had turned hostile.[56] Similar reports poured in from other districts as well. In response, some of the recalcitrant *zamindars* were removed and replaced by men worthy of trust. However, the policy of dispossession wasnot very effective as many powerful *zamindars* continued to hold sway in their respective *zamindaris* like those of Bogri and Palamu.[57] In case of Ghatsila, the Company even reinstated the recalcitrant *zamindar* to his *zamindari* because it knew that Gatseela will not be settled or free from disturbances so long as Jagganatt Doll is deprived of the zemindarry and inhabitants are prepossessed in his favour knowing him to be the lawfull [sic.] inheritor of Gatseela.[58] Besides, some of the replacements also proved to be tactless and incapable of keeping the *zamindari* under their proper control as they did not enjoy the confidence and attachment of most of the subjects as in the case of Palamu.[59]

55 Firminger (ed.), *BDRM*, vol. 2, L.N. 348, p. 70.

56 WBSA, *GGC*, vol. 56, L.N. 427, P. 267.

57 *Ibid.*, vol.74, Extract from the Proceedings of the Committee of Revenue, dated 5 May 1783. In Bogri, Zamindar Jadu Singh was replaced his son Chattar Singh, but still Jadu Singh continued to exercise his control over the zamindary 'in Contempt and defiance of the Authority of the regular Government.' Similarly in Palamu, although Gopal Roy, the former raja of Palamu, was confined at Patna, he was particularly instrumental in exciting his adherents to rebellion, by assuring them that it was the only means to obtain his release. *Ibid.*, vol. 55, LN. 283.

58 WBSA, PCRB, vol. 15, letter dated 3 June 1776, p. 64.

59 Virottam, *Op. Cit.*, p. 106. Gopal Rai was made the *zamindar* of Palamu but was unable to control it. Therefore, on the recommendation of Gopal Rai himself, the government decided that the revenue affairs be entrusted to Sugandh Rai and Gajraj Rai, relations of Gopal Rai until the conditions improved. The change eventually restored Palamu to its former prosperity.

In the wake of all this, the British authorities came to believe that the only means to ensure steady obedience and subjection of the inhabitants of the Jungle Mahals, without incurring a heavy cost on account of maintaining troops and sending expeditions, was by making them civilised. They attributed the rebellious disposition of the citizens to their uncivilised state. The British policy makers believed that the inhabitants could be civilised by being induced to take up cultivation, which would provide them with a stable means of subsistence and obviate the necessity of depredations and other forms of violence. While deliberating on the plan to appoint civil collectors in the jungle districts, the government emphasised their role to provide encouragement to agriculture and commerce. It was remarked, 'By Measures of this nature, the Country will not only be enriched, but civilised, and its Dependence on the Government better Secured than merely by the presence and awe of a military force.'[60] Therefore, various methods were adopted to promote agriculture such as grants of waste lands with nominal assessments, etc. In Bogri, the government made advances under the head of *Bazee Jungul Serinjam* to keep the poor people employed and prevent them from having recourse to improper methods of obtaining subsistence.[61] These measures brought dual benefits to the company; on the one hand it pacified the 'violent' inhabitants, and on the other it improved the revenue. However, the

---

60 WBSA, *GGC*, vol. 8, L.N. 17.

61 WBSA, *CR*, vol. 47, letter dated 16 November 1784, p. 185. *Bazee Jungul Serinjam* were advances made at proper season on the part of the government for various crops, which when collected are sold and carried to the account of the revenue.

implementation of these methods was somewhat restricted due to certain inherent difficulties like poor fertility of the soil and adverse climate. For instance, with regard to the state of agriculture in Ramgur, the collector remarked, 'From the nature of the Country being so very hilly there are very few spots that will admit of cultivation - they have only One Crop in the year.'[62] Thus, although the British authorities perceived agriculture to be the only solution to the problems; in reality it was the poor state of cultivation which was the root cause of all the problems. Resource mobilisation through plunder was just another means of procuring subsistence. In fact, raiding was a recurrent feature of relationship between the hills and the plains, contributing both to the economy as well as the political power of the polities of this region.[63] In the context of the Jungle Mahals, violence, therefore, had a much deeper implication than what was understood by the Company. In the name of civilising the country, the British authorities attempted to simply substitute one form of subsistence with another.

In reality, the British officials wanted the forest dwellers to adapt more to the habits and occupations of the plain country, not because they considered the plain people civilised, but because they didn't pose much threat to the Company and were easy to control. In fact, James Browne in his India Tracts described the inhabitants of the plains as 'wretched' and 'spiritless' people who were 'neither formidable by character or situation'. The

62 WBSA, *GGC*, vol. 44, letter dated 28 August 1778, p. 382.

63 Alavi, Seema, *The Sepoys and the Company Tradition and Transition in Northern India 1770-1830*, OUP, 1995, p. 164.

British government, thus, developed an altogether different understanding of the term 'civilisation' to suit their needs, which was used merely as a tool to reduce 'disobedient' and 'violent' inhabitants into obedient and profitable subjects. For most British officials, the difference between tribes and castes was, therefore, not the one between the civilised and the wild, it was rather about different forms of wildness.[64]

Late 18th century, thus, represents a formative phase when the EIC was still trying to develop an effective strategy to establish its control over the Jungle Mahals. Even though it resorted to military tactics in the beginning, gradually it gravitated more towards a diplomatic approach. The shift not only proved to be more economical, but also proved to be very effective in the long run. Simultaneously, it also provided the British with the much needed time to get acquainted to the unfamiliar terrain and people and learn the basics of jungle warfare. It was this knowledge which later enabled the British to develop a better strategy to subjugate this region and counter the revolts which occurred in the later centuries. Simultaneously, it is also important to acknowledge the fact that even though the resistance offered by the inhabitants of the Jungle Mahals were scattered and sporadic, nevertheless, they were effective and slowed down the pace of the British advance. These acts of resistance not only kept alive the desire for autonomy and dignity among the jungle inhabitants, but also laid down the foundation for subsequent uprisings.

64 Skaria, Ajay, 'Shades of Wildness Tri.e. Caste and Gender in Western India', in the *Journal of Asian Studies,* vol. 56, No. 3, August 1997, p. 727.

REFERENCES

O' Malley, L.S.S., *Bengal District Gazetteer Bankura (BDGB)*, Calcutta, 1995, p.42

Marshall, P.J., *Bengal: The British Bridgehead Eastern India 1740-1828*, Cambridge, 1987, p. 42.

Chaudhari, B.B., 'Tribal Society in Transition: Eastern India 1757-1920' in Munshirul Hasan and Narayani Gupta (ed*) India's Colonial Encounter*, Manohar, Delhi, 2004, p. 105.

Munda villages by batches generally of 12 came to be grouped together as a patti with the strongest and most influential amongst the headmen as the Manki or the patti chief. (Sarat Chandra Roy, *The Mundas and their Country*, Asia Pubishing House, 1968, p.73) Similarly, in Oraon villages, Parha was a federation of 7, 12, 21 or 22 villages, over which there was a raaja who was the headman of one of the villages. (Sarat Chandra Roy, *The Oraons of Chota Nagpur*, Ranchi, 1915, p. 30

Virottam Balmukund, *The Nagbanshis and the Cheros*, Munshiram Manoharlal, New Delhi, 1972, pp.23-24.

Sinha, Surajit, State Formation And Rajput Myth In Tribal Central India *in Man in India*, vol. 42, No. 1, 1962, pp 41-42.

According to tribal traditions, the founder of Chotagpur Raj was a son of a Munda Chief, whereas according to Brhamnical traditions he was a son of a certain Pundarika Nag who took the shape of a Brahman. According to K.S. Singh, Chotanagpur Raj was founded by one of the scions of Dravida Kawardha Nagbanshis (Chattisgarh-Vidarbha Region) when they were ousted by the Gonds in the 14th century. (KS Singh, 'The Chhotanagpur Raj, Mythology, Structure and Ramification' in Surajit Sinha (ed) *Tribal Polities And State Systems In Pre-Colonial and North*

Eastern India, Calcutta, 1987, p. 62.

They were originally the dissident gops who belonged to a ritually unclean pastoral caste. (Hitesranjan Sanyal, *Social Mobility In Bengal*, Calcutta 1981, p.82.)

For example, while the brahmanical tradition of Mallabhum projects projects the first Malla raja as the son of a Rajput Kshatriya raja from the north; the Bagdis (semi-aboriginal group) regard him as one of their own. (Hitesranjan Sanyal, 'Mallabhum', in Surajait Sinha (ed) *Tribal Polities and State Systems in Pre-Colonial Eastern and North Eastern India*, Calcutta, 1987, p.77) Similarly, in case of the Nagbanshis, the tribal traditions project the first king as the son of the daughter of a Munda Chief while the brahmanical tradition portray him as the son of a certain Pundarik Nag who took the shape of a Brahman. The process of hinduisation among the tribes simultaneously resulted in their departure from their tribal roots in their genealogy.

Sinha, *Op. Cit.*, p. 73.

ibid, p. 44-46.

Roy, *The Mundas*, p.88

Sanyal, *Op. Cit.*, pp.86- 87. *Ghair amli zamindars* were the *zamindars* who by imperial decree enjoyed the right of ruling their territory hereditarily as autonomous landlords paying a fixed amount of money by way of tribute.

Ibid, p.81.

Firminger, W.K., (ed.), *Bengal District Records Midnapur (BDRM)*, vol. 1, Calcutta 1914, no. 109,p. 82.

Pri.e. J.C., *Notes on the History of Midnapur*, Calcutta, 1876, p. 37.

Ibid., p. 41.

Firminger (ed), *BDRM*, L.N. 109, pp. 36-37.

Pri.e. *Op. Cit.*, p. 51.

West Bengal State Archives (WBSA), *Provincial Council of Revenue at Burdwan (PCRB)*, vol. 8, letter dated 10 June 1775, p. 189.

WBSA, *PCRB*, vol. 8, letter dated 10 June 1775, p. 189.

Ibid.

Ibid.

Ibid.

WBSA, *PCRB*, vol. 13, letter dated 4 March 1776, p. 84.

WBSA, *PCRB*, vol. 22, L.N. 302, dated 22 November 1777, p. 113.

WBSA, *PCRB*, vol. 27, L.N. 314, dated 17 December 1778, p. 201.

WBAS, *PCRB*, vol. 5, letter dated 14 December 1774, p. 4.

WBSA, *Governor General Council (GGC)*, vol. 172, letter from Mathew Leslie, Collector of Rampur, dated 14 July 1789, p. 2166.

WBSA, *GGC*, vol. 20, L.N. 259, p. 463.

Hunter, W.W., *Bengal MS Records*, Vol. 1, 1782-1793, London 1894, p. 100.

WBSA, *Committee of Revenue (CR)*, vol. 52, letter dated 3 March 1785, p. 50.

Firminger (ed.), *BDRM*, vol. 2, Calcutta, 1915, L.N. 379, p. 96.

WBSA, GGC, vol. 96, letter dated 10 March 1986, p. 216, L.N. 180.

Firminger (ed.), *BDRM*, vol 2, No. 359, p. 78. Captain Charles Morgan, In charge of the Jungle Mahals in 1768 described his experience in the following words, '...they have not the least idea if fighting; they are like a parcel of wasps: they endeavour to sting you with their arrows and fly off. It is impossible almost to kill any of them, as they always keep at a great distance and fling their arrows at you, which, you may suppose, seldom or ever to any execution. As the thing is to frighten these fellows as much as possible, I wish you would send one of the one-pounders with a pair of the new wheels as soon as possible. It will be necessary to keep that gun... which I believe will be of more service than an extraordinary company of sepoys.'

Firminger, *BDRM*, vol. 1, Calcutta, 1914, No. 127, p. 97.

Pri.e. *Op. Cit.*, p. 43.

WBSA, *GGC*, vol. 57, L.N. 493.

Ibid., vol. 56, L.N. 433.

Ibid., vol. 172, letter dated 14 July 1789, p. 2163.

Ibid., vol. 200, L.N.3, P. 39.

Dirks,Nicholas B., 'From Little Kings to Landlord: Property, Law and the Gifts under the Madras Permanent Settlement', in *Comparative Studies in Society and History*, CUP, vol 28, No. 2 (April 1986), p. 312.

WBSA, CR, vol. 32, letter dated 20 September 1783, p. 264.

Sen, Social Banditry, p. 24.

Das, Civil Rebellion, pp. 66-68.

Marshall, Bridgehead, p. 97.

Sen, Ranjit, *Social Banditry in Bengal: A Study in Primary Resistance 1757-1793*, Ratna Prakashan, Calcutta, 1988, pp. 32-46.

Pri.e. *Op. Cit.*, p. 67.

WBSA, *CR*, vol. 33, dated 3 October 1783, p. 249.

Sen, *Op. Cit.*, p. 102.

WBSA, *GGC*, vol. 162, letter dated 20 June 1789.

Firminger (ed.), *BDRM*, L.N. 532.

Virottam, *Op. Cit.*, pp. 136-138.

WBSA, *PCRB*, vol. 24, letter dated 28 March 1778.

Firminger (ed.), *BDRM*, vol. 2, L.N. 348, p. 70.

WBSA, *GGC*, vol. 56, L.N. 427, P. 267.

Ibid., vol.74, Extract from the Proceedings of the Committee of Revenue, dated 5 May 1783. In Bogri, zamindar Jadu Singh was replaced his son Chattar Singh, but still Jadu Singh continued to exercise his control over the zamindary 'in Contempt and defiance of the Authority of the regular Government.' Similarly in Palamu, although Gopal Roy, the former raja of Palamu, was confined at Patna, he was particularly instrumental in exciting his adherents to rebellion, by assuring them that it was the only means to obtain his release. *Ibid.*, vol. 55, LN. 283.

WBSA, PCRB, vol. 15, letter dated 3 June 1776, p. 64.

Virottam, *Op. Cit.*, p. 106. Gopal Rai was made the *zamindar* of Palamu but was unable to control it. Therefore, on the recommendation of Gopal Rai himself, the government decided that the revenue affairs be entrusted to Sugandh Rai and Gajraj Rai, relations of Gopal Rai until the conditions improved. The change eventually restored Palamu to its former prosperity.

WBSA, *GGC*, vol. 8, L.N. 17.

WBSA, *CR*, vol. 47, letter dated 16 November 1784, p. 185. *Bazee Jungul Serinjam* were advances made at proper season on the part of government for various crops, which when collected are sold and carried to the account of the revenue.

WBSA, *GGC*, vol. 44, letter dated 28 August 1778, p. 382.

Alavi, Seema, *The Sepoys and the Company Tradition and Transition in Northern India 1770-1830*, OUP, 1995, p. 164.

Skaria, Ajay, 'Shades of Wildness Tri.e. Caste and Gender in Western India', in the *Journal of Asian Studies,* vol. 56, No. 3, August 1997, p. 727.

CHAPTER 4

A Priest and a Prince
Defining Self and the Other

Vandana Madan

Anthropology has been called the study or science of man and primitive cultures, or what has been in our discipline often called the 'Other'. The word Anthropology has been used in an academic sense from the 17th century onwards. Towards the middle of the 19th century, Anthropology came to be seen as a discipline that studied the emergence and development of man from the physical, cultural, and social points of view. To make the social sciences more acceptable, there was a general tendency to make them more 'scientific' in their outlook. So too it was for Anthropology. It turned to already existing theories of evolution, the study of language and semantics as well as statistical documentation, all of which seemed a good way of rooting the discipline in more acceptable 'scientific' terms. To understand how the discipline emerged, it may help to take a brief look at its growth, which has been intrinsically bound with colonial expansion.

In the 15th century, the era of world discovery began under the European powers. We all know that this exploration and discovery ranged from the Americas to Asia and Africa.

Following industrialisation, the agents of industry i.e., trade and commerce, began a search for raw materials and the new markets to sell their goods. This search often sent the Europeans far and wide. As economic activity grew, it also gradually set the base for political expansion and domination. At the same time the agents of imperialism also recognised the need to study the way of li.e. the languages, customs, and practices of the people over whom they were trying to establish control.

Besides this need to know for the political dominion and administrative purpose, there was also the desire to proselytise the unknown 'Other'. Thus, some of the earliest information was gathered not only by the travelers, explorers, and administrators, but also by missionaries who accompanied these expeditions.

So, if we look at India from the 14th to the 16th century, travellers, and explorers such as the Portuguese Duarte Barbosa or the Frenchman Jean Baptiste Tavernier described not only the India that they saw, marvelling at its caste system and religious practices, but also seeing the colonised as savage and barbarian. There were other works by administrators like Sir Charles Metcalfe and Sir Thomas Munro, who in the 19th century, wrote of India as a land of self-sufficient village republics. Their documentation work played a critical role in influencing the colonial and administrative policy in India.

By the 19th century, we find that these 'primitive/other' societies had not only become the meeting ground of the colonising imperialists and missionaries, but also raised the curiosity of the European philosophers who saw these societies as prime examples of man living in a state of nature. This idea helped strengthen the European notion of superiority that enabled these powers to dominate other nations.

It is this image of the 'savage other' that beckoned scholars to distant shores, and it is their initial attempts at understanding the unknown land and those 'Other' communities that inhabited these lands, which eventually gave birth to the discipline of Anthropology as we know it today. Towards the end of the 19th and in the early 20th century, the branch of social anthropology had begun to take shape and the method of fieldwork leading to ethnographic writing was emerging. Many significant contributions made this possible.

For instance, James Hunt in 1863 founded the Anthropological Society, which was expected to concern itself with the collection of facts and the identification of natural laws that explained the diversity of humankind as also the study of the physical as well as the cultural aspects of humans. No scholar is, however, believed to have made the whole European world more conscious of the 'Other' than Sir James G. Frazer, a Scottish social anthropologist, who made governments aware of the need to know the value of the culture they colonised and thus, governed. In his *The Golden Bough,* Frazer assimilated data about themes of myths and rituals found among the ancient Greek and Latin works and then defined them as common to simple societies. Frazer's work deeply influenced the lives of young scholars in England, some of whom took it upon themselves to engage in ethnographic research of the most detailed kind.

While anthropologists were thus, establishing themselves in the field as experts on primitive cultures, not all who made anthropology what it is today were trained to be anthropologists.

There was an interdisciplinarity that was central to the foundation of Anthropology. Significant contribution came from what is known as the Torres Strait expedition in 1898, under the leadership of A.C. Haddon.

This was the first anthropological expedition with a view to cover all aspects of the life of a community in New Guinea. Haddon was both an anthropologist and ethnologist. He was accompanied by his daughter, Kathleen, and colleagues. Among them was a doctor, W.H.R. Rivers. Rivers was trained in psychology and was interested in carrying out neurological studies on the natives of the Torres Strait islands. During his wanderings on the islands, Rivers began collecting family histories and constructing genealogical tables. Little did he know that his diary notings would one day give birth to seminal work on native kinship systems in the field of Anthropology.

There are many other examples of such brave scholars. I call them brave, for they travelled into the length and breadth of the accessible and the inaccessible, describing what they saw, sometimes reflexively, sometimes judgmentally, sometimes even losing life and limb, but all the while committed to the mission of gathering and sharing information about new cultures and communities that made up the world of the unknown 'Other'.

The work of these early scholars made seminal contribution to the growth of Anthropology because of their use of the ethnographic method. This method, which is the corner stone of the discipli.e. was refined and dominated by the contributions of two scholars who gave it its present character and influenced the future of the discipline. These were Bronislaw Malinowski and Sir A.R. Radcliffe-Brown.

The British anthropologist, Sir A.R. Radcliffe-Brown, was

deeply influenced by the evolutionary theory and the analogy between biological systems and social organisms. He believed that the anthropologist's duty was to seek a functional unity between parts of a whole and this unity could be seen or understood only by living in a society and observing its parts, by doing fieldwork. Radcliffe-Brown also has the distinction of bringing to the world the Andaman Islanders with whom he spent two years (1906-1908), highlighting their diverse language, religion, culture and social organisation. His work, *The Andaman Islanders. A study in Social Anthropology*, published in 1922 was devoted to understanding the Andamanese, not as fragmented groups, but as parts of an organic unity. He was also the teacher of many significant future scholars including M.N. Srinivas.

On the other hand, Bronislaw Malinowski, a Polish anthropologist, is credited with some of the most significant ethnographic work in the discipline and pioneering the method of personal diary and record keeping. Malinowski was a student of James Frazer and Radcliffe-Brown. While Radcliffe-Brown was studying the Andaman Islanders, Malinowski was busy in the same years working among the Melanesians in Papua New Guinea.

His study of these islanders and their way of life became a passion for him and from his fieldwork emerged some of the most in-depth studies of a society and its customs and culture. In 1914, he travelled to Papua New Guinea and was stranded on the islands due to the outbreak of the WW I. Malinowski was not allowed to return to Europe, and Australian authorities gave him two options: to be exiled to the Trobriand Islands, or to face internment for the duration of the war. Malinowski chose the Trobriand Islands. It was during this period that he conducted his fieldwork on the methods of economic and ritual exchange among the islands, and advanced the practice of participant observation and keeping a diary. His work and methods, remain to this day, the hallmark of ethnographic research found enshrined in his monumental work on the *Argonauts of the Western Pacific.*

There were others too like Franz Boas, the American regarded as the father of modern anthropology, who published his *The Central Eskimo* in 1888 and set the highest standards for ethnographers. He lived among the Eskimo from 1883-1884; E.E. Evans-Pritchard who began his career with field work in 1926 with the Azande, a people of the upper Nile; Leo Frobenius who made significant contribution to ethnographic research under the German tradition and engaged not only in travels, but also collected significant artifacts for ethnographic museums. In fact, his collection of about 4700 pre-historical African stone paintings is currently in the museums in Germany.

Boas, like Frobenius, spent a large part of his career collecting artifacts for American museums. However, while Frobenius was fascinated by the idea of collecting artifacts as representing cultures, Boas was deeply critical of this act of displaying artifacts in museums and he found strange ways of protesting. It is believed that in 1894, he even placed himself on exhibition in the Smithsonian Museum diorama, reenacting a ceremonial dance of the Kwakiutl Indians.

And we think public and 'live' installations are a modern idea!

As can be seen, fieldwork for these scholars like many others was an emotional and moral engagement with people, not just an act of data gathering. As fieldwork and ethnographic studies began to take shape, interesting facts and personal experiences began entering into the diary of the fieldworker. Reflexivity gave the fieldworker a more human and personal face while at the same ti.e. it made the anthropologist more self-critical in his aim to stay objective.

Over the 20th century, the colonial knowledge-power thesis that argued how there was a clear connection between anthropological knowledge and the expansion of colonialism, received much attention in western academia. For instance, in 1965, the famous French sociologist, Claude Levi-Strauss, in an address to the Smithsonian Institute spoke of the legacy of Anthropology as emerging from a colonial and racial mind. He said that Anthropology was the daughter to an era of violence. Similarly, Talal Asad, the historian, argued that Anthropology was rooted in an unequal power encounter between the West and the Third World. It is important to remember that such encounters were nevertheless critical because they allowed ethnographic and historical knowledge of the colonised domains to be gathered and enabled the colonisers to 'know' and administrate territories, albeit at the cost of freedom and equality.

This brings us to the second part where the focus is on India. Anthropology was established in India by Sarat Chandra Roy, lawyer and anthropologist. He was close to the missionaries and administrators, but he still questioned the colonial mindset.

Roy spoke of the need to have empathy for the subjects rather than be dependent on western tools. He argued that we need to remember that India and her 'tribes' of primitive people were not of a single kind and not easy to describe nor define because of the fluidity of their social, cultural, and geographical boundaries.

Not far behind was the work and contribution of the anthropologist Nirmal Kumar Bose who joined the Calcutta University in the 1920s. He was trained in Geology and then Anthropology. Bose was closely associated with the freedom movement and Gandhian politics. As a scholar, he believed in the importance of fieldwork and in its scientific spirit that encouraged his students to be deeply engaged with their work. He believed that academics had a critical role to play in bringing about social change and transformation. Influenced by scholars like Franz Boas, he stressed that the anthropologist must engage in cross cultural comparison to enable social reconstruction. Writing on tribes in India, he argued that they were closely related to the Hindu society and were assimilated over time through a process of acculturation or what he called as the Hindu method of tribal absorption.

When examining the relationship of tribes with the wider society, archive documents often tell us of how the British opened up tribal areas to missionaries, money lenders and merchants. New descriptions of the tribal communities emerged from such contact, describing their isolation and assimilation in relation to a wider society that Bose had also written about. Often the idea of isolation raised the question of whether these communities were really isolated making it difficult to know the 'Other' or was it a convenient way of not having to understand the social structure or cultural world of the Other? Or was it just easier to club the communities together into the Other that was 'savage and barbarian' and opposed to the more civilised 'Self' rather than attempt to understand this world of different identities and ways of life. A world where there were spirits, gods and ancestors for illness and well being;

where there were shamans, sorcerers and witches that blessed and begot. However, everyone who worked on this world was not of the same thought. Many engaged with the tribals not just as academics or administrators, but also experientially.

In this context, two scholars were directly associated with the tribes of Central and North-East India. The engagement that these scholars had with India in academic and administrative capacities played an important role in defining how they perceived the tribal world and, in the process, also shaped their personal lives.

Verrier Elwin was a British priest and writer whose involvement with the tribal people highlighted the opposing viewpoints held within the Indian scholarly society. Elwin was the son of a Bishop. He studied Theology and English at Oxford. In 1926, he was ordained and joined the Anglican Seminary. Instead of taking a scholarship that Oxford offered him, he chose to join the Christa Seva Sangh and came to India. This was an offshoot of the Church of England and focused on indigenising Christianity. Soon, he had joined Gandhi and the Indian National Congress. In 1932, wanting to spend his time working with the people, he went to live among the Gonds in Madhya Pradesh. While he was there, he felt a deepening sense of rejection of both Gandhian ideals and Christian values. As he got more engaged with his new world, between 1936 and 1955, he published critical ethnographic studies and two novels on the cultural lives and customs of the Gonds. He published works about the Baigas in 1939, the Agaria Gonds in 1941 and other works on tribal li.e. agriculture, social and familial practices. His work spoke for the voiceless tribals. The more he lived with them, the more he saw the world through their eyes, eventually marrying Kosi and later Lila, both Gondis. He lived in Bastar from 1940-42 and then in Orissa from 1943-48, constantly searching for tribes to study and protect. Deeply troubled by what he experienced as he traveled, he drew attention to how the tribal or hill people had been ignored.

In 1954, Elwin became an Indian citizen and was also appointed Advisor to the Indian government with reference to the tribes of the hills of the North-East Frontier and moved to Shillong. Elwin was a great supporter of hill tribal traditions and spoke up against government policy and Hindu nationalists. As Nehru's policy maker on the tribal situation, Elwin believed that a higher truth could be found by looking at the 'Other' and preserving their cultural identity. He proposed that the tribal regions of the North-East be declared Excluded Areas where the plainsmen could not interfere. His Philosophy for NEFA in 1957, outlined what the government could do to protect the tribes of the NE.

Not understanding that Elwin spoke from living within the tribal world, many leaders and Indian scholars reacted calling him an isolationist or exclusionist, whose ideas were aimed at keeping the tribes of the North-East away from development. Elwin also had a confrontation with social reformers who wanted to stop tribal dances, other rituals and cultural differences.

Between 1940-50, he had several debates with Indian scholars, of which the most violent one was with the social anthropologist G.S. Ghurye. Ghurye's motivation was his nationalist desire to challenge and correct what he saw as the mischievous misinterpretation of Indian society and history by colonial scholars. He wrote a book on the situation calling it the *Burning Cauldron of the North-East.* He believed that Elwin was artificially separating the tribes of the North east from the Hindu Society. While Elwin was a protectionist, Ghurye, an integrationist, accused him of wanting to create 'anthropological zoos'.

According to his biographer, Ramchandra Guha, Elwin was gravely misunderstood for he only saw himself as a man '...poised between two worlds and well placed to interpret one to the other' (2007, p. 335). For Elwin, the tribals were not laboratory specimen. He firmly believed that the work of the scholar was to lead administrative reform and improve the lives of the people he studied otherwise it is failed work. He also believed in the importance of living with the people and joining in their distress and celebrations. Guha quotes Elwin stating that for him Anthropology did not just mean fieldwork but it was his whole life as an experience of engaging with the people. Elwin is believed to have remarked, 'You cannot observe mankind from the howdah of an elephant' (ibid, 341).

Another such scholar was Christoph von Furer Haimendorf. He was born to an Austrian elite upper-class (and so the reference to him as a prince). In 1927, he entered the Theresianische Akademie of the University of Vienna to follow courses in Anthropology and Archaeology. Among the German stalwarts who taught him was also Leo Frobenius, who has been mentioned before.

Haimendorf was a Research Assistant in Vienna between 1931 and 1934. He was keen to work in India and went to the London School of Economics where scholars like Bronislaw Malinowski were also present. Although inspired by Malinowski, Haimendorf was also critical of the functional approach. He left London for

India in 1936, hoping to work among the Nagas of Assam.

Haimendorf worked in the North-East region for over two years, but after 13 months of field-work he returned to Austria. Not happy there too, he soon returned to India, not realising how Malinowskis's life and his were entwined experientially. While on his way to the Naga hills to carry out new research, the Second World War broke out. When Malinowski found himself in the Trobriand Islands during the First World War, he chose to remain there and produced some of his most brilliant work. Haimendorf had a German passport and was detained by the authorities. He was sent off by the British to the Hyderabad State under the jurisdiction of the Nizam. He may have not chosen to be among the Gond but he did end up being where Elwin started out.

Given his background and engagement with the people, he soon found himself appointed the Advisor for Tribes and Backward Classes to the Nizam's government. From 1941 onwards, Haimendorf spent several years among the Raj Gonds in this district. Like Malinowski in the Trobriand islands, while he was among the Gonds, Haimendorf is believed to have done some of his best ethnographic work among tribal communities such as the Chenchus, Reddis and Raj Gonds.

Haimendorf may have had to leave the North-East but his ethnographic work, engagement with the people and intellectual curiosity left an indelible mark. His deep engagement with the cultural lives and social welfare of the tribal communities was so significant that the government offered him the post of Special Officer and Assistant Political Officer to the North-East Frontier Agency. He was now able to go back and do fieldwork among the remote areas. This is where he produced his critical work on the Apa Tanis of the Arunachal Pradesh. He conducted in-depth fieldwork in 1944 and 1945.

All of his work, whether on the Gonds region or the North-East region, was critically acclaimed in terms of the richness of the reflexive description of the lives of the people he studied or chose to be with. Haimendorf was a deeply curious man and this enabled him to, as it were, 'get between the sheets'. However, often, he was accused like Elwin of getting too involved with his subjects.

There is an anthropological 'urban myth' that says that decades after he had left India, some inquisitive anthropologist came to work on the Nagas. One of the questions asked, of course, was whether they were head hunters. It is believed they replied they once were but had given up. However, if a man called Haimendorf ever came back, they would go straight back to head hunting and begin with him because of the questions he asked them and his ethnographic inquisitiveness.

The trajectories of the lives of Elwin and Haimendorf were such that where one ended, the other began. So, while Elwin began among the Central tribes and married Kosi, and then Lila, the daughter of a Gond Pradhan, he lived in the North-East till he died in 1964 and his ashes are immersed in the Siang River in Arunachal Pradesh. On the other hand, Haimendorf began his career in the North-East and ended up among the Gond. He did not marry a Gondi woman, unlike Elwin, but he and his wife Elisabeth's ashes are entombed according to Gond custom in Marlavai village, Adilabad district that was home to the Haimendorfs when he did his ethnographic work among the Gonds. The tribals have built a statue of the couple in Marlavai village.

This chapter highlights how as an ethnographer one had to struggle to be objective and acknowledge one's effect on the society being studied and at the same ti.e. find connections with those one was studying. Of course, much of ethnography stresses on the importance of distancing from the subject/Other, keeping roots in objectivity, but ultimately, the life of the ethnographer shapes the outcome of their research as does their research shape them, often making the anthropologist a more empathetic interpreter in cross-cultural dialogue.

In some way, the anthropologist's reflexivity allows the ethnographer in him to become emotionally and physically involved with his subject matter and gives the subject and its interpretation a new meaning.

Ethnographic writing is an anthropological journey; more than just a piece of fact gathering and research; more than just an exploration of those under scrutiny; it becomes, so to say, an outlet for the anthropologist/author to reflect back and forth, sometimes excluding oneself, and at others, immersing oneself in a delicate balance of storytelling.

REFERENCES

Alsop, Christiane K. (2002, September). Home and Away: Self-Reflexive Auto-/Ethnography

[55 paragraphs]. Forum Qualitative Sozialforschung / Forum: Qualitative Social Research [On-line Journal], 3(3). Available at: http://www.qualitative-research.net/fqs/fqs-eng.html https://www.researchgate.net/publication/251821590_Home_and_Away_Self-Reflexive_AutoEthnography

Cohn, Bernard.S.(1988). *An Anthropologist among the Historians and other essays.* New Delhi: Oxford University Press.

Deshpande, Satish, Uberoi Patricia and Sundar Nandini. (Eds). (2007). *Anthropology in the East: Founders of Indian Sociology and Anthropology.* (Ed.) New Delhi: Orient Blackswan Pvt.Ltd.

Digitalcommons.macalester.edu. 2022. [online] Available at: <https://digitalcommons.macalester.edu/cgi/viewcontent.cgi?article=1549&context=himalaya> [Accessed 13 March 2022].

Elwin, Verrier. (1992) *The Agaria.* New Delhi: Oxford University Press.

Elwin Verrier. (2007). *The Baiga.* New Delhi: Gyan Publishing House.

Frazer, James.G.(1987) *The Golden Bough: A Study in Magic and Religion.* New York: Random House Publishing.

Fürer-Haimendorf, Christoph von. (1990). *Life Among Indian Tribes: The Autobiography of an Anthropologist.* Delhi: Oxford University Press.

Ghurye, G.S. (1980). *The Burning Cauldron of North-East India.* New Delhi: Popular Prakashan.

Guha, Ramchandra. (1999). *Savaging the Civilized: Verrier Elwin, His Tribals, and India.* Chicago: University of Chicago Press.

Guha, Ramchandra. (2007). Between Anthropology and Literature: The Ethnographies of Verrier Elwin. In Satish Deshpande, Patricia Uberoi and Nandini Sundar (Eds), *Anthropology in the East: Founders of Indian Sociology and Anthropology (pp.330-359)*. New Delhi: Orient Blackswan Pvt.Ltd.

Manuscripts, A., 2022. *Christoph von Fürer-Haimendorf.* [online] Therai.org.uk. Available at: <https://www.therai.org.uk/archives-and-manuscripts/obituaries/christoph-von-fuerer-haimendorf> [Accessed 13 March 2022].

Radcliffe-Brown, A.R. (1922). *The Andaman Islanders. A study in Social Anthropology.* Cambridge: Cambridge University Press.

CHAPTER 5

The Tribes of Bengal A Colonial Perspective

Sanjukta Naskar

The ethos of tribal history is manifested within its attitudes, cultures and aspirations. Tribes are universally considered to be the original inhabitants of any land. An entire cultural ethos has grown and developed around tribal lives and settlements. Tribes always have and some still continue to maintain a unique identity of their own. However, in the fast paced life of constant change, there is very little left for the tribes to express, or to find a voice in the cacophony of modern life. This saga of constant struggle began centuries ago, yet it continues to persist till today. The problem is not just of visibility, but carries a long history of exploitation and ruthless land grabbing. The initial inquiry (in the 19th century) into the state of the tribes in India along with collections in folklore and folk culture of the indigenous people was initiated by the British administrators. Along with governmental data collections were personal accounts, both professional and amateur, official accounts by colonial administrators, which became part of a huge body of documented literature. There were multiple reasons for making this huge library of information, namely administrative, gradual disappearance of rituals and cultures due to multiple factors, making additions to the library of the Folklore Society in London for a comparative study of various features of indigenous races and tribes. The census was introduced in England, Scotland and Wales in the early 19th century (1801) in order to settle the debate about population (Harvie and Mathew 2000:10). The census in India was also introduced to assess the population and the first census based on a direct survey of the population took place on 1 January 1853, in the North Western Province (which also covered present day UP) (Samarandra 2011: 5). An important and relevant observation was made with the Census:

> The late census showed how rapidly the old aboriginal faiths are being effaced, and what progress is being made in the absorption of the primitive races in the great system of Hinduism. At the same time the opening of communications, the increase in the facilities for travel, and the spread of education, are tending to obliterate the land-marks of the Hindu faith, to slacken the bonds of caste, and to provide occupations unknown to the ancient polity. There is nothing to be gained, and much to be lost, by postponing this important work. If it is not undertaken now, a mass of information of unsurpassed interest will be lost to the world (Risley 1892: iii)

Census was not just a document of statistical information but provided important insights into the caste system, of human habitat, ritual practices, and social order. The above statement makes it amply clear that the factors for the eroding of tribal cultures were manifold. The administrative process was pillared upon acts of documentation, which was the source of both control and understanding; and policies were made real and practical through a project as vast and as consuming as the census. True to its nature, a country as geographically vast and diverse as India with its multiplicity of culture and ethnicity could only be deciphered through close, intimate and detailed documentation. The systematic survey completed through immense toiling produced large body of literature which was handed down to posterity. An attempt has been made to understand the nature of the accumulation and documentation specifically like *The Tribes and Castes of Bengal* by H.H. Risley carried out extensively in the province of Bengal in the years 1885-1891. Risley's work has been particularly significant due to the scientific methodology that he applies in his analysis of the castes and tribes of Bengal. Risley's seminal work concerns the physiological differences that tribes would have created due to inter-tribal movement. It is also concerned with social mobility among the castes and tribes which would have generated a dilution of purity among them.

Collecting, Collating and Documenting

The approach to any kind of study of indigenous cultures and people began with the fundamental action of collecting, compiling and cataloguing. Conceived towards the beginning of the 19th century, a call for worldwide collection and compilation of indigenous cultures (as a marker for nation building) became a predominant debate among a new crop of investigators who may or may not have been directly involved with the indigenous cultures.

> The roots of ethnography lie in anthropological studies that focused on studying social and cultural aspects of small communities in foreign countries. The researchers lived among the inhabitants with the purpose of understanding the culture that these people shared. Thus, the classic anthropologists were foreigners in their field sites. (Eriksson and Kovalainen 2008, P. 149)

Age old rituals, songs, stories, marriage practices, divorce customs and cultural remnants of any kind were rigorously collected and researched upon. However, who were the principal researchers? And what inspired them to pursue such intensive and rigorous hunt for folkloric/anthropological material? Western education introduced formally by *Macaulay's Minutes* in 1835 in the British Parliament was a step towards consolidating and implementing a 'project for the refiguring and restructuring of society' (Mohan 829) through the introduction of English education. The spread of education, and through it enlightenment, became an attractive proposition among the educated youth of Bengal and among the British administrators, which led to a larger and more personalised involvement with the indigenous masses.

> As practitioners of the enlightenment theory of knowledge, the British civil servants began a scientific exercise of enumerating and classifying Indians. The underlying belief was that control of society depended upon a precise knowledge of the composition and location of its taxonomic system. The colonial administrator turned ethnographer began the comprehensive and time-consuming process of counting through census maps, statistical tables and

> pigeonholing and classifying people into races, tribes and castes. (Mohan 2002, P. 829)

However, within a global scope, it is understood to have started with 'an engagement of middle-class intellectuals, poets and writers with the narratives and songs that were common among the majority populace of a society, namely Germany, in transition from feudal to modern systems, and from small principalities to a nation' (Naithani 2010: 1). Therefore, most of the primary material collected was used either for a comparative study across cultures or had a strong socio-political implication creating national boundaries through cultural signifiers. Europe, which spearheaded the collection of the signifiers of the indigenous people became a guideline for similar efforts outside the European boundaries. India, on the other hand, projected a completely different scenario. By mid-19th century, India as a country was beginning to feel the impacts of colonisation. Across the Indian landscape, Christian missionaries and European traders were making inroads and impacting both social and religious life. However, anthropological documentation of indigenous life was hardly a concern among the people of the country. Feeble attempts were made as an emulation of their European counterparts. Educated men like Rev Lal Behari Day, Natesa Sastri towards the latter half of the 19th century began to collect folkloric material in the form of folktales and folklore. Lal Behari Day was well aware of the western scholarships which were being propagated in the field of folk literature, and therefore, he utilised his own association to western scholarship to promote textual accuracy, thereby conforming to certain western biases.

Never has folklore occupied itself with such active human imagination as the way it did during the 19th century. Many reasons and causes have been sighted and adequately established by folklore scholars regarding the significant upsurge, yet these scholarly interventions have always been limited by the fact that the 'folk' have led a neglected and marginalised existence. This phenomenon is common to not only the primary British-coloniser folklorists, but is also significantly obvious even among the subsequent native folklorists. The pedagogical approach to folklore was aimed to ascertain homogeneity that bound the people together and subsequently laid the basis for exploring nationalism through folklore. These collections made more than a century ago, have evolved, 'during which folklore has become transformed from a rather conservationist exercise in collection traditions to a radical enterprise which explores the dynamics of folk reproduction in the study of a variety of expressive forms' (Appadurai, Korom and Mills 1991: 4). The alternative 'expressive forms' becomes juxtaposed with the 'conservationist exercise' and thus, emerges the discourse of folklore.

However, the narrative of a national culture augmented through the cultural signifiers of folktale or folkore was not a preoccupation that was under consideration among the native folklorists in the 19th century, the few involved continued to do so probably in emulation of their western counterparts. The collection and compilation of indigenous cultures was actually taken up by the colonial administrators posted in various parts of the sub-continent due to multiple reasons. The discourse of nationalism, however, emerged only during the early decades of the 20th century, which was expressed through the projection of a pristine past signified through texts and stories of yore. The failure of the Revolt of 1857 became a legitimate reason for the politicians of the British Parliament to pay greater attention to the affairs of India. Another important dispensation of the occupation of the British administrative hegemonic legacy was the creation of tomes of data about the native population. This, as has been discussed by scholars, had multiple connotations: ethnographic data creation, better administration, application of the scientific methodology of ethnographic research, and so on.

Indigenous tribal and folkore collections, therefore, face an interesting twist in which folklore which is essentially globally taken as a document of national representation was documented in India by outsiders. Such material, therefore, in the initial stages at least did not aim to become representative of a national culture, it was only during the late 19th and early 20th century that scholars realised the potential of an unadulterated pristine past being spoken about. The 19th century is, therefore, dominated by collections made by colonial administrators, their family members, and by sporadic indigenous collaborators or in an individual capacity.

One of the major concerns of all tribal studies is defined through the narrative of loss and revivalism. Beginning from the 19th century with the concerted efforts of British administrators posted in various parts of the geographical landscape of India, research related to tribes and tribal affairs like that of folklore studies has been dominated by the doctrine of what has been lost and what are the means of recovery. In collaboration with the Folklore Society at London, a massive endeavour was launched in order to explore the indigenous cultures of India.

However, the research yielded at times rigorous study of the people, their cultures, and their position in society depending upon their caste, rituals and customs. Many questions and queries were developed during the process of exploration since a cultural outsider would have to be deeply involved in order to be a researcher. The caste system being one of the biggest hurdles and since so much of social life is incumbent upon caste affiliation that an in depth understanding was required. Part of the exercise of collection and compilation was also about being acquainted with the people, about being closely associated and also developing a sense of affinity and trust.

Methodology

Ethnographic research in India during the 19th century conducted by well-established ethnographers like H.H. Mai.e. Risley, Ibbetson have always maintained a systematic scientific approach stemming from their own training in the field.

> Most of the barbarous and semi-barbarous tribes which come under observation in India are at the present day fairly accessible, and the inquirer can as a rule get together as many specimens of them as he wants without undergoing excessive trouble or hardship himself. (Risley 1891: 238)

India continued to remain a land for providing pure data. The intermingling of races and castes as Risley concludes had not become a pressing reality and the threat of interracial marriages did not seem too emergent either.

> The institution of caste breaks up the population of the continent into a countless number of mutually exclusive aggregates of homogenous composition, and forbids a

> member of one group to marry within any group but his own. (Risley 1891: 239)

This homogeneity, at least among smaller groups or communities has over the centuries cocooned 'racial purity', which had drawn the attraction of the European ethnographers.

Risley, in his introduction, gives a very detailed account of the manner in which the research has to be done. He is very categorical that the entire duration of the collecting and compiling has to be done by a single officer. Also, in order to completely secure his preparations for collecting information, Mr Risley visited Mr Denzil Ibbetson, the Director of Public Instruction in the Panjab and Mr. J.C. Nesfield who was the inspector of schools in Oudh both of whom were experienced men in the field. In a conference held from 18-22 March, 1885, the aim for the collections was clearly stated:

> One chief object of our deliberations was to secure, so far as might be possible, that ethnographic researches carried on in different Provinces of the Bengal Presidency should proceed on the same general lines in order that their results might be of some service to students of comparative ethnology in Europe. (Risley 1892: iv)

Questionnaires were drawn out with the objective of extracting as much ethnographical details about the tribes of India as possible. Though the approach was heavily influenced by European standards and theories, yet they approached the research mechanism keeping in mind the conditions of India. The series of questions or heads of enquiry that was followed was the one prepared by a committee of Anthropological

Institute of Great Britain and Ireland in 1874. Risley also took as reference the set of questions prepared by Mr. C.L. Tupper's volume on *the Customary Law of Panjab*. The set of questions prepared explored minute issues with utmost detail that it would sometimes be difficult to distinguish between administrative utility and scientific interest.

Some of the key areas of research and probe were:

1. Early history of marriage
2. Development of family
3. Modes of relationship
4. Early history of inheritance
5. Growth of property in land

These areas of research were meant to throw light on ethnological problems of research that were already in discussion in Europe.

The relations of different castes to the land, their privileges with respect to rent, their relations to trade, their social status, their internal organisation, their rules to marriage and divorce—all these matters were intimately concerned with practical administration and its dispensation. Risley cites the example of distribution of famine relief material, which can be done more efficiently only if there is an adequate knowledge about caste dynamics. Food and its consumption (the manner in which food is served and what is being served indicates social structures and hierarchies within the family and outside) is an important indicator of Indian social orders. Therefore, it becomes amply clear that 'the more Government officers know about the religious and social customs of the people of their districts, the better able they will be to deal either with the possible social problems of the future, …' (Risley 1892: ix)

The methodology applied was a fully approved one by the members of the Lahore Conference and the execution equally meticulous. The entries were written in local vernacular of the census enumerators, which were then transliterated into English by the temporary clerks, who oftentimes wrote from dictation instead of reading the transcript. This was then set up in type from manuscripts and copied from transliterations. The local translator or sometimes scribes were also employed but rarely mentioned in the text. This, however, was not a fool proof method and opened doors to all kinds of errors of judgement since anything misread by a clerk might get transformed beyond all recognition. A thorough and meticulous documentation became essential and made the administrator cognizant of the importance of the role he played in the entire scheme of documentation.

The general perception regarding the collection and compilation was relegated to better and more efficient administration. Risley, however, stands to differ. He perceives that Indian administration will not be made more efficient by the 'elucidation of historical or pre-historic problems' (Risley 1892: vii), which he eventually also refutes. Compiling of such data did not have any direct bearing upon actual work of colonial administration and was considered to be the general perception. The general rule of administration, however, involves a direct and intimate association with socio-cultural condition of the people. Government rules are created and implemented effectively only after there is a close knowledge of people's social behaviour. The governmental requirement of systematic and practical policy-making factors cannot be fully ignored. Legislative and executive action, in order to be effecti.e. must touch upon the ethnographic relations in a fully satisfactory manner. Therefore, a record of the customs of the people plays a vital role in executing land reforms or land survey. The census, therefore, played a key role in providing necessary statistics.

Genealogy of the Tribes

However, collecting data and analysing it led to key questions being asked about the genealogy of the tribal people, their customs, cultures and rituals. Of what remained as an extant from being heavily influenced by surrounding Aryan, Hindu, Islamic cultures due to cultural assimilation happening for many centuries. The key areas of disruption in following the practices of primitive behaviour were also identified.

> It was apprehended that the rate of spread of education, and the growth of practical intelligence in India, may lead within the next generation, to the abandonment of many practices which were of special interest to ethnologists. (Risley 1892: vi)

The issue of Hinduisation was real and practical one.

> A whole tribe of aborigines, or a large section of a tribe become gradually converted to Hinduism without … abandoning their tribal designation. This is what is happening among the Bhumij of Western Bengal. Here a pure Dravidian race have lost their original language, and now speak only Bengali: they worship Hindu gods in addition to their own (tendency being to relegate the tribal gods to the women), and the more advanced among them employ Brahmans as family priests. (Risley 1892: xvii)

Cultural assimilation and social mobility became significant reasons for a gradual movement among tribal people to the mainstream. The caste based Hindus were definitely more dominant in the social order and a search for a better life is assumed to be the chief cause for the tribal aboriginals merging with the Hindus.

> There exists now in Orissa a caste, called Chattar-khai, recorded in the lists of 1881, which is made up of people who lost their caste in 1866 for eating in relief-kitchens (chattras). The caste is divided into an upper and a lower sub-caste marry within that group, irrespective of the caste to which they belong; but no intermarriage is possible between members of the two sub-castes. ... All Chattar-khais are entirely cut off from their original castes. (Risley 1892: viii)

There are many such examples in which new castes are formed due to social disruptions like the one mentioned above. As mentioned above, this trend can also be traced among the Bhumij and the Rajbanshis. During the time when Risley would have been making his field study, the Bhumij still retained some of their totemistic exogamous subdivisions, but with the passage of time and the rapid appropriation the Bhumij were beginning to forget their totems in favour of more aristocratic designations.(Risley 1892: xviii)

> The tribe would then become a caste, and will go on stripping itself of all customs likely to betray its true descent. The physical characteristics of its members will alone survive. (Risley 1892: xviii)

With the multiple reasons for appropriation, eventually, distinctive customs fall into disuse and the tribe after its promotion into the rank of a caste, breaks up into a number of endogamous groups like Tamudia or Tamara Bhumij, Haladipokharia Bhumij, Teli Bhumij and Desi or Dehuri Bhumij identified by the different traditional occupations. (Risley 1892: Foreword)

For Risley, the crucial point of distinction was the facial features and differences, which could be drawn despite inter-caste/tribe marriages. Typically, it would take two generations to completely dilute the original features. Rajbanshis and Bhumij are two instances of tribes in an early stage of transition whose antecedents could be traced accurately. The 19th century, therefore, becomes a crucial juncture of historical documentation. It is, however, also important to remember that Aryan invasion and assimilation has been happening for centuries and documentation of this kind carried out by the colonial administration occurs only in the 19th century. The process of dilution has been happening for a much longer period. It is only with the island inhabitants that any kind of purity of racial and tribal behaviour can be identified. The bifurcation into castes is not limited to the evolution of a single caste, 'but the tribe itself, after its promotion to the rank of a caste, breaks up into a number of endogamous groups, each of which practically forms a separate caste.' (xix) However, it is the unique physical characteristics which distinguished a tribe and according to Risley, a scientific methodology defining physical characteristics makes it possible to guess a man's caste within, of course, certain limitations. The fragmentation and the combining into castes was achieved through bonds of sympathy or interest which would have initially drawn the families together.

J. C. Nesfield in his *Brief View of the Caste System of the North-Western Provinces and Oudh* (1882) mentions that it was functionality alone which was the sole reason for the caste system. By functionality, Nesfield probably was referring to the role that the caste system played in society.

> It presupposes an unbroken continuity in the national life from one stage of culture to another, analogous to what has taken place in every other country in the world whose inhabitants have emerged from a savage stage. It assumes, therefore, as its necessary basis, the unity of the Indian race. (Risley 1892: xx)

Nesfield's theory was based on multiple levels of pre-suppositions, drawing primarily from historical documentation and linguistic variations. Risley, however, firmly believed that facial appearances were the true test of race. Risley successfully proceeds with his research by using the 'anthropometrical' methodology. His findings further consolidate his opinion that Indian conditions actually favour anthropometry. Anthropometry is a scientific study of measuring the human body. It was first developed in the 19th century as a method to study the variation and evolution of the human body. The inter-racial marriages would be appropriate to provide important clues to the study:

> In a society thus organised, a society sacrificing everything to pride of blood and the idea of social purity, it seemed that differences would find a peculiarly favourable field for its operations. (Risley 1892: xxvii)

This would ensure a successful documentation on racial purity since intermixing would be largely eliminated and racial purity would be assured. The proselyting influences of Hinduism was a real challenge as Risley observed that conversion to Hinduism actually erased much of the customs and rituals earlier prevalent among the tribes, '... but every tribe that passes within the charmed circle of Hinduism inclines, sooner or later, to abandon its more primitive usages or to clothe them in some Brahmanical usages.' (xxvii). However, the Aryan and aboriginal intermixing was least influenced among the lower castes, who were seen to still carry the primitive cultures, 'just as the oldest geological formations contain the simplest forms of organic life.' (Risley 1892: xxvii-xxviii)

The transformation in society was remarkable and the ease of exchange was equally distinguishable. The ability to discard old customs and embrace new ones gradually led to the rituals being lost to time. Tribal gods are conveniently replaced by the Hindu pantheon, though certain gods are able to retain some of their tribal leanings and appear in a hybridised manner. A common example is the brother-sister trio of Jagannath, Balaram and Subhadra at Puri, which is a very important centre of pilgrimage among Hindus. Looking at the idols, one cannot ignore the remnants of an influence of tribal gods. Social changes are equally pointed, infant marriages are introduced, widows are forbidden to marry again, and divorce which was a very important and vital component of tribal society is summarily discarded. These changes have a very deep impact on the domestic life of the people. The concept of pilgrimages is introduced and travel becoming a possibility with the introduction of railways, led to a further homogenisation with Hindu doctrines.

> Pilgrimages become more pleasant and more popular, and the touts, who sally forth from the great religious centres to promote these pious excursions, find their task easier and their clients more open to persuasion than was the case even twenty years ago. (Risley 1892: xxix)

H.H. Risley's contribution is invaluable in the context of understanding the finer issues of intermingling among the tribes and their appropriation into the caste fold. The history of tribal behaviour is well understood and these key points of movement are cogent with the history of racial intermingling in Europe. This scientific approach has helped in reaching important social and political conclusions, which would perhaps not have been available if the documentation remained unattempted. Differences of customs, rituals, religion and social status would not have been identified in the context of tribal cultures if not understood in the context of social order and behaviour. Risley's primary concern was the racial differences that would have appeared due to racial intermingling. The appearance of newer castes simply makes additions to the long list of castes in India. Sub-tribes, which would have emerged due to inter-caste or inter-tribal marriages continue to exist as individual castes and have been able to sever their relations with the parent group and stand forth as individual tribes and castes. India provides a plethora of such tribes and castes and a 'functional or territorial name disguises their mixed descent, ...' (Risley 1892: xxxvii)

Upon Risley's death, his fellow colleague J.D. Anderson commented in *Man* that Risley's anthropological work 'was performed officially, and with all the advantages that official authority and prestige confer in India' (Fuller 2) despite his considerable administrative work. Risley's contribution, however, carries a controversial tag giving his theories related to facial configuration, a notoriety of reputation. More recent scholars have never shied away from criticising and dismissing Risley's works due to its controversial nature and imperialistic agenda. In the short piece titled *The Study of Ethnology in India* (1891), H.H. Risley identifies the historical and social structure of the societies among the rural peasants, providing a foreground to the issues and concerns that would have helped him to configure a historiography of his observations.

> A society thus organised, whatever may be its social and political peculiarities, clearly offers in some respects a peculiarity favourable field for anthropological research, especially for that branch of science which is known as anthropometry. (Risley 1891: 241)

Thus, H.H. Risley determines remnant facial appearances (structure of the nose) as identifying factors among tribes which have intermingled and assimilated with the mainstream. Risley's contribution stands as an important landmark in initiating a dialogue in identifying factors that lead to further classification of trends in tribes. Subsequent efforts have been put in to further document the nature of evolution among the tribes. The 20th and, particularly, the 21st century a period which is marked by struggle among the tribes to assert their voices which is subdued by land reform laws and mining, leads to issues of sustainability among the tribal people. In the current nature of study, it is essential to be cognizant of where we stand in identifying the threshold of responsibility and the right to a dignified life among the tribal people since most efforts, governmental or otherwi.e. lay a lot of emphasis on configuring tribal identities. It is always particularly easy to museumise and create pedestals of reverence, but to live a life of respect and one close to nature is always the way forward. It is, thus, important to not stop at only documentation but ensure that rights are upheld and a respect for diversity and trust is maintained. Risley's work is important as a point of start, but we must move ahead in identifying and ensuring that right of land and natural resource is not compromised in our rush for modernisation in the postcolonial world. Whether it is in the 19th or in the subsequent centuries, tribal welfare continues to be controversial. Even today, most governmental involvement in terms of welfare and documentation is carried out by bureaucrats being part of official duty. However, it is literary works like that of Mahashweta Devi's that will continue to draw our attention to the plight and exploitative nature of association with the tribes.

REFERENCES

Appadurai, A., Korom, F., & Mills, M. (1991). Gender, Genre, and Power in South Asian Expressive Traditions. University of Pennsylvania.

Eriksson, P., & Kovalainen, A. (2008). Qualitative methods in business research.

Fuller, C. (2017). Ethnographic inquiry in colonial India: Herbert Risley, William Crooke, and the study of tribes and castes. *Journal Of The Royal Anthropological Institute, 23*(3), 603-621. https://doi.org/10.1111/1467-9655.12654

Mohan, K. (2002). The Colonial Ethnography: Imperial Pursuit of Knowledge For Hegemony in British India (Late 19th to 20th Century). *Proceedings of the Indian History Congress, 63*, 827–836. http://www.jstor.org/stable/44158151

Naithani, S. (2010). *The story-time of the British Empire.*

Ota, A., Mohanty, S., & Barad, H. (2014). *Bhumij.*

Risley, H. (1892). *The tribes and castes of Bengal.* The Bengal secretariat Press.

Risley, H. (1891). The Study of Ethnology in India. The Journal Of The Anthropological Institute Of Great Britain And Ireland, 20, 235. https://doi.org/10.2307/2842267

Samarendra, Padmanabh. (2011). 'Census in Colonial India and the Birth of Caste', Economic and Political Weekly

CHAPTER 6

Tribalism, Buddhism and Pan-Indianism The Membas of Arunachal

Krishna Kumar Sharma

Who are the tribal people, and what are their socio-cultural characteristics? Anthropologists have laid down some theories in the last five-six decades. Scholars have tried to understand primitive or tribal peoples from economic, political institutions, religious and magical points of view. During the colonial period, British scholars started to study about Tribal peoples with the purpose to control them. In the post-colonial period, many Indian Anthropologists-Sociologists contributed to the field of tribal studies. In the context of Indian tribes, analysing approaches are very contentious within the scholars from colonial to the present. We can categorise the scholar's obtuseness of views into two groups: One is *'Isolated Primitive Condition'* in which tribal people have separate entities from start to end. This theory remains the politico-intellectual weapon for the people inspired by Marxist-communist ideology at present. They deny any camaraderie with the culture of Sanatana. The new generation of communist ideology and some political groups also try to benefit from this static theory. Another group emphasises 'Cultural assimilation from the neighbour community through the process of Sanskritisation and peasantisation'. Scholars like M.N. Srinivas, G.S. Ghurye, F.G. Bailey, and others talk about cultural commutation. G.S. Ghurye describes tribal people as backward Hindus. However, what we find in the case study of Membas, some similar Hindu cultural activities in the primitive life of Membas even without any liaison to Sanatana belief of plain areas. It does not mean that Memba is related to Hindus in any way, nor is there any such attempt. However, after Buddhist influence on the tribes of the Eastern Himalayas and establishment of its material culture through monasteries and land consumption, the spread of Indian cultural elements in the region intensified.

Arunachal Pradesh has a territory of 83,743 square kilometers, which is highly precipitous and has a varied terrain and acts as the natural boundary for the different communities that inhabit there. The altitude of Arunachal Pradesh varies roughly between 100 and 7000m. Arunachal Pradesh has diverse forest types and climate with tropical to alpine diverse ecological habitat. Arunachal Pradesh is one of the top 12 global biodiversity hotspots and is rich in biodiversity, flora and fauna. The origin of the tribes of Arunachal Pradesh is mysterious. There are 26 tribes and 110 sub-tribes that inhabit the land of Arunachal Pradesh. There is no conclusive data about their early history and migration. It is believed that some tribes came from the triangle of Burma and some from Tibetan areas. Some tribes are followers of Buddhism. Some tribes are related to Mahayana, and some are followers of Theravada. Mahayana followers are in western Arunachal, settled in the Tawang and West Kameng districts. Memba and Khamba tribes inhabit the higher reaches of the central part of the state. Theravada followers settled in the Eastern part of the state. Due to unstable political conditions, as C.K. Borpatragohain mentioned in his article, hostility between the Gelukpa and Nyingmapa sects in Tibet was the leading cause of the migration of different tribes, including Membas. The Memba tribe is a follower of the Nyingmapa school of Tibetan Buddhism. The language of the Memba tribe is included in a list of UNESCO Atlas of the World's Languages in Danger of Disappearing. The Memba have their own Tibetan origin script called *Hikor.* Memba people mainly live in Shi-Yomi, West Siang, and Upper Siang districts. The population of Memba in the present time is near about 5000 (4395-2011 census). The Buddhist tribes of the Western and Eastern parts of Arunachal Pradesh are studied by scholars working on Buddhism of Arunachal Pradesh extensively. Hence, the less researched Buddhist tribe the Membas, has been studied.

The Memba society is patriarchal and follows endogamy, but they establish relationships with neighbouring tribes in exceptional cases. The slave system has been part of the Memba tribe. The Memba enslaved people from the neighbouring tribes. Membas have their socio-political institution controlling the entire community and settling disputes (Head of the socio-political institution – *Deb*). The Tibetans identified early Memba as *Neh-nang* (people living in the holy place). The term 'Memba' is used in British colonial government records. With the migration from Tibet to other parts of the Eastern Himalayas, the Memba tribe settled as agriculturists and traders. Under some chieftains (i.e.-*Sugin Gombo*), the Memba tribe tried to institutionalise their socio-political practices.

In the absence of any solid political system and a class

hierarchy, the Memba was a community that believed in nature worship and Bon culture. Gradually, Memba came under the influence of Buddhism through the guidance of Buddhist lama monks. Their mother language belongs to the Bodic group of the Tibeto-Burman branch of the Sino-Tibetan language family. But in the current ti.e. they understand Hindi and English and mostly use Tibetan for religious and commercial occasions. Memba dress is made of animal skin and fine quality silk. Before modern engineering, Memba built houses made of stone and wood. In addition to various fruits, the Memba community has been fond of different non-vegetarian foods and addicted to tobacco and alcohol. Modern education has created awareness in the Memba community, and the new generation is getting separated from the clutches of drug abuse.

There are more than 20 clans in the Memba tribe. They are settled in a different part of the Eastern Himalayas, and farming and trading are their main occupations. Memba society was divided into three groups:

a) Lama, whose primary duty was to do ritual performances;
b) Bureaucrats who performed administrative tasks;
c) Commoners who engaged with domestic work and agricultural or trade.

Comparing the family structure of different tribes of North East India, we find that the Memba family is very similar to the typical family of Northern India, where males and females both have importance and generally, the males manage and handle family. Endogamy is prevalent in Memba, but in some cases, in a wealthy family, or as we see in North Indian families, we find more than one wife.

Coincidence or any historicity, Memba marriage is close to north Indian Hindu marriage custom. Just like the eight types of Ancient Hindu marriage, as mentioned in Hindu Dharmashastra: Brahma marriage, Daiva marriage, Arsa marriage, Prajapatya marriage, Asura marriage, Gandharva marriage, Rakshasa marriage, and Paisacha marriage; out of which, the last four are not advocated by the scriptures. Memba society recognises seven forms of marriage. The first form is the arranged marriage (similar to Brahma marriage). The second is love marriage (which is identical to Gandharva marriage). The third marriage is by escape. The fourth marriage is by capturing the bri.e. which is very similar to Rakshasa form of marriage. The fifth marriage is by service. The sixth marriage is by exchange and the seventh is widow remarriage. However, in the present times, arranged marriage is mostly followed by common Memba. In the customs followed by the Hindu families, astrological calculation is essential.

An instance of the co-existence of pre-Buddhist principles and Buddhist practices is visible among the Membas along with some other tribes such as Monpas of Tawang area also. During the construction of a house, the practice of hoisting flags corresponding to the colours of indigenous deities considered to be reigning over the four directions is still followed. As per their belief, Jang Doindup, a green coloured deity rules the northern si.e. the east by a white coloured deity named Sher Dorjee Shamba, a red coloured deity named Nup Nagothaia rules the west and the south is administrated by a yellow coloured deity – Rinchin Jungne. While in the monasteries of the area, the four directions are believed to be guarded by the four *dikpalas*, who are worshipped there. The concept of the four dikpalas is integral to Mahayana Buddhism (Gyalchen zhi). Rinjun Lhantrab/Vaishravana, the guardian of northern direction and leader of the guardian deities; Pag Pi Kye Bo/Virudhaka, the guardian of the Southern direction and king of the Kumbhanda; Yul Khor Srung/Dhritrashtra, the guardian of the eastern direction and king of the Gandharvas; Chen Mi Zang/Virupaksha, the guardian of the western direction and the king of the Nagas (snakes).

Similarly, in Vajrayana (a part of Mahayana Buddhism), the concept of eight Dharmapalas (Chos Kyong) exists: Mahakala (Nagpo Chenpo); Yama (Shinje); Yamantaka (Shinje Shed); Hayagriva (Tamdrin); Vaisravana (Kubera); Shri Devi (Palden Lhamo); Tsangs-pa Dkar-po (White Brahma); and Pranatma (Begtse). The names of these Dikpalas, Dharmapalas and guarding deities indicate certain interactions between Buddhist and pre-Buddhist social beliefs. It is also noticeable that these names have a Sanskrit-like resonance to them, which may have been a consequence of the influence of ideas of Hinduism. In the traditional worship, the Sun was perceived to be the strongest manifestation of nature and worshipped accordingly. Snakes were viewed as the symbol of death and worshipped as well. Rituals of the faith were directed towards warding off demons and evil spirits who were believed to bring misery and sickness to mankind. It was this Tibetan influence which transformed Buddhism into a strong tantric cult of its own. Goddess Tara, a deity well known to Indian tantricism, is the presiding deity of many spiritual concepts and principles of metaphysics and religious philosophy in Bhutan, Tibet, Arunachal Pradesh and Assam. The rituals that are followed have the influence of Hinduism too, such as the lighting of the *diya*, burning of the incense sticks and offering in the name of the lord.

In a Memba family, if there are two or more boys, they choose any one occupation, either a Lama for religious work or administrative work, or they live as commoners for household work. Memba students generally read the Buddhist sacred text about medicine, astronomy, etc. Apart from *Kangyur* and *Tangyur*, the Buddhist canon, *Cheik*, and *Neik*, both are essential works of Memba that contain history, origin and about sacred law and pilgrimage place of Memba society.

Memba follows the Buddhist funeral ceremony, similar to Hindu rituals. According to Hindu shastras, all matter is composed of *Panchamahabhutas* (five elements), where the properties of earth, water, fire. wind, and space are in here. These elements have importance in Buddhism also. There was a different funeral method in Tibetan Buddhism, including cutting the dead body into several pieces for birds or thrown into water for aquatic organisms. But due to the availability of wood in Arunachal Pradesh, fire cremation is famous in the Memba community. Like Hindu pandits, Buddhist monks carry out these rituals. After the funeral of a person, Memba prohibits non-essential works and performs rites guided by a monk for 49 days, the same as *Kazia* or *Shraadh* of Hindu families.

Unlike the north Indian women, Memba women have been free from all restrictions and malpractices. The Memba women exercise their rights in almost all cases, except in some matters such as receiving education in Buddhist monasteries and other related works. At present, Memba girls receive modern education under the different state and central government schemes.

The Memba community celebrates Buddhist festivals such as *Losar* (New Year festival) in the months of December-January and *Bham-Mesh* in May-June, related to agricultural works. Another ceremony is Torgya which is performed for the village community's welfare under the guidance of Buddhist monasteries and Lama. *Broh* is the folk dance of Memba. Apart from this, *Pissh* (arrow shooting game), *Of-Tong* (Wrestling), *Chonje* (High jump), *Gyuje* (Running race) are the games for the amusement of Membas.

Deb, as an officer, was appointed by Tibetan higher authority for maintaining law and order and for revenue collection. Another appointment was *Dung-yek* as personal secretary and record keeper of day-to-day activities of Deb; *Gozo-Karma* as the personal bodyguard of Deb and *Chim* as village headmen assisting Deb. Tibetan aristocratic families depended upon the revenues. Therefore, revenue collection was very important in the Tibetan control areas. Memba had to pay taxes either in the form of kind such as agricultural and forest products. Those who engaged in trading activities were paying in cash mostly. There was a penalty system for those who did not pay taxes on time.

Membas migrated from Tibet along with some traditional or customary law by which they used to settle disputes within the community with the help of the village headman, *Chim*. Apart from the fact that Membas of Arunachal Pradesh were bound by Tibetan state law which dealt with serious matters like murder crimes or cases related to revenue, Membas also had some traditional customs similar to Hindu traditions but originally belonged to the pre-Buddhist culture of Tibet. Oath-taking is one of them. Generally, Membas take oath in the name of Gods. A method called *Terih* seems to be the primitive method of oath-taking. It is very similar to other tribes of the rest of India in which they check the loyalty of a person by cauterising the accused's hand with a hot iron. During the treaty between Memba people or different tribes, they swear by drinking chicken blood, a pre-Buddhist practice. There were two types of punishment for crimes in the Memba community, individual-level and collectively.

Apart from spending their life in jail with heavy fines levied on the person accused of a heinous crime like murder, the villagers also had to pay compensation in the form of silver coins from the village to which the offender belonged. In other offences, the accused were charged a fine as prescribed by the officials or the village arbitrament. We found many records and writings that mentioned the tribal conflict in Arunachal Pradesh during the colonial period (from 1826). They fought for inhabitation areas, animals and agricultural products. They used to capture slaves for different motives, i.e., sacrifice for deities, household works, or women for sexual amusement. One can easily guess the horrific condition of various tribal women and children in this dire past. Some records and writings of the colonial period have pointed to practices in which women, girls, and child slaves were exchanged through the barter system. The Memba's relations with neighbouring tribes have been partly peaceful and primarily full of conflict. Due to their socio-economic reasons, the Memba have faced conflict situations with their neighbouring tribes such as the Ramo, Pailibo, Bokar, Tagin, etc. Memba performed human sacrifice rituals and consumed human flesh to ward off divine wrath and various diseases. These activities were primitive and tribal, which differed from Buddhist faith and ideology. This example is helpful to show that the Memba community was theoretically attached to Buddhism whi.e. in practi.e. their daily lifestyle was dominated by primitive tribal culture.

The land ownership of the tribal areas of Arunachal Pradesh was considered to be the claim of the Tibetan noble family. Various tribes used to pay cess for living on this claimed land. Different tribes inhabited the whole region of Arunachal Pradesh. Gradually, the claims of the Tibetan royal families over land proprietorship weakened, and the tribal's ownership became stronger. The Memba classifies their land into forest land, agricultural land, township land, etc.

Membas follow the traditional methods of Jhum or shifting cultivation. They domesticated goats, sheep, and pigs for food and sacrifices; and dogs for hunting. Hunting and fishing have been part of the daily needed necessities of the Memba community. Tawang monastery has played an important role in the socio-economic life of Buddhist tribes and that of the Membas. As a Buddhist monastery, Tawang monastery has always been on the lookout for the interest of these Buddhist tribes. Membas gathers forest products for self-consumption and sale. Besides that, they engage in growing bamboo, timber, and make leather products for commercial activities.

The Buddhism of Arunachal Pradesh has been iridescent whose effulgence intersperses through the beliefs of different tribal groups. Tribal people came to Arunachal Pradesh from Tibet and Burma (Myanmar) for various reasons. Some tribes entered the present area of Arunachal Pradesh with Buddhist values and culture, and some others gradually adopted Buddhism. Some tribes are still following the pre-Buddhist culture and other religions. Memba people migrated from Tibet to different parts of Arunachal Pradesh during the 16th-17th century. When they got influenced and came close to Buddhism, they started to follow the empiricist adoration of Buddhism. The pre-Buddhist culture of Memba easily concords with the occultist methodology of Buddhism that is known as Tantrayana or Vajrayana. Although the Nyingmapa school of Tibetan Buddhism guides every aspect of the lives of the Memba people, their attachment to the pre-Buddhist Tibetan Bon culture and customs is visible during the Memba's ongoing process of assimilation into Buddhism.

The advent of various Buddhist monks and tribal beliefs, such as Guru Padmasambhava's journey into the valley, gave stability and strength to Buddhism in Arunachal Pradesh. The Memba, who expressed their faith in Buddhism, established the Tibetan Lamaism practice in the valley. The Memba community consists of unmarried male Lamas who lived in Buddhist monasteries called *Drup-da Gaih* Lama and the married Lamas who live with their families, known as *Tachok-Gaih* Lama. As I have mentioned earlier, the Memba tribe is a male-dominant society, we did not see any female Lamas or nuns. Memba Lama is bound by rule and regulation, which is illustrated through Buddhist monasteries and gonpas. Monasteries are essential within the Buddhist tribal people as they control the socio-religious and moral life of Buddhist followers in the valley. Monasteries and Gonpas have their right on a piece of forest and agricultural land, one of the primary sources of income for religious institutions in Arunachal Pradesh. Apart from this, household members daily donate money and necessities to these institutions. In a more profound and comparative analysis, we find a similar fascination of Brahmanical temples also coming from these Buddhist viharas.

Although the Buddhist sect has primarily influenced the Memba and other tribal people through their philosophy and rituals, glimpses of pre-Buddhist primitive culture are visible in arts and handicrafts, music, stone carving, statue making, etc. Pilgrimage and holy places known as *Neh* are more popular and important in the Memba community. Memba sacred places such as Gompas and Stupa (Charten) related to miracle Buddhist saints, lamas. rivers, mountains and lakes are essential for them as these are believed to be the residence of God. One should note here that these natural sites were also crucial in pre-Buddhist Bon culture. Therefore, it shows the gradual assimilation of non-Buddhist elements in Buddhism. A religious manuscript called *Naik* has information about sacred places and pilgrimage of Arunachal Pradesh. In the Memba community, registering your presence by visiting pilgrimage sites is considered essential for your needs and benefits as well as for the peace of the departed souls of your family. Like other Buddhist tribes, the Memba community performs worship, charity, and dakshina for blessings and prosperity from supernatural powers.

Rinpoche's presence is considered necessary for all these rituals to be completed. Rinpoche which literally means 'precious one' is used in the context of Tibetan Buddhism to show respectability towards lamas or teachers. The chanting performed by Rinpoche is deemed essential for the rituals to be successful. Memba collected drinking water and other materials from Buddhist holy places by the belief that they contained medicinal qualities and supernatural power, which is welfarist for his family. Volunteers, known as Jinda in the local language, are also selected from the Memba community to assist the devotees on pilgrimage and holy places. There are some examples of pilgrimage for Memba: *Karte-Neh* (in January), *Sekar Bumchoe-Neh* (in the first week of March), *Neh-Pema Shel-phu* (in the third week of March), *Pema- Ziling Neh* (in April and October), *Chandan-Takpa* (in September), *Tse-da-sha, Tsari Neh*, etc. These all pilgrimages hold different important holy places for Memba people. Some religious festivals are celebrated enthusiastically by the Memba, i.e., *Sonam Losar*; *Tse-chu*. They celebrate the birth anniversary of Guru Padmasambhava during *Tse-chu* celebration.

People solemnise the birthday of Lord Buddha through Saga Dawa; Memba celebrates Gaden Ngachen to mark the death anniversary of Lama Tsongkapa; during the celebration of Torgya, Memba performs mask dance which was part of pre-Buddhist Bon culture. The Buddhist rituals of the Memba community that is for the happiness and prosperity of society and the salvation of departed souls include everything included in Hindu worship. Whether it is charity or the observance of Buddhist rituals out of respect to the Gods, the Memba, like the Hindu community, follows all the rules that the Lama directs. It reminds us of the Hindu sacerdotalist system, where the delusions between deity, bhakta, brahmanas are very enlaced. I want to mention some rituals of Memba such as *Chok – Kor* performed to Goddess *Gelium Dorjee Phagmo* for the forgiveness of the sins of the deceased person's soul, *Men – Drup* in which Lama uses human skulls as an instrument for controlling evil spirit for well being of villagers; *Songway – lah* performed by Lama which is associated with sexual pleasure, increases active energy and prevents illness. There are so many rituals for Membas. This community worships Buddhist deities and local deities such as *Dorjee dak-Tsen, Gyalchen Kunga, Nima Tsengoue*, etc.

The concept of Pan-Indianism flourished in the Eastern Himalayas, despite the tribal communities not belonging to Sanatan beliefs are visible from the case study of Membas. We can say that in the context of tribes, especially Membas, apart from two major concepts – *'Isolated Primitive Condition'* and *'Cultural assimilation from the neighbour community through the process of Sanskritisation and peasantization'*, the similarity of some cultural elements with Hindu beliefs, no matter how coincidental, binds the whole of India and Indianism in one thread.

The mutual rivalry of the tribes due to socio-economic inequalities and difficulties resulted in the migration of different groups from Tibet during the medieval period, which settled in other parts of the Eastern Himalayas. One of these tribes was the Memba, who had the customs and practices of the pre-Buddhist primitive culture. Some tribes migrated to Arunachal valley from Burma sides. The adoption of Buddhism by the Membas and other tribes who followed the pre-Buddhist Bon culture is significant. The form of the Buddhist sect initially originated from India, changed further, structurally, as it travelled from China to Tibet. The entire world's civilisation has welcomed new religions in their ways where religions and their Prophets have tried to liberalise religious philosophy according to the local culture. Buddhist religion has also been no exception to this. The acceptance and vast mass base that Lord Shiva has received in the Himalayan region as belonging to Hinduism, certainly the followers of Gautam Buddha have also tried to give him the same stature in Tibet and the entire Himalayan region through mythological legends and the welfare works of the monasteries. The incorporation of non-Buddhist elements into Buddhist culture in the Eastern Himalaya region is a part of this process in which Tibetan Buddhist religious leaders have been largely successful. The ritual activities of the Memba community were first recognised in the course of their joining the Buddhist sect, which is congruent to the ideals of Tantrayana-Vajrayana.

The Tawang monastery and various local Gonpas served as shelter, food, and financial support for the Memba community and other Buddhist tribes. They sustained their daily lives through Buddhist practices and customs. Various Buddhist missionaries who came to Arunachal valley from time to time also tried to get local recognition of the philosophy of Mahatma Buddha in Memba and other tribal communities by miracles, narrations, and stories of salvation. On one si.e. where the Memba community adopted Buddhist culture and their pre-Buddhist practices and beliefs, the Buddhist sect happily accepted non-Buddhist elements to gain acceptance of the people of Buddhism, despite the differences. Buddhist philosophy has worked to connect the Eastern Himalayas with Pan-Indianism.

Today, the Memba community worships all Buddhist deities and visits places of pilgrimage and holy sites; however, for fear of some bad omen, it performs all ritual activities under the guidance of the Buddhist Lama. At present, the Memba is the identity of Buddhism in Arunachal Pradesh, where he represents being an ideal follower among other tribes of Northeast India.

REFERENCES

Bailey, F.G (1957). *Caste and the Economic Frontier: a village in highland Orissa.* Manchester University Press.

Barpujari, H. K (1981). *Problem of Hill Tribe of North East Frontier 1873-1962.* Spectrum Publications.

Chakravarty. L. N (2007). *Glimpses of the Early History of Arunachal.* Directorate of Research, Government of Arunachal Pradesh.

Dai, Mamang (2009). *Arunachal Pradesh The Hidden Land.* Penguin India.

Dutta, D. K (2006). *The Membas: Arunachal Pradesh.* Directorate of Research Government of Arunachal Pradesh.

Dutta, P. C. & Duarah, D. K (1997). *Aspects of Customary Laws of Arunachal Pradesh.* Directorate of Research Government of Arunachal Pradesh.

Ghurye, G.S (1943). *The Aborigines 'so called' and their future.* Gokhale Institute of Politics and Economics.

Huber, Toni & Blackburn, Straut (2012). *Origins and Migration in the Extended Himalayas.* Imprints Brills.

Hui Kalita, Pallabi. '*Biodiversity of Arunachal Pradesh*', National Institute of Technology Arunachal Pradesh Yupia, http://nitap.ac.in/storage/pdf/0d2e3e8226096158b227619bd8e22221.pdf, accessed on 16-2-2022.

Chhomu. (1970, January 1). Socio economic and cultural life of the monpas of Arunachal Pradesh, unpublished Ph.D Thesis, Department of History, Gauhati University, Guwahati.

Srinivas, M.N (1952). *Religion and Society Among Coorgs of South India.* Oxford, Claredon Press.

Sharma, D. D (2000). *Peculiar Customs and Rites of Himalayan People.* Mittal Publication.

Sharma, Krishna Kumar (2019). Women in Eastern Himalaya with Special Reference to Sikkim, *Samvedna*, Vol-1, Maitreyi College, Delhi, pp 13-21.

Sharma, Krishna Kumar (2021). Non-Buddhist Elements in Buddhism of Sikkim, in Lanukumla Ao (ed.) *Northeast India Readings in Cultural Li.e.* Research Press India, pp. 77-93.

Tamak, Chera (2018). Understanding the Political History of Memba Tribe of Menchuka in Aruncahal Pradesh, India from 1866 to 1951AD, *Saudi Journal of Humanities and Social Sciences (SJHSS)*, vol-3, Issue- 1A, pp 5-10.

Thakur, Amrendra Kumar (2003). *Slavery in Arunachal Pradesh.* Mittal Publication.

Thakur, Amrendra Kumar (2014). *History of Arunachal Pradesh (Early times -1972 AD).* Institute of Distance Education, Rajiv Gandhi University, Itanagar in association with Vikas Publishing House Pvt. Ltd.

Thakur, Amrendra Kumar (2016). Cultural Development in Buddhism of Arunachal Pradesh: Probing Through Arts, in Sudhir Kumar Singh and Ashan Riddi (eds.), *Pre-Colonial History and Traditions of Arunachal Pradesh*, DVS Publishers, Guwahati, pp.26-42.

Thakur, Amrendra Kumar (forthcoming). Buddhism in Arunachal Pradesh, in C. A. Mawlong and Tejimala Gurung Nag (eds.), *Religions of Northeast India,* D V S Publications, Guwahati.

SECTION II

TRIBAL REPRESENTATIONS
TEXTUAL, ORAL, AND VISUAL

CHAPTER 7

Resistance, Performance and Cultural Labour

Srestha Bhattacharya

A trenchant critic of inequality and oppression, author and activist Mahasweta Devi uses her writings to draw attention towards the ordinary, unsung heroes who are neglected by mainstream discourse and remain outside the common consciousness as a result. As she herself had once remarked:

> I have always believed that real history is made by ordinary people. I constantly come across the reappearance, in various forms, of folklore, ballads, myths and legends, carried by ordinary people across generations . . . The reason and inspiration for my writing are those people who are exploited and used, and yet do not accept defeat. For me, the endless source of ingredients for writing is in these amazingly noble, suffering human beings. (Devi, 1986, as cited in Bardhan, 1990, p. 24)

For an author like Devi, who herself is very much a part of the privileged socioeconomic 'elite' class, the representation of the subaltern can be a potentially contentious enterprise, there is a constant risk of reducing them into either uneducated 'savages' who partake in outdated superstitious rituals or hapless subjects who silently endure the oppression inflicted upon them by the mainstream population. However, as one observes, Devi manages to avert such risks by featuring multiple instances of organic subaltern resistance in her works. As Sanatan Bhowal notes, while '*The Right of the Forest*', '*Bashai Tudu*', '*Hulmaha*', '*To the Call of Shalgira*' and '*Draupadi*' represents [sic] the voice of aggression and revolt [,] '*Chotti Munda and his Arrow*' [speaks of] resistance [against] restricted action.' (Bhowal, 2016, as cited in Saxena, 2016, p. 419). To achieve this organic representation, Devi chooses to focus on the indigenous cultural practices of her tribal subjects. Myths, rituals and tribal culture form the core of subaltern resistance and emancipation in her 'tribal' novels.

This chapter proposes to analyse the performance of tribal culture with reference to two such novels, namely, *Aranyer Adhikar* (*The Right of the Forest*, 1977) and *Chotti Munda Ebong Tar Teer* (*Chotti Munda and His Arrow*, 1980). In these narratives, both of which focus on the Munda tribe, it becomes virtually impossible to separate the aesthetics of song and dance performances and cultural rituals from the immediate socio-political ramifications of the tribal populace's marginalised existence. In other words, the culture of the Mundas is not merely a de-politicised form of aesthetic expression, but rather a mode of asserting political resilience that challenges state-sponsored violence against their marginalised tribal identity. Consequently, the Mundas in Devi's novels end up enacting what Brahma Prakash, following Sharmila Rege, has termed as 'cultural labour' (Prakash, 2013, p. 13).

At the very outset, it is important to clarify what 'cultural labour' means in the context of this chapter. The term was first coined by Sharmila Rege, who used it in her study of Lavani and Powada in Maharashtra to argue that cultural performances that arise from Dalit-Bahujan spaces have long been neglected in favour of 'bourgeois theatre' (Rege, 2002, p. 1040). In his work on the cultural practices of the various marginalised sections in India, Brahma Prakash demonstrates the applicability of Rege's region-specific observations to a variety of marginalised folk cultural forms (like bhuiyan puja and bidesia) to establish 'cultural labour' as a conceptual category. Prakash questions the commonsensical assumption that views 'culture' and 'labour' as antagonistic concepts. To counter this hegemonic view, he puts forth the idea of 'cultural labour' as a category. Prakash defines cultural labour as 'popular cultural performances which are embedded in the materiality of caste and labour and are constitutive of manual labour in Indian society' (Prakash, 2013, p. 13).

By equating the materiality of labour with art, Prakash not only highlights the revolutionary purpose of the art practices, but also acknowledges the active role that the marginalised may play in the production of culture. Such an idea of culture is integral to the understanding of folk performances and rituals in Devi's novels, whereby the aesthetics of tribal culture are inextricably tied with questions of oppression, exploitation and survival. This chapter explores the concept of cultural labour as deployed by Devi in *Aranyer Adhikar* and *Chotti Munda Ebong Tar Teer*. Following Prakash's concept, my chapter studies how tribal cultural practices (as depicted in Devi's novels) disrupt bourgeois ideals of art and aesthetics. As a wider concern, my chapter also addresses how the cultural labour of the Munda tribe can provide a useful category to help us reconfigure our understanding of 'modernity' and 'progress'.

Performance as Resistance in *The Right of the Forest*

Set against the backdrop of the 19th century Munda Revolution, *The Right of the Forest* chronicles the birth, life and death of Birsa Munda, the mytho-historical leader of the Munda tribe inhabiting the Chotanagpur Plateau region. The novel in particular focuses on the Great Munda Rebellion, or the Ulgulan, in which the Mundas, led by Birsa, fight back against the systematic marginalisation meted out to them. Devi depicts how the corrupt practices of the British government and their Indian allies, the *dikus* (the eli.e. 'upper class' group, composed mostly of landlords and moneylenders) threaten to displace the Munda tribe from their land and culture by interfering with their socio-economic existence.

The ritual of *khutkatti*, in which the tribals left their earlier settlement once overpopulation disturbed the ecological balance and demarcated their new settlement by simply cutting the trunk of a new tree, without any legal interference from the outsi.e. comes into direct conflict with the feudal and the legal system introduced by the British government. Consequently, the Mundas lose their claim to their own natural habitat as the *dikus* continue to usurp their lands. Moreover, the prospect of losing their rituals, consisting mainly of simple nature worship that is fundamental to their tribal identity, to the totalising order of organised religions, whether Hinduism or Christianity, through conversions further contribute to their identity crisis.

The rebellion then, for the Mundas, is a movement of resistance against colonisers both internal and external.

The novel opens with its protagonist's death. Having endured excruciating torture at the hands of the colonial jail officers, Birsa Munda—the young, fearless tribal leader is seen to succumb to his multiple injuries right at the beginning of the novel. As the narrative progresses, the reason behind Birsa's imprisonment and his subsequent death comes to the fore. Devi makes use of techniques like literary flashbacks to show how the Mundas, under Birsa's leadership, begin to cultivate a sense of self-identity. This new awareness among the Mundas finally goes on to take the form of Ulgulan, or The Great Rebellion. While the colonial government manges to officially 'crush' the rebellion and imprison many of its leaders, the Ulgulan nonetheless registers the assertive political presence of the tribal subjects. Taking the Great Munda Rebellion as its focal point, Devi's narrative serves as a literary documentation of this historic event.

This resistance is made possible chiefly through the performance of cultural labour. The members of the Munda tribe in Devi's narrati.e. become heroes not in spite of, but rather, because of their cultural identity. For the author, the tribals and their folk culture embody the essence of human existence. In the preface to the novel, Devi locates in the dance movements of the various tribes around the world 'a universal rhythm', a rhythm, which according to her, is natural – 'the earth was undivided once'. (Devi, 1977, p. 12). Nature indeed permeates the consciousness of the Mundas. In fact, the title of Devi's book literally translates into 'the rights of the forest', and not to 'the rights of the land', the struggle for which is usually thought to have sparked the rebellion. It seems that for the Mundas, nature, rituals and politics are virtually indistinguishable from one another. As his tribe anticipates cultural extinction, Birsa realises that the only way for the Mundas to reclaim their spaces back is to vehemently reassert their identity. To realise his vision of the Ulgulan, Birsa turns the protest into a ritual, he seeks to inculcate in his followers a sense of pride in their Munda identity. Therefore, singing, dancing and playing instruments was as integral part of the movement as was the act of developing strategies to defeat the enemy. The narrator remarks that Birsa could 'stir the blood of his people just by singing' Devi, 1977, p. 29). Through their cultural performances, the Mundas seek to move back to their roots, which in turn re-establishes their organic bond with nature. In fact, Birsa's self-deification, which he does by aligning himself to nature by becoming the *Dharti-Aba*, or the Father of the Earth, has to do with the greater goal of mobilisation against their oppressors: 'I'll bring happiness to everyone, I'll be a God! I'll turn into *Dharti-Aba*! The Mundas will live on because of me!' (Devi, 1977, p. 75)

Reassessing Modernity

It needs to be noted that in Devi's novel, there exists a clear distinction between traditions and superstitions. The ancient beliefs and practices of the Mundas, including their tribe's patron deity Sing-Bonga, is subjected by Birsa to as much scrutiny as Christianity or Hinduism, and once they are found to be lacking in credibility, they are promptly discarded. Scientific temperament and folklore go hand in hand for Birsa; he deftly uses his knowledge of medicine, which he acquired from his missionary education, to further solidify his place as the new 'god'. Empty rituals hold no significance for him, so he goes on to modify the old customs of his tribe so that they remain in tune with the spirit of the revolution: 'Usually, Mundas light a fire on Holi and sing and dance around it. This time too, a fire was lit, songs were sung. But the songs this time were not of celebration' (Devi, 1977, p. 141). Instead, the songs were of revolution, songs that talked about overthrowing the oppressive regime of the British as well as the *dikus*. Instead of being a constricting force, then, traditions become a source of liberation against injustice perpetrated by outsiders. By portraying the 'black-skinned, almost naked' (Devi, 1977, p. 19) Mundas, united by nothing but a sense of community through their shared cultural values, as an organised collective capable of challenging the very foundations of the empi.e. Devi challenges the arbitrary standards of progress which place more value on superficial markers of modernity.

Birsa's deification also greatly owes itself to the tradition of the oral. As Devi declares in the preface to the book, Birsa could become a legendary figure because 'he got a place in the oral tradition within his lifetime' (Devi, 1977, p. 14). Orality is present at several levels in the text. The function of characters like Shivan, Sunara, Dhani, Bharmi and Sali is primarily choral in nature. The novel begins with Birsa's death, and it is through the dialogues of these characters, and not through omniscient third person narration, that his li.e. vision and works are unravelled before the reader. It is almost as if Birsa gets resurrected from death and comes alive before the reader as they reminisce about their 'god'. In addition to that, Birsa also remains a constant presence in the popular imagination of the

Mundas as the subject of the songs that the Birsaites compose and sing as they prepare for the Ulgulan. These repeated oral references to Birsa take him out of his flesh and blood existence and transform him into a myth, a legend, an idea. As his corporeal identity gradually gives way to his mythification, Birsa attains a sort of immortality that is indispensable for his ideas to live on even after he passes away. That Birsa is well aware of this himself becomes evident when he says to Sunara, 'You [the Mundas] will not survive as long as I do not leave this body. Don't lose hope. Don't think that I abandoned you all. I have given you the ideas, use them to struggle and survive' (Devi, 1977, p. 29). The realisation of his vision is testified by the Mundas, including Shiva, Dhani and Sali, who at different points of time declare: 'Ulgulan doesn't end! God doesn't die' (Devi, 1977, p. 30). Birsa dies, his legend lives on.

The Continuity of Cultural Labour in *Chotti Munda and His Arrow*

The immortal quality of Birsa's legend is further underscored by Devi in *Chotti Munda and His Arrow*. In some ways, *Chotti Munda* can be read as a sequel of *The Right of the Forest*. Like *The Right of the Forest*, *Chotti Munda and his Arrow*, too, narrates the story of a resilient tribal leader, the eponymous protagonist, who, like Birsa, becomes somewhat of a living legend within his lifetime as he navigates through the multifaceted workings of institutionalised victimisation in both, colonial and postcolonial India. This striking similarity, however, is not coincidental; as Gayatri Chakravorty Spivak has rightly observed, Chotti, despite being born 15 odd years after the Ulgulan, serves as a 'figure of continuity, from the Ulgulan, to the Emergency, and post-Emergency' (Spivak, 2003, p. ix). Mythmaking becomes the continuum that connects these two figures otherwise separated by generations between them. Actively inspired by the mythical Birsa's heroic deeds, Chotti, a young Munda archer, grows up to transcend his corporeal presence and become an extension of his predecessor's fabled persona. This section studies how the politics of cultural labour operates in Devi's *Chotti Munda and his Arrow*, with special reference to the acts of mythmaking and storytelling as depicted in the novel.

Chotti in Devi's novel is exceptionally skilled in archery. For him, his lifelong commitment to the sport is not merely a matter of recreation. Rather, it becomes a well thought-out mode of political assertion. This was, however, always not the case. As a young boy, Chotti's first brush with archery occurs when he meets Dhani Munda, his sister's grandfather-in-law, known for his remarkable talent in archery. Keen to win the archery competition in the village tribal fair, Chotti requests Dhani to teach him the craft. However, what begins as a leisurely and somewhat frivolous pursuit for Chotti soon becomes a vital part of his and his tribe's political subjectivity. Chotti's initiation into this new form of political awareness is aided by his teacher Dhani. An aide of Birsa in the cause of Ulgulan, Dhani is acutely aware of the fact that archery, which used to be an indispensable part of the Munda culture, has gradually started waning, largely because of the Mundas' subjugation and their consequent loss of their sense of self:

> Dhani was always crazy, at the time of the Santal Hul Dhani was a lad of twenty. The Kherwar revolt, the Mulkoi revolt of the Sardars, and then Birsa's revolt. Armed struggle is

> also an addiction. He went to all the revolts in the hope that Mundas would establish villages in forest and arable land and farm rightfully and in peace, and that other adivasi groups would do the same. But looking at the peaceful farming Mundas he understood that he had not wanted this peace. (Devi, 2003, p. 11)

With a desire to make him aware of the radical potential of a quintessentially tribal form of cultural expression, Dhani Munda regales Chotti with the stories of the Ulgulan and other tribal uprisings; he stirs Chotti's consciousness by repeatedly emphasising upon the present misfortunes of the Mundas under the regime of the government-*diku* nexus. This, in fact, is a conscious exercise of cultural labour on Dhani's part that motivates Dhani to impart archery lessons to the young Chotti, as the narrator remarks, '[t]here's something drives Dhani inside' (Devi, 2003, p. 12).

Dhani's actions mark the beginning of Chotti's lifelong association with the politics of culture. As Chotti's brilliance as an archer soon elevates him to the status of quasi-mythical figure, everyone around him his skills to be a product of magic and attributes his repeated wins at the archery competitions to the supernatural. Unlike Birsa, whose self-mythification was a conscious strategy to organise and orchestrate the Munda uprising, Chotti's initial inclusion as the subject of tribal myth and lore is largely inadvertent on his part. In fact, he even tries to dissuade the other Mundas from regarding him as a magician. His skills, he insists, come from nothing but practice. However, as the Mundas are confronted with several forms of oppression, be it perpetrated by the British Raj, the *diku* moneylenders and landowning zamindars, or the post-independence Indian government, mythmaking becomes a deliberate political strategy that engenders subaltern resistance. Each of these instances becomes a story about Chotti Munda's life; as the narrator repeatedly states throughout the course of the narrati.e. 'everything is a story in Chotti's life' (Devi, 2003, p. 23). The first of such examples is when Lala Baijnath, the local landowning moneylender, calls Birsa, Chotti's father, a Mahajan (moneylender). Perceiving it as an insult, Birsa enters into an argument with Baijnath, provoking the latter to lodge a complaint with the police that ultimately leads to Birsa's arrest. However, interestingly, the rumours surrounding Chotti's 'spelled arrow' effectively strikes fear in the heart of the powerful moneylender: 'As soon as he heard [the Munda village head Pahan mention Chotti's magical arrow], Lala thought of the spelled arrow. Lordy lord! Mountain from a molehill—if life goes?' (Devi, 2003, p. 29)

This altercation between Baijnath and Birsa, however, eventually culminates into Birsa's suicide. Baijnath, fearing Chotti's magical vengeance, decides to leave his business to his son Tirathnath and relocate to Banaras, where he eventually meets his death by an accident and ends up further strengthening the lore surrounding Chotti's magical powers. While Chotti's life is filled with many such oral legends, two of them need to be mentioned. The first of such examples is the case of Dukhia. One of Chotti's students, Dukhia, slays his boss, the Nakata King's manager after the manager insults his tribal heritage. This leads to Dukhia's inevitable arrest even as his identity of being Chotti's archery student further solidifies the mythical nature of the Chotti's arrow. In another such incident, the tribal inhabitants of the Kurmi village take massive loans and commit themselves to a life of bonded labour, only to convert to Christianity *en masse* (which frees them from the obligations of their contract) and leave their village. This act of strategic manoeuvre, too, gets attributed to Chotti Munda and his magic arrow by Chotti's fellow tribals.

These incidents merit a closer analysis for at least two reasons. Firstly, the process of myth formation is directly related to orality, a quintessential characteristic of Munda culture. Since the Munda language does not have a written script, it is through the oral legends and songs that Chotti's legends remain documented and get circulated from person to person. As Devi herself mentions in her interview with Gayatri Chakravorty Spivak: 'What I can do must also be woven into a song and sung, this song continues, then another phase, another song, these songs are sung here and there—that it continues to li.e. this is also resistance.' (Spivak, 2003, p. xi). Secondly, the legends of Chotti accomplishing impossible feats with his arrow are a direct result of socio-political upheavals surrounding the Mundas. More importantly, all of these situations involve a Munda or a group of Mundas securing a victory over their oppressors. The argument between Lala Baijnath and Birsa, for example, ends with Birsa successfully escaping prison time while managing to elicit fear in his more powerful adversary. In the case of Dukhia, he manages to slay his exploitative employer (the manager) and voluntarily hands himself over to the police. The strategic planning of the Kurmi villagers not only helps them dismantle the existing hold of the bonded labour system over them, but also enables them to trick their oppressor out of his money. All of these incidents surrounding

Chotti's lore denote a significant event where the tribals and the untouchables manage to win against their privileged tormentors. It needs to be noted that the involvement of Chotti in the last two cases is indirect at best; yet his name seemingly manages to get intertwined with all other instances of tribal resistance in Devi's novel. Various events of successful subaltern resistance therefore get condensed and coalesced within a single figure, namely, Chotti Munda, who wields a magical arrow. By creating an infallible, all-powerful mythical figure, whom they derive inspiration from, the Mundas manage to forge their own symbol of resistance against the various manifestations of power that seek to commodify and subdue them. Interestingly, while the other Mundas celebrate the 'magic' of their leader, Chotti himself repeatedly rues his helplessness and points out the irrationality behind the idea of his so-called magical spell. The following instance makes it clear. Talking to the Daroga, a symbol of authority, a tribal man exclaims: 'There's an adivasi here, our pride and joy, a magician with the arrow, knows everything about all the Mundas of the region, and that is Chotti Munda' (Devi, 2003, p. 128). Chotti's mythification, then, ceases to be an act of mere make-believe by 'uncivilised', 'savage' tribals and instead represents a tactfully constructed mode of subaltern self-subjectification.

Chotti's Strategic Mythmaking

The political currency generated by Chotti's mythification reaches its culmination in the novel's climax. As *Chotti Munda and his Arrow* illustrates, the marginalisation of the tribals continues to take place well after India attains independence. Nivedita Sen and Nikhil Yadav note how 'Devi's diatribe on the government and administration is central to her questioning of what the nation in the post-independence era has done for its people' (Sen & Yadav, 2008, p.15). Several manifestations of institutionalised power, including the unscrupulous party workers of the Youth League (which ironically rose to power by capitalising on the tribal 'vote bank'), the inefficient post-independence Indian bureaucracy and the *diku* moneylenders and landowners, seek to retain the pre-independence social hierarchies. Consequently, when the government at the centre prohibits the practice of bonded labour, the highly casteist *diku*-administration nexus try their best to prevent the implementation of the ban. A struggle breaks out between the tribals and the *dikus* which ultimately leads to the death of Swarup, the adivasi rights activist who comes to support the tribal-untouchable resistance. Chotti and his group retaliate and avenge Swarup's death by killing and injuring a number of adversaries (including Romeo and Pahlwan, the notoriously casteist and misogynist lumpens of the Youth League Party).

In a bid to catch the killers, the administration arranges for the archery competition to identify the person who shot Romeo and Pahlwan. It is at this moment that Chotti finally partakes in his own mythification. He participates in the competition and hits his target, while prohibiting all his followers from doing so, thereby identifying himself as the killer. However, instead of turning himself over to the poli.e. Chotti stirs up a remarkable show of solidarity, and the novel ends with 'Chotti on one si.e. S.D.O. on the other, and in between a thousand bows upraised in space. And a warning announced in many upraised hands' (Devi, 2003, p. 288). It is at this moment that the man and the myth converge into one single entity. Chotti channels the cultural practices to unite the subaltern population, who rise in unison to protect their mythical leader. The transition from the cultural to the political is, therefore, complete.

Towards an Alternative Historiography

The performance of cultural labour in Devi's novels transcends its immediate contexts. For the Mundas, who lie at the periphery of the society, it is only by 'performing' history that they can construct their own historiography. Highly significant events like The Munda Uprising of 1899-1900, that have consistently been relegated to the margins of mainstream Indian history, in fact, survive only through the performance of cultural labour. Under such unfavourable circumstances, the tribals in Devi's novels engage in what Adrienne Rich calls 're-vision' (Rich, 1971, p. 18), whereby indigenous modes of knowledge production give rise to a subversive form of discourse that questions dominant modes of storytelling. By portraying the tribals as politically aware agents who actively forge their unique mode of resistance, Mahasweta Devi deliberately complicates commonplace categories like 'tradition', 'modernity', 'centre' and 'periphery'. As the author compels her readers to confront the issues which are as pertinent at present as it was in Birsa Munda and Chotti Munda's times, her fictionalised portrayal of the tribal uprisings manage to become extensions of the oral tradition that surrounds these events.

REFERENCES

Bardhan, K. (1990). Introduction. In Kalpana Bardhan (ed.), *Of Women, Outcastes, Peasants, and Rebels: A Selection of Bengali Short Stories* (pp. 1-49). University of California Press.

Devi, M. (1977). *Aranyer Adhikar* [The Right of the Forest]. Karuna Prakashani.

Devi, M. (2003). *Chotti Munda and His Arrow* (G. C. Spivak, Trans.). Blackwell Publishing. (Original work published 1980)

Rege, S. (2002). Conceptualising Popular Culture: 'Lavani' and 'Powada' in Maharashtra. *Economic and Political Weekly, 37*(11), 1038-1047. https://www.jstor.org/stable/4411876

Rich, A. (1971). When We Dead Awaken: Writing as Re-vision. *College English, 34*(1), 18–30. https://doi.org/10.2307/375215

Saxena, A. (2016). [Review of *The subaltern speaks: Truth and ethics in Mahasweta Devi's fiction on tribals*, by S. Bhowal]. *Sociological Bulletin, 65*(3), 418–420. http://www.jstor.org/stable/26369550

Sen, N. & Yadav, N. (2008). Introduction. In Sen, N., & Yadav, N. (Eds.), *Mahasweta Devi: An Anthology of Recent Criticism* (pp 11-40). Pencraft International.

Singh, B. P. (2013). *The Performance of Cultural Labour: A Conceptual Framework for Understanding Indian Folk Performance* [Doctoral dissertation, Royal Holloway, University of London]. EThOS. https://ethos.bl.uk/OrderDetails.do?uin=uk.bl.ethos.603539

Spivak, G. C. (2003). 'Telling History' Gayatri Chakravorty Spivak interviews Mahasweta Devi. In *Chotti Munda and His Arrow* (G. C. Spivak, Trans., pp. ix-xxiii). Blackwell Publishing (Original work published 1980).

CHAPTER 8

Popular Bengali Thriller Genre Exploring Tribal Cultures

Durba Mandal

This Chapter studies the representation of tribal cultures and practices in popular Bengali thriller fiction. The domain of *Rohoshyo-Romancha* and *Kishore Sahitya* or young adult mystery-thrillers, has always been one of the most popular threads of Bangla literature; even in the 21st century it remains a genre loved by not only adolescents, but also young-adult and mature readers. This popular genre often tends to appropriate certain aspects of tribal systems such as religious practices, rituals, gods and goddesses or folklore, as plot points. Particularly in horror/suspense thrillers, we see either the indigenous individual or some romanticised tribal practice stereotyped as the exotic site the uncanny that motivates an adventure-seeking urban protagonist to confront the limitations of his rational approach towards a material world, or the lack of proper engagement with the tribal cultures that are made to fade into the background.

Often penned by upper-class urban men, works of Bangla thriller fiction present the tribal essence either as a site of horror and potential danger, or manifesting as exotic 'others' who live in self imposed isolation away from modern society. The deeper implications of a popular tradition of vernacular genre fiction interacting with unknown cultures and unfamiliar populations should be noted as an attempt to delve into the complications of indigenous representation in young-adult Bangla popular fiction.

The deployment of the word 'tribe' in India has had its problems. In colonial India, the British colonisers were not very clear about the word tribe. Virginuis Xaxa mentions the category of tribe is to be seen as a 'colonial construct' (Xaxa, 2008, p. 14). The word could be associated with more than one concept regarding different communities that trace their descent back to singular ancestral bodies. Howevr, the usage of the term in a sense of 'barbaric' people living under primitive conditions of life beyond normative state control is what dominates anthropological documentation. Practised religions, obscure languages, taboo customs, naming traditions, defiance to state order, technological deficiencies—these have all become facets of differentiating the indigenous tribes from the rest of us.

Particularly in the Indian context, castes and tribes are often intermingled. Xaxa notes, 'Tribes are said to have accepted the ethos of the caste structure and to have become absorbed within it.' Bengal is no different. Pre-colonial and post-colonial Bengal always seems to gloss over the issue of differentiating castes and tribes. Most data available is either in the form of census lists, or reports by land revenue departments. The official website of the tribal development department of West Bengal makes a list of the 40/41 tribal communities that can be encountered in the state. However, no widely accessible contemporary list is invested in actually detailing the differences that these tribes share nor is there a deeper investment in exploring their lifestyle choices. Such stereotypes seem to linger even today, and literature is definitely one aspect that perpetuates imaginary ideas about subjective experiences of individuals belonging to certain 'tribes'.

Bangla young adult fiction has always been associated with some of the biggest names. There is a nostalgic attachment most of us share with the genre. Growing up, all Bengali children have read one or the other of these stories and novellas, maybe in widely available popular children's magazines and periodicals, and have nostalgic attachment with the genre as I myself can confirm. It would not be fair to consider it a conscious attempt on part of the authors to sustain stereotypes that they can then pass on to their large reader base, but it is indeed easier to succumb to popular stereotypes in such speculative genres whether as a reader or a writer. Even in the works of some of the most prominent authors of Bangla thrillers the tricky issue of tribal portrayal can come up, especially as we re-read these novellas as adults. I will provide some examples in the chapter.

In Bibhutibhushan Bandopadhyay's novella *Mishmider Kavach* (The Amulet of the Mishmis), detective fiction turns supernatural when the murderer blames the unexplainable evil powers of an amulet he stole from the body of a deity worshipped by the Mishmi tribe in Assam for bringing his downfall. In another story by him titled '*Rankini Devir Khorgo*' (The Sword of the Goddess Rankini), the author takes us to the temple of Goddess Rankini in the Manbhum region, who was once worshipped by Adivasi tribes that lived in the area before the Hindus came. The Hindu rites of worship are clearly differentiated from the ways of the savages who would incorporate rituals like human sacrifice and ornament the Goddess with actual human skulls. In the second story of *Taranath Tantric*, Bandopadhyay clearly notes how the woman who comes to visit his guru at night and who later turns out to be the yogini sub goddess Madhusundari is very much different in her appearance from local santal girls, she appears to be 'boro ghorer meye' or a woman from an affluent household because of her beauty and appearence. Even when it is not the central plot point in Bibhutibhushan's stories, often, the adivasi essence is explored through shallow stereotypes and a sense of superiority when compared to the non-tribal characters.

In arguably the most popular novel from Sunil Gangopadhyay's Kakababu series, *Sobuj Dwiper Raja* (The King of the Green Islands), the adventures are centered around the Jarawa community in Andaman and Nicobar islands. Popular opinion about the jarawas in the novel is widely negati.e. the word *hinghshro* is repeatedly used to describe them. There is a sense of wild, animalistic savagery attached to this word. The outsiders consider this tribe to be filled with whimsical killers who attack anyone who tries to get closer to them with poisoned arrows. The story takes a patriotic turn when we find out that their king is a bengali freedom fighter named Gunoda Talukdar who had broken free from Cellular Jail and chose to remain in bliss amongst the savages who saved him, away from the chaos of colonial clutches.

Even though Gangopadhyay ends his story with a much more sympathetic attitude towards the tribe the fact does not change that the Jarawas are denied much agency. They are interpreted through this cultured upper class man, an outsider who has somehow risen to the position of their monarch.

Now that man becomes their mouthpiece and vouches for the revocation of the tribe's 'savage' status. The Jarawas are but a homogenised bunch of certain stereotypical features who are obedient to this enlightened patriot who chose to live freely amongst uncultured noble savages rather than go back to an India that remains under western control. Choice is the keyword I argue; Talukdar has a choice to live the tribal life or go back to the world he came from and he chooses to go back in the end. However, is a similar choice available to the people of the tribe? The idea of a hierarchy is subtly infused in the story.

In Himadri Kishore Dasgupta's horror story 'Mosmai Orchid' from his *Bhoy Bhoyankor* collection of thriller stories and novellas, a man from Khasi community grows orchids that suck blood and he hunts victims for that purpose. In *Durgo Rahasya* (The Castle Mystery), one of the novels from Sharadindu Bandopadhyay's ever-popular Byomkesh series, the migrant bede community is portrayed as a whimsical population associated with poison and snake venom.

The murderer even manages to get his hands on the poison for the murder weapon he crafts from these unpredictable and somewhat dangerous people. Often, it is not only the Indian tribal communities but tribal populations all across the world that get appropriated in Bangla horror and adventure fiction.

There are mentions of Spanish hybrid communities who use tarantula spiders for addiction in Byomkesh's '*Makorshar Rawsh*' (The Spider's Juice). Most of Himadri Kishore Dasgupta's popular adventure thriller novels like *Sunda Dwiper Shonar Dragon* (The Golden Dragon of Sunda Islands) or *Burundir Shobuj Manush* (The Green Men Of Burundi) are set in obscure locations miles away such as in Africa or Indonesia where exotic communities like the primitive pygmies or the islanders of Sunda protect some exotic artifact or endangered creature and the adventure seeking urban heroes help them. In '*Ekshringo Ovijaan*' (The Adventure towards The One-Horned) from Satyajit Ray's Shonku series, the fictional scientist Trilokeshwar Shonku has to deal with Tibetan Khampa bandit tribe who have murdered his fellow researcher professor, Willard, and are known to be ferocious, merciless raiders running around with their wild mastiffs.

It is to be noted that by going beyond geographical limits and incorporating tribes that would be considered global in the plot development, the risk of appropriation might get diluted, though at the cost of wider homogenisation. The concept of civility might also get relative when considering ethnicities that go beyond national boundaries. Nevertheless, the fact remains that the idea of aboriginal presence continues to be exoticised and otherised. These people continue to be clearly detached from the world the readers come from.

The other approach widely followed regarding dealing with tribal representations in Bangla thriller fiction is to maintain a much clearer distance. Readers do not come across well-known authors in the popular young adult genre who come directly from aboriginal backgrounds. Bangla literature clearly lacks representation when it comes to authors from diverse communities. It can be problematic for an upper class writer if he chooses to impersonate a tribal protagonist. Such distancing we see in the works of Manabendra Pal or Sasthipada Chattopadhyay. Such cases risk subscribing to ready-made stereotypes and even getting racist.

In Manabendra Pal's stories, the adivasis do not directly

become a site of horror, instead what stands out is how they are distanced from a subjective horrifying position and sometimes pushed to victimisation. They thrive in their own superstitious belief systems. Often in his stories, the intruder is a foreigner, a condescending sahib. He sets many of his stories in areas occupied by tribal communities, but a distinct tribal presence is never central or of much importance. With Sashtipada Chattopadhyay's horror stories, like '*Boraler Shei Raat*'' for example, we see a lot of stereotyping. Sometimes the adivasi communities are portrayed in a way that valorizes their bravery. They are physically quite different from soft-hearted, protected metropolitan outsiders. Sometimes his use of stereotyping gets quite racist as darker skin tones or ways of dressing are incorporated in plot development.

As Bangla thriller fiction evolves, the contemporary developments in the genre witness tantra and folklores becoming more and more popular. There is an element of secrecy that gets attached to the genre. Different tribal populations and their clandestine ways of life become the site of study. In many stories of lower tantra, Buddhist tribes like the Ningma sect, for example, appear as practitioners of the dark arts. The trends of depicting unfamiliar tribes and communities, that used to be more subtle, are now becoming more and more pronounced as the domain of folk occult horror evolves and finds strong fanbases. Bangla horror fiction genre has found a potent launchpad in youtube audio stories. These audio stories become important as they are easy to access and also capable of more clearly bringing out certain power dynamics through mocked accents and more such subtle hints. Successful productions like Areen Sen's 'Manot' on the channel Midnight Horror Station, or Ranadip Nandy's 'Ispaa' available on the channel *Thrillerland* take up tribal rituals, savage gods and such to present these elements as inseparable parts of the tribal existence. As audio stories dramatise the written text very well, there is a different force in their deployment and staging of realism.

This kind of otherisation through popular fiction goes on to serve a few purposes. Firstly, in such romanticised stories, the idea of dispossession is ignored. In Bandopadhyay's novella, the murderer even while blaming the amulet to justify his wrongdoings never considers his act of stealing a community artifact to be immoral. Secondly, such othering of unfamiliar communities based on their remote living conditions and 'savage' practices (like human sacrifice or unfamiliar eating habits) establishes a binary between a world of modern science and another of ancient superstitions.

The onus is put on the tribal peoples who appear to have chosen to embrace a backward lifestyle. The fact is ignored that probably these communities never got to choose what land they live on. Thirdly, the tribal population is homogenised badly. There is hardly ever a protagonist who comes from an adivasi background; the hero or speaker is always an intruder. He might be assisted by a tribal representati.e. but the inherent hierarchy in their roles is clearly established. Any kind of resistance is romanticised in an attempt to overlook potent inherent identity politics. The gender issue never materialises. The tribal woman is either seen as an ultimate victim of all kinds of atrocity, or her resistance is imagined through a masculine gaze as the victim is raised to a goddess of revenge, possibly motivated by male violence.

It is interesting how among the words for 'tribe' in Bangla

probably the most well known one is *upojati*, which would literally translate to sub-community. This word has a built-in sense of inferiority that properly captures the active opinions about tribal experiences that the Bengali community at large finds engraved in what Gramsci would call the 'bourgeoisie common sense'. The lack of direct contact and communication with the unfamiliar populations being depicted, is the cause for a Kolkata-centric authorship to blossom. To play it safe and keep up the image of a progessive educated society, deeper political issues like those of caste and class are brushed under the carpet.

The utopian idea of equal access for all is promoted, but the power structures can never truly be hidden. In most of these stories, the educated protagonist seems well aware that his station is superior in some sense and that is why while conversing with a tribal person, he uses the pronouns 'tui' or 'tumi', which lack the connotation of respect that the pronoun 'apni' used by the adivasi character, usually a servant or an inferior associate, directs towards the protagonist. When the pronoun 'tui' is casually deployed for the protagonist, it points at the lack of culture that the tribal individual suffers from, and is often followed by a 'babu'. 'They' are otherised from 'us' through very different everyday pronouns. Close study of the dialects and conversational styles in these stories disclose how permanent power structures are infused in the most basic rhetorics. 'Otherness' is commodified and maintained. Bell Hooks talks about how the differences that the 'other' presents become a site for pleasure in commodity culture as they can be more satisfying than the usual mundane ways of everyday life. The manufacturers and consumers in the genre of popular fiction who like to venture outside their comfort zones through such portrayals of a different world, risk treading very closely towards fetishisation and appropriation.

In adjacent genres like thriller, suspense, detective fiction, mystery or horror, the 'other' is an important existence. Since most of these genres either tread very closely or completely with speculation and fantasy, the 'other' becomes the one who falls outside our familiar systems, and thus, the site that produces the sense of wrong that needs to be corrected. Usually these are genres assumed to be enjoyed by younger audiences who will be entering or have recently entered the social sphere. So these stories serve as moral lessons as well as light entertainment reads. The figure of the other becomes so important here for this very reason; the other does things that are not to be emulated or followed. I keep coming back to my primary point that either by directly showing tribal characters as sites of horror or by maintaining a safe politically correct distance from them what is assured in popular fiction is that a particular sect is positioned outside the domain of culture and modernity.

Even when the tribal presence is revered by being equated with nature and glorified for their pristine ways of li.e. as done in *Sobuj Dwiper Raja* for example, the truth is that major biological and economic issues are glossed over. The Jarawas are never considered Indians as such. These uncultured tribals killing intruders is seen as a mere act of wanting to be left alone in their land of choice. The idea is not considered that maybe because of the lack of connection with the outside world, they do not have bodily immunity to certain diseases an outsider may bring in and even a cough and cold can be deadly for them. Also, the government officials working to make sure the community stays in peace are not exactly sympathetic to the causes that a closed tribe like the Jarawas might have, they just want to respect government's decrees for the sake of respecting them. Also, even after Gunoda Talukdar who considers himself a part of the Jarawa faction makes it clear that he does not want to leave them and come back to civil society, he is requested time and again to come back to live among civilisation. His sensibilities as a patriot are evoked to make him come home. At the end, even Talukdar is not allowed to remain as a part of 'them', he is brought back to 'our' civilised world.

By pretending that the tribal individuals intentionally obstruct their amalgamation into the mainstream, a neoliberal community suffering from a deep colonial hangover like the bourgeoisie Bengali society can keep up a facade of distant inclusivity and egalitarianism. These depictions hardly take into account the contemporary dilemmas that indigenous communities encounter; indeed these portrayals are very much in tandem with primitive colonial concepts regarding the other. As Said notes in his seminal treaty on Orientalism, during the era of colonial occupations, the west had certain homogenised romantic ideas and exotic stereotypes about the orient and the people who lived there.

The process of such psychological otherisation had helped them convince themselves that they are superior and the inferior other, a site of exaggerated differences, has to be conquered. Even though it has been more than half a decade that the British have left our country, certain innate colonial after-effects which are at large boosted by the ever present Brahmanical dilemmas of the Indian societal hegemony are ever present in the society we inhabit today. Since we are expected to repress the manifestations of our inner conservatism and colonial hangover, such silly popular genres for children can become harmless outbursts of certain internal sets of belief. What often happens with tribal representation in popular Bangla young adult fiction, is an example of that happening. The stereotypes that we grow up with regarding the tribal communities help the hierarchies grow in capillaries. Perhaps through the study of the portrayals of unfamiliar tribal cultures in popular young adult fiction, we come to understand that Bengali society is still not completely out of its deep-rooted colonial hangover.

However, that is not all. Tabish Khair, talking about the origins of Indian racism in an interesting column for The Hindu, says it would not be fair to blame it all on 'colonial inheritance and neocolonial cultural ramifications,' there is a need to confront our internal issues as a society. He goes on to add, 'Before the British brought us stories of 'African' cannibalism, we had our own stories of cannibalism-associated, from classical texts down to some current Chitra comics, with dark-skinned, non-'Aryan' looking creatures.' (Khair, 2017) As long as we don't tackle our inherent racism and casteism, there is no way for us to do justice to fictional portrayals of otherised lives. This is one issue that goes beyond authorial intent and readers' preference; unlearning and overcoming the micro processes that have internalised prejudices and stereotypes can be difficult, time-consuming yet achievable.

To conclude, I would like to look into a way of coming out of the problems of such fictional representations. Do we completely stop setting the stories in cultures that we do not know about? That seems a bit too much. After all, we learn things from these accounts as well. Maybe the answer lies in doing sufficient research before penning stories or trying to create protagonists who fit the bill, without cultural appropriation. That is not an easy task, I understand, but maybe the most important thing to do is not limit such genres to younger unsuspecting audiences and take it easy with important political sensibilities.

REFERENCES

Bandopadhyay, B. (2018). *Mishmider kavach.* Createspace Independent Publishing Platform. Bandopadhyay, B. (2018). Rankini devir khorgo. In Rupak Chattoraj (ed.), *Aloukik O Bhoutik Golpo* (3rd ed.). (pp 114-120). Dev Sahitya Kutir.

Bandopadhyay, B. (2018). Taranath tantriker dwitiyo golpo. In Rupak Chattoraj (ed.), *Aloukik O Bhoutik Golpo* (3rd edition). (pp 77-94). Dev Sahitya Kutir.

Bandopadhyay, S. (2007). Durgo rahasya. In *Byomkesh Samagra* (10th ed.). (pp 282-344) Ananda Publishers.

Bandopadhyay, S.(2004). Makorshar rawsh. In *Byomkesh Samagra* (10th ed.). (pp 90-102). Ananda Publishers.

Chattopadhyay, S. (2015). Boraler shei raat. In Paulami Sengupta (ed.), *Anandamela Bhuter Golpo Sonkolon.* (pp 154-162). Ananda Publishers.

Dasgupta, H. K. (2015). Burundir shobuj manush. In Sudhangsu Sekhar Dey (ed.), *Adventure Samagra.* (pp 11-115). Dey's Publishing.

Dasgupta, H. K. (2015). Sunda dwiper shonar dragon. In Sudhangsu Sekhar Dey (ed.), *Adventure Samagra.* (pp 115-153). Dey's Publishing.

Dasgupta, H. K. (2019). *Bhoy Bhoyankar.* Dev Sahitya Kutir.

Gangopadhyay, S. (2014). Sobuj dwiper raja. In Subirkumar Mitra (ed.), *Kakababu Samagra* Vol. 1(13th ed.). (pp 89-181). Ananda Publishers. 2014.

Hooks, B. (1992). Eating the other. In *Black Looks: Race and representation.* (pp 21-41). South End Press.

Khair, T. (2017, April 16). *The Roots of Indian Racism.* The Hindu. https://www.thehindu.com/opinion/columns/the-roots-of-indianracism/article18061795.e%20c

Midnight Horror Station. (2020, September 16). *Manot* [video]. Youtube. https://www.youtube.com/watch?v=6YFvn74XJv4

Pal, M. (2014). *Bhoutik Omnibus.* Dev Sahitya Kutir.

Ray, S. (2012). Ekshringo obhijaan. In *Shanku Samagra* (11th Ed.). (pp 251-186). Ananda Publishers.

Said, E. (1978). *Orientalism.* Pantheon Books.

Thrillerland. (2020, June 17). *Ispaa.* [video]. Youtube. https://www.youtube.com/watch?v=-HHOca9VODo&t=1931s

Tribal Development Department. (n.d). *Scheduled Tribes of West Bengal.* https://www.adibasikalyan.gov.in/html/st.php

Xaxa, Virginius. (2008). The Transformation of Tribes: The Terms of Discourse. In *State, Society and Tribes: Issues in Post-Colonial India.* (pp 13-27). Pearson Longman.

CHAPTER 9

Liberal Goddesses Feminine Agency in Tribal Hindu Mythology

Jisha Ponnachan

Ancient mythology, folklore, and legends have always been a part of many cultures and civilisations, and they are still considered to be the foundations of many. Most of these tales which were later published in the form of sacred texts were entrusted in the hands of the upper caste men who have interpreted and disseminated the same in a manner that not only accommodates their caste, but also favors their masculinity. The contemporary writers, seeing the need to challenge these hegemonies, often present a retelling of these epics that are more inclusive in nature. It is, therefore, not uncommon for these to be revisited and re-visioned in contemporary times with hundreds of different versions differing in terms of language, region and performative traditions. Such a polyphonic nature of these epics should, therefore, not be considered as a constraint, but rather as a domain of limitless possibilities (Tharuvana, 2021).

Observed in a similar light is an oral rendering observed amongst the tribal communities of India that provide a more nuanced understanding of the epics as practised by those who are forced to live on the periphery of Indian society.

The *Mahabharata* and the *Ramayana* hold a significant place in many Indian tribal lore and are often derived from multiple oral traditions. They have been heard and told for ages and are intimately woven into India's cultural fabric. Their popularity has survived for over two thousand years and more, over the entire Indian subcontinent. The peculiarity of the tribal versions of these epics is that they incorporate a lot of natural and supernatural elements in their story and are mainly more feministic or women-centric in narrative. This study focuses on the Adiya tribe of Wayanad and the tribal Bheels' (or Bhil's) interpretations of the *Ramayana* and *Mahabharata*, respectively. For the same, two texts that provide an English translation of the compilation of tales from these two tribes will be used as primary texts. These books are *Painted Words: An Anthology of Tribal Literature* which is edited by G. N. Devy, and the *Living Ramayanas: Exploring the plurality of the epic in Wayanad and the World* by Azeez Tharuvana. These are one of the few texts that document the tales of these tribals in English. Devy's text is an attempt to present various literary genres ranging from epics, long heroic prose, tribal songs, autobiographical writings, and a tribal drama. Tharuvana, on the other hand, explores the various versions of *Ramayana* that exist amongst the locals of Wayanad. The focus of this chapter will be on Devy and Tharuvana's compilation of the *Bhilli Mahabharat* and *Adiya Ramayana* respectively. The chapter will examine how female figures like Draupadi and Sita are free to express their own feminine agency through these tribal interpretations. They are presented as being more empowered, are more assertive about their sexual demands and break away from the traditional expectations that come from being a woman. The tribal creation myths appear to play an important role in developing positive power dynamics shared between a man and a woman.

The Bhilli Mahabharata

The Bhils are India's second-largest tribal population and the largest in the Rajasthan-Gujarat region. Bhil people are mentioned in the ancient Hindu epics *Ramayana* and *Mahabharata*, making them one of India's most ancient tribes. For them, the *Mahabharata* is crucially significant. The Bhil version of this epic is presented in discontinuous episodes rather than as one continuous narrative and different events from the epic are recited at key moments based on the social context and the episode's relevance in the same. The performance is a sacred ritual in and of itself, and it is worth noting that the epic can be recited by either a male or female storyteller who must adhere to certain rites and abstinences before and during the retelling (Patelet al., 2012). Such an oral rendering is not meant for entertainment, but is an integral part of the tribe's traditional and social customs.

An attempt in foregrounding this oral narrative into written form was made by Bhagwandas Patel in his text titled *Bhilo Ka Bharat*, which is a compilation of tales documented from the Doongri Bhil version of the *Mahabharata*. The overall narrative of the tales in this collection runs parallel to Vyasa's version of the epic, but the characters and their characteristics have been altered based on the tribal worldview. The women we encounter in the *Bhil Mahabharata* are more empowered and stronger, and play an equally important role in the epic. According to the Hindu code of Dharma, women had only one duty, which was to 'obey the father when unmarried, the husband when married and the son when widowed' (Pattanaik, 2006). Women in the *Bhil Mahabharata,* however, are not defined by their relationship with the males around them and a prime example of this is the role of Draupadi in this tribal epic. Vyasa's tale merely looks at Draupadi as the wife of the five Pandava brothers and as the one who was humiliated at the hands of the Kauravas.

The Bhil's *Mahabharata* goes beyond the popular narrative and presents Draupadi, referred to as *Dhofa,* as an individual with a mind of her own and as someone who has power over her husbands. Her beauty is still unmatched as she manages to catch the eye of Vasuki, the serpent king of the netherland. After being enamored by Draupadi's golden hair, Vasuki decides to restlessly search for her. Because of his misbehavior with her, Draupadi hurls curses at him and does not mind questioning and offending him. When Arjuna returns to the palace, he learns about the intentions of Vasuki who by then desired to sleep with Draupadi. A duel ensued between the two leading to the eventual defeat of Arjuna. The latter was then tied to a rod in front of his own bed and watched as his queen and the serpent king made love to each other (Patel et al., 2012). Draupadi in this version accepts the serpent king as her lover and after copulating with him, she prepares a large meal for him followed by 40 nights of love making. She, in the process, is not portrayed as a victim, but rather as a consenting sexual partner.

Another version of the tale also describes this incident as one where Draupadi herself asks Vasuki to make love to her so as to teach Arjuna a lesson because he had been arrogant to her. She is portrayed as a woman who has mastered the art of manipulating the men around her so as to get what she wants. She does not see the need to satisfy the masculine ego by waiting to be saved by her husbands and neither does she see a flaw in being desired by men outside her marriage. Her refusal to forgive Arjuna and punish him for his negligence indicates how women in the tribal mythology had space to express their sentiments overtly. Arjuna, after realising his mistake, worships her as *Adi-Shakti*. She, unlike in the standardised version of the epic, is not presented as an *abala* woman, without any strength, waiting to be rescued. Her empowerment is accompanied by the awareness of her rights, which she does not hesitate to execute explicitly, even in the presence of men. The peculiarity of *Bhil Mahabharata* is also that it does not observe Draupadi's sexual practices or desires as a disgrace. Either she entirely gives in to her desire or she engages in intimacy with the intention of making her husband recognise his mistake. Sexual longing, irrespectively, is seen as primal and instinctual, with no stigma or punishment accompanying the same. Moreover, Draupadi's depiction in this tribal epic defies the long-held patriarchal notion that a woman can have sexual relations only with her husband or whoever he selects for her. She becomes the creator of her own definition of morality and does not let her husbands' or the society's perspective hinder her from fulfilling her own desires.

Draupadi is in complete control of the situation and holds authority within the nature of their male-female interaction.

Arjuna's act of worshiping Draupadi and the latter's active involvement in the decision making demonstrates the power and magnificence she holds and hints at a plausible matriarchal culture observed amongst the Bhil tribals. A different tale in the *Bhil Mahabharata* also details how Yudhishthira who instead of consummating his marriage with Draupadi, fears her and worships her. He is aware of her magical nature and therefore kneels before her and performs her *aarti* (Chaitanya, 2009). Women in the *Bhil Mahabharata* are not merely put on a pedestal and considered goddesses. They are also treated like one. Bhil's *Mahabharata,* therefore, has the power to entirely make the readers forget that Draupadi was used as an instrument, her body merely observed as a site of establishing the male dominance by the men in Vyasa's epic. The tribal version of the epic, therefore, witnesses a role reversal in the power structure shared between men and women.

The Adiya Ramayana

The *Ramayana* is yet another epic that despite being composed centuries ago, still continues to thrive and exist in multiple versions. A. K. Ramanujan claims that these versions cannot be considered as a 'retelling' of Valmiki's *Ramayana*, in that they are not variants of the text, but are rather their own 'telling' (Ramanujan et al., 2013). Wayanad *Ramayanas* are not new to this tradition. The Wayanad region in Kerala is largely isolated by mountains on all sides and, therefore, the inhabitants of this district have developed their own culture. Their *Ramayana* presents the epic as being part of their history (Tharuvana & S, 2021). Their tales, however, consist of supernatural elements that separates itself from the events of their history. The Adiya community comprises tribal inhabitants that belong to this culturally rich Wayanad district of Kerala. The name Adiya has its roots in the word *Adiyaan* which means slave and it is believed that the inhabitants were mostly agricultural slaves in the ancient times. Many of the events in the epic are said to have occurred in and around Wayanad region, according to the oral traditions of Wayanad tribes. A popular belief about the propagation of the epic amongst the tribals is assumed to be through the upper-caste Ambalavasi community. The Adiyas may have witnessed dramatic enactment of the epic and may also have overheard discourses around the same through their overlords. Nonetheless, their version of the *Ramayana* is a far cry from Valmiki's *Ramayana*, and the characters are represented as tribals who lead a primitive lifestyle and are closely linked to nature. Characters such as Rama and Sita are also subjected to the same brutalities that other marginalised people face. However, the most notable feature of their tales is their feministic stance.

It is impossible to talk about the *Ramayana* without mentioning the key character of Sita. Like most epics, the war in the *Ramayana* too, happens over a fight for the woman who is desired by more than one man. The woman in the tale, although epitomised for her virtues and chastity, is still objectified, even by her own husband and father. In the *Adiya Ramayana*, the narrative mostly revolves around Sita. Their tale begins with Sita being presented as a tribal and is asked to leave Pulpally by the lord of the area. What is worth noting here is the communication that takes place between a lord and a tribal woman. Such interactions were often rare in the ancient times when women were kept out of every important decision. The epic presents a rustic image of Sita who soon leaves Pulpally and travels over hills while also carrying all her belongings.

Ram and Lakshman meet her on the way and the former

falls in love with her even though she barely notices him. She meets Ravana later who immediately wins her heart and takes her to Lanka. Even when Hanuman burns down Lanka, she has no idea about Ram or his doings. The Adiya tribal *Ramayana* also stands out specifically because it excludes mentions of any chariots or carriage. When Ravana and Sita travel to Lanka, they commute in a bullock cart and manually cross a river together. This is unlike Valmiki's *Ramayana* where Sita had to be escorted on a chariot by a man. This rustic image of Sita gives her the identity of a commoner, a local deity that is relatable and can be worshiped by the Adiya tribals.

There is an instance in the *Adiya Ramayana* that describes how Sita first encountered Hanuman while on her way to Lanka with Ravana. To reach Lanka, one had to go beyond the river for which a bridge was needed. Hanuman and his friend, the Bear built one by carrying huge blocks of stones. In the process, however, Hanuman felt greatly offended by the fact that a female Bear was able to carry the stones with one hand easily while he had to use both his hands and still struggled to lift the stones. Enraged, he threatened to pull down the hill. Sita, having heard the threat, requested Hanuman not to do so or they shall be buried under the Earth. She instead blesses him and the monkeys that they shall henceforth only eat the fruits of the trees and drink the freshwater from the streams (Tharuvana & S, 2021). This hints at how women in the Adiya society often carried the burden of providing for their families and maintaining the sustenance of their natural resources. From an eco-feminist perspecti.e. the patriarchal notion of masculinity that Hanuman holds is threatened when the female Bear challenges his strength. The rage produced as a response to this challenge could have exploited and led to the degradation of natural resources. The intimate relationship that the tribal Sita shares with nature, allowed her to be more sensitive to the preservation of the bountiful nature and its sanctity.

Sita in the tribal telling is also a woman who is portrayed as someone who is perfectly capable of making and exerting her own choice. Despite falling in love with Ravana and travelling with him to Lanka on her own free will, she asks him for a vow that he shall not touch her body or her clothes for 12 years as she mediates and that she will marry him only after that period. Ravana, here, is not in a position to make any demands and agrees with the condition (Tharuvana & S, 2021). Men and women in the *Adiya Ramayana* are presented as equal partakers of life. If anything, the women are almost given god-like status and their greatness is recognised by the men around them. Even after Hanuman convinces Sita that Ravana is not a good man and that Ram is in love with her, Sita decides to leave only when her mind says so. She does not randomly decide to marry Ram. Only after he declares his love for her and describes his wanderings in search for her, does Sita appreciate his effort, and she decides to marry him. What one observes, therefore, is a strength of character in Sita. She is unwavering with her choices and is not fearful of making men work hard to convince her. Here, the age-old tradition of the *swayamvar* is also not mentioned. Such a tradition is not observed amongst the tribals and this is reflected in their telling of the epic.

Like any other fairy-tale wedding, Ram and Sita encounter several disagreements in the course of their marriage. Sita misses the luxuries she enjoyed in Ravana's palace and she longs for the company of maids and companions (Tharuvana

& S, 2021). Often in our reading of the *Ramayana,* we find Sita as a mute and lonely character. Be it her abduction by Ravana in Lanka or her abandonment by her husband who doubts her chastity. However, in the *Adiya Ramayana*, this loneliness is given an expression in the form of her neglect and lack of interest in her household duties. In her melancholy, Sita has prioritised her emotional expression over her duties towards her husband. Such a subversive representation not only challenges the derogatory stereotypes associated with women's roles and responsibility in the society, but also highlights and lays emphasis on the mental state of a woman in an unhappy marriage. When confronted, Sita also retaliates and breaks her silence. For the same, Ram orders Lakshmana to slay Sita, who because of his utter devotion for his sister-in-law, refuses to perform such a sin and lets her and her kids live in hiding. The Adiyas, thus, portray their Sita as a woman who breaks the stereotype of the Sati-Savitri. She is unlike Valmiki's Sita who is silent and obedient towards her husband. When pushed away by her husband, Sita even manages to convince Lakshmana to let her live. Yet again, this is an indication of the fact that tribal mythologies were crafted in a manner in which the female characters had the ability to communicate with the males around them with the intention of getting them convinced in their cause.

Lord Ram is considered to be the epitome of an ideal husband and is a central figure amongst the Gods in Hindu mythology. The *Adiya Ramayana,* however, presents him as a commoner who is not flawless. In their epic, Ram was not the first man to fall in love with Sita and he is the 'other man' in the story. He is portrayed as someone who will move mountains in order to make Sita his own. His role as a saviour is, however, challenged when one questions whether Sita was his to be saved in the first place. Ravana's character becomes questionable, not through his actions or intentions but through Hanuman's testimony of him. Events of insult and control of Sita followed after she was married to Ram. Sita's retaliation makes the flaws in her husband's character more prominent as he reveals himself to be a harsh and insensitive husband who is a far cry from the ideal man. However, there is no space in Valmiki's account of the *Ramayana* to explore the shortcomings of a man who is placed on such a pedestal. On the other hand, the Adiya version recounts a scene where Rama and Lakshman are bound to a tree and interrogated by tribal leaders regarding Rama's desertion of a pregnant Sita (Tharuvana & S, 2021). Here, the close-knit tribal community acts as a counsellor for the couple. Their faith in the local leaders re-emphasises the idea that Lord Rama and Sita are not godly individuals but tribal commoners who rely on the help of their community to solve their differences.

Tribal Creation Myths

The Hindu creation myths for the longest time were seen as a barrier in women's empowerment. The Hindu society assumes Brahma to be the creator of the universe who manifested as a golden egg that encompassed everything. Brahma then splits himself into two and from his second half a woman is formed (Pattanaik, 2006). According to one version of the tale, Brahma granted himself the ability to reproduce, then turned into a stag and made love to his daughter. For the same reason, he was punished by being struck by an arrow. His seeds later took the form of a lake. The male is always described as the powerful creator whereas the females are described in relation to the men—originating from or created by men, made to complete men and created to satisfy men's pleasure. Power resides in such a creation myth and it is only reasonable to assume that it is likely to be motivated by a thirst for political power and control. They have an overall effect on various streams of thought (Ogdoc-Gascon, 2016). More often than not, humans derive their identity and orientation in the world from these creation myths. Their fundamental patterns of life and living are influenced by these myths.

Unfortunately, so many use the same to exert power and dominance in the society. The idea that the universe was created by a male God and the fact that women were created from the body of a man, is used to justify much of the misogyny in the Hindu society. In the Hindu culture, therefore, women are considered to be inferior to men. Their individuality is reduced and they are observed merely as a property of their husbands. Man is equated to culture whereas woman is equated to nature. Nature, too, is valued only when it gives natural resources.

The tribal creation myths in this respect are like a breath of fresh air. Unlike the Sanskritised texts that believe that culture can exist only when nature is domesticated, the tribal versions of the same do not see nature (or women) as a threat to culture. They believe in the thriving of culture and society but not at the cost of nature. It observes, instead, a harmony between nature and culture. A variation of the creation myth of mankind in the Adiya tribe involves both Shiva and Parvathy carefully making human figures out of clay. Both man and the woman are equally involved in the creation of man. In addition to this, dogs also play a significant role in the creation of mankind because every time Shiva and Parvathy fell asleep, Goddess Bhadrakali smashed the figures that the couple made. To prevent this from repeating, the couple created a dog out of clay who would guard the forms of humans. So every time the goddess arrived, the dog would alert the couple by barking (Tharuvana & S, 2021). The tribal creation myths, therefore, see a united participation of the male and the female and also incorporate other elements of nature in the creation of mankind. Gender is viewed as a societal construct that is challenged by the fact that the female goddess is not perceived as any less powerful than the male one.

As a result, it is clear that women in tribal Hindu mythology resist the gender norms and responsibilities imposed on them by society. The tribal versions of the epics make space for women to feel liberated, have a voice of their own and express themselves in ways that challenge the patriarchal hegemony of the society. The readers are given a chance to get acquainted with the perspective of these women who were portrayed as mere spectators of the injustice perpetrated against them in the Sanskritised versions of the epics. However, despite the mythology and folklore of these Indian tribes being so women-centric, the tribes mentioned in this chapter, by nature, are considered to be patriarchal with men ruling their household and females being married off by the age of 15. Carl Jung in his *The Phenomenology of the Spirit in Fairytales: The Archetypes and the Collective Unconscious* states that the archetypes portrayed in art, literature and mythology are a reflection of the 'collective psyche' of a community. The tales express the unconscious element of a person's psyche (Jung & Hull, 2014). These creation myths, therefore, have set the foundations regarding gender roles and attitudes in the minds of the people of these tribes. These ideologies have emerged from the collective unconscious of the tribal men and women. It is only reasonable to assume, then, that the alterations that one witnesses between preaching and practise in these tribes is not inherent but is rather inculcated because of their interactions with non-tribal communities. Alternative research can, therefore, be conducted to explore the kind of influence that non-tribal communities have over tribal politics, their culture and worldview. However, this would involve a rethinking of the entire complex of the knowledge-power conundrum because they are so intrinsically linked to one another.

Nonetheless, the women in the tribal mythology are an inspiration to today's tribal women. Learning about empowered, fierce women in a matriarchal system encourages women to accept the fact that they too can become what their female ancestors were. Thus, an inventory of one's own past has the power to help the tribal women perceive themselves as strong individuals.

REFERENCES

The Adiyas, Tribal Sects, Wayanad, Kerala, India. Kerala Tourism - Wayanad. (n.d.). Retrieved 26 January 2022, from https://www.keralatourism.org/wayanad/adiyas-tribe.php

Anil, K. M. (29 December 2018). *The Plurality of Ramayana: In conversation with Prof. K.M.*

Anil. Sahapedia. Retrieved 26 January 2022, from https://www.sahapedia.org/the-plurality-of-ramayana-conversation-prof-km-anil

Bhattacharjee, D. (2020, February 1). *Hinduism and women: Glimpses from a feminist perspective.* Welsh Women's Aid. Retrieved 26 January 2022, from http://www.welshwomensaid.org.uk/2020/01/hinduism-and-women-glimpses-from-a-fem inist-perspective/

Brandmaier, G. V. (2015). *Patriarchy and the Power of Myth: Exploring the Significance of a Matriarchal Prehistory.* Bard Digital Commons. Retrieved 26 January 2022, from https://digitalcommons.bard.edu/cgi/viewcontent.cgi?article=1350&context=senproj_s20 15

Chaitanya, S. (13 September 2009). *Women, gender and power in Bheel Mahabharata 1.*

Women, Gender and Power in Bheel Mahabharata 1. Retrieved 26 January 2022, from https://satyachaitanyas.blogspot.com/2009/09/women-gender-and-power-in-bheel.html

Chaitanya, S. (13 September 2009). *Women, gender and power in Bheel Mahabharata 2.*

Women, Gender and Power in Bheel Mahabharata 2. Retrieved 26 January 2022, from https://satyachaitanyas.blogspot.com/2009/09/women-gender-and-power-in-bheel_13.ht ml

Chakravarty, K. K. (2009). *Text and variations of the Mahābhārata: Contextual, regional and performative traditions.* National Mission for Manuscripts, Indira Gandhi National Centre for Arts.

Godbole, D. (8 October 2018). *Why were the male heroes 'masters' of both women and nature in Hindu mythology?* Feminism In India. Retrieved 26 January 2022, from https://feminisminindia.com/2018/10/09/hindu-mythology-male-women-nature/

Joshi, A. R. (2006). Fieldwork Report: The Dangi Ramakatha: An Epic acculturated? *Indian Folklore Research Journal, 3*(6), 13–37.

Jung, C. G. (2014). The Phenomenology of the Spirit in Fairytales. In R. F. C. Hull (Ed.), *The Archetypes and the Collective Unconscious* (2nd ed., pp. 207–254). essay, Routledge.

K, H. (2016, March 20). *When Surpanakha Beevi almost seduced Rama.* Times of India Blog.

Retrieved 26 January 2022, from https://timesofindia.indiatimes.com/blogs/tracking-indian-communities/when-surpanakha-beevi-almost-seduced-rama/

Kriti, H. (8 September 2021). *Women in Hindu mythology: Is their space too a myth?* Feminism In India. Retrieved 26 January 2022, from https://feminisminindia.com/2021/02/26/women-hindu-mythology-space/

Lal, A. (17 February 2007). *The Maha Tradition.* The Economic Times. Retrieved 26 January 2022, from https://economictimes.indiatimes.com/the-maha-tradition/articleshow/1630272.cms

Lal, A. (3 November 2011). *The Spectre of A.K. Ramanujan.* The Economic Times. Retrieved 26 January 2022, from https://economictimes.indiatimes.com/opinion/et-commentary/the-spectre-of-a-k-ramanuj an/articleshow/10588424.cms

Madhavan, A., & Narayana, S. (2021). Violation of land as violation of feminine space: An ecofeminist reading of Mother Forest and mayilamma. *Tattva Journal of Philosophy, 12*(2), 13–32. https://doi.org/10.12726/tjp.24.2

Ogdoc-Gascon, D. (2016). Gender socialisation in creation myths. *International Journal of Culture and History (EJournal), 2*(2), 83–86. https://doi.org/10.18178/ijch.2016.2.2.043

Patel, B. (2004). *Bharata of the Bhils*. Mahabharata Resources. Retrieved 26 January 2022, from http://mahabharata-resources.org/variations/BharataoftheBhils.html

Patel, B., & Devy, G. N. (2012). From the Bhilli Mahabharat. In A. Dandekar (Trans.), *Painted words: An anthology of tribal literature* (pp. 13–36). essay, Purva Prakash.

Pattanaik, D. (2006). *Myth = Mithya: A handbook of Hindu mythology*. Penguin Books India.

Ramanujan, A. K., Dharwadker, V., & Blackburn, S. H. (2013). *The Collected Essays of A. K. Ramanujan*. Oxford University Press.

Ramayanas of Wayanad. Sahapedia. (14 March 2018). Retrieved 26 January 2022, from https://www.sahapedia.org/ramayanas-of-wayanad

S, P. (5 August 2020). *Wayanad, Where Stories of 'the Ramayana' Come Alive*. The Hindu.

Sen, N. D. (1997). *When Women Retell the Ramayana*. Retrieved 26 January 2022, from http://manushi-india.org/pdfs_issues/PDF%20file%20108/5.%20When%20Women%20R etell%20the%20Ramayan.pdf

Singh, V. (2017). Reclaiming Female Identity: Feminist Retellings of the Hindu Epics. *The Criterion: An International Journal in English, 8*(II), 380–386.

Tharuvana, A. (2021). *Exploring the Plurality of the Epic in Wayanad and the World*. (O. E. S, Trans.). Eka.

Tharuvana, A. (21 October 2021). *Adiya Ramayana: An oral tradition of Wayanad sees the main figures of the epic as Tribals*. Scroll.in. Retrieved 26 January 2022, from https://scroll.in/article/1008155/adiya-ramayana-an-oral-tradition-of-wayanad-sees-the-m ain-figures-of-the-epic-as-tribals

Tharuvana, A. (29 October 2021). *Ramayana and the world: Kerala academic Azeez Tharuvana explores plurality of the epic.* On Manorama. Retrieved 26 January 2022, from https://www.onmanorama.com/news/kerala/2021/10/28/azeez-tharuvana-epic-ramayana-world-plurality.html

Tharuvana, A. (1 November 2021). A Thousand Flowers Bloom. *The Caravan.* Retrieved 19 November 2021, from https://caravanmagazine.in/religion/many-muslim-versions-ramayana.

CHAPTER 10

Nagas in the Frame

Pouriangthanliu

With the advent of the British along the North east Frontier of India, visual materials constituted an important medium in knowing and recording the territory and its inhabitants. During the 19th and first half of the 20th century, colonial administrators, anthropologists, soldiers, surveyors, and Christian missionaries were quite prolific in producing textual accounts as well as visual records of their journeys, encounters, and observations in the Naga Hills. These photographic collections, such as those of the German anthropologists Furer-Haimendorf and Hans Eberhard-Kauffmann have received attention in recent times (Jacobs, 1990; Opitz, 2008). Milada Ganguli's collection may also be a valuable contribution towards a visual history of north-east India as it provides a rich context of post-British Naga Hills.

Born on 10 July 1913 in Czechoslovakia, and educated in Prague and London, Milada Ganguli came to India in 1939 as the wife of the Bengali writer Mohanlal Ganguli, a close relative of Rabindranath Tagore. Her earliest opportunity to visit the areas inhabited by the Nagas came in 1963. This visit was made possible by the Manipuri princess, Maharaj Kumari Binodini Devi, who arranged an Inner Line Permit for her to travel to the Naga Hills. Between 1963 and 1988, she visited the state around 18 times. As she travelled across the Naga Hills, she amassed photographic records and information of the Nagas (Ganguli, 1984). Her collection is remarkable in the sense that she was able to gain access into the Naga Hills during a time when it was officially closed to outsiders due to the prevailing political unrest and was undergoing immense changes. Based on these visits and secondary sources/ findings/ publications etc., she published *Pilgrimage to the Nagas* (1984). Its preface is written by Christoph von Furer-Haimendorf, and it is a field-based literature of the post-colonial period, providing a comprehensive representation of the Nagas. In contrast to the interest on colonial visual materials, there has been a surprisingly relative lack of research on Milada Ganguli's photo collection. The collection comprises well over 300-400 'field photographs'. Mostly in black and whi.e. these provide a rich record of Naga social life and material culture in the post-British period. Its contents depict a range of aspects of the Naga society, including villages, houses, *morungs* or youth dormitories, ethnographic illustrations, dances, scenes of war parties, agricultural work, crafts, domestic activities, weapons, musical instruments, dance, textiles, clothing, headdresses, ornaments, architecture, customs, tattoos, ritual practices, etc. This photographic record is in large part the result of her concern to make an 'in-depth' study of the beliefs, customs and ways of life of some of the 'exotic' Naga 'tribes' (Ganguli, 1984). The collection presents a unique context to study people caught in a moment of tremendous changes in post-British India. This study will try to analyse the dissemination of photographic images from camera to archive to mass viewership, and the forms, meaning and history of this memorialising process.

Photography is an important recording tool for inquiry as exemplified in the ground-breaking work of Margaret Mead and Gregory Bateson in *Balinese Character* (1942). Bateson and Mead employed photography as a tool for observing and recording everyday Balinese interaction through visual ethnography. This method was popular among anthropologists, particularly during the first few decades of the 20th century in which fieldwork, the central practice of the discipli.e. came to be used as a basis for constructing the 'Other'. It was subsequently employed by anthropologists to document 'vanishing' cultural practices of non-western cultures and peoples resulting in a realist recording of 'exotic' images of people and cultures as can be seen in Franz Boas's photography, Evans-Pritchard's photography in *The Nuer* (1940), and Mead's and Bateson's detailed collection of still images of the Balinese. With this, the 'exotic' was reduced to 'objective' data couched in a temporal, 'ethnographic present' (Fabian, 1983, cited in Aloysius Ma. L. Canete, 2008) that reified the cultural practices of the other by transforming the subject of photography into an object (cited in Aloysius Ma. L. Canete, 2008).

Studies on photography have provided new and exciting insights in underlining the role of photographic materials and their use in studying and reconstructing the cultural past of a given society. It has drawn our attention to complex ways in which photography became a necessary element in the colonial enterprise of recording, documenting, and classifying 'the people of the empi.e.' making them visible and understandable (Ryan,

1997; Karlekar, 2005; Pinney, 2008). Besides, photographs also provide us a glimpse of a moment in history. Photographic images, as Christopher Pinney suggests, 'are pieces of evidence in an ongoing biography or history' (Pinney, 2006, p. 166). In *Camera Lucida*, Roland Barthes (1981) argues the usage of photographs as 'power' where photograph travels across time and space, and in the process the intended meaning behind the image changes as it moves from one context to another. For example, colonial administrators took photographs of their subjects for the purpose of asserting their hegemony over them. Conversely, it can also be argued that subjugated people may appropriate the same photographs to reassert their identity and power in the post-colonial context (Van Schendel: 2002; Rycroft: 2004).

Hence, 'the authority of the photograph resides not in the stilled object itself, but in its capacity to make the apparent blurred, the strange familiar, and the hidden visible. In this context, photographs are not passi.e. but dynamic representations of reality that are constituted in/through the lived experience and milieu of the photographer and the viewer', it perpetuates the past while it is being reproduced (consumed) in the present, the transformation of the 'there-then' into the 'here-now' (Ma. L. Canete, Aloysius, 2008, Roland Barthes, 1981).

Many of the anthropological and ethnographic writings present continuities and 'changing continuities' that have taken place in Naga communities, cultures, and customs. As Verrier Elwin notes, all writings and records do not present a correct picture, but were illustrative of how the Nagas were viewed by the outsiders (Wouters & Henei.e. 2017, pp 1-2). It has to be noted that 'none of the writers represented here were professional anthropologists', while 'some of them wrote better anthropology than many of the supposedly [anthropologically] 'trained' young men of the present.' Most of the ethnographic detail of early colonial writings were written during trying circumstances, often under 'military escort' and amidst hostilities. Skirmishes along the way also meant that 'precious notes and documents were lost and in spite of their defects we should be astonished that, under the circumstances, they collected so much information and wrote as well as they did' (Ibid 2017, pp 5-7). This archive of the colonial and post-colonial helps us to re-evaluate the Nagas in context. There are various projects by universities, museums which continue to showcase Naga skulls, spears, headgear, and a host of other artefacts.

In 2000, the Hornbill festival was first launched. It was a weeklong celebration of traditional Naga ritual re-enactments, dances, handicrafts, and food traditions, and inspired critical scholarship which coincided with a new discourses in museum studies, centred on the ethics of colonial acquisition (Thomas, 1991), the politics of repatriation (especially of sacred objects), the contemporary relevance of 'curiosity box' curatorial practices, and perhaps more presciently, the cultural and historical relevance of indigenous material culture amid a worldwide re-genesis of indigenous cultural and identity politics (Arnold-de Simi.e. 2013; Barrett, 2011; and Bennet, 2004). As colonial collections re-emerge, curators and scholars wrangle over correctly portraying continuities and discontinuities, but also, in a sense, seeking to educate visitors (and readers of associated write-ups) about the fraught history of orientalist portrayals (West 2011, 1999). Under the Digital

Himalaya project developed by Alan Macfarlane and Mark Turin at Cambridge University, there was the Naga project, which 'was intended for use in a variety of educational contexts and encourage a critical engagement on the part of the user. This small endeavour is part of a wider project to experiment with various methods to 'return culture', contribute a little to the preservation and public understanding' (Mark Turin and Alan Macfarlane, pp. 372, 375-76). There was a resurgence on Naga visual and material culture not only among the European but also by Naga scholars and scholars of South Asia such as Alban van Stockhausen, Michael Oppitz, Arkotong Longkumer, Dolly Kikon, Vibha Joshi, Richard Kunz, Aditya Arya and others (Wouters & Henei.e. 2017).

Relating to the new genre of pictographic works echoing the conscious effort and reinvigoration, for instance, the coffee-table books do not have scholarly implication yet their pursuit of the 'exotic give us some idea of the continuity of some traditions and thus, counter the pessimistically styled writings of some Western scholars who consider that Christianity has led to the destruction of people's culture and a feeling of shame about past cultural practices. These books capture a resurgence of interest among the Europeans' (Joshi, 2012, p. 260). There is also a project initiated by the Pitts Rivers Museum (PRM) on Naga material culture, which focuses on community engagement with the photographs of Naga objects in the PRM's colonial collections and the repercussions and reverberation of the effect of such information being brought back to the community. The ongoing collaboration has already resulted in two indigenous publications and a visit of members of the women's group to PRM (Joshi, 2018).

A study of the images, whether colonial or post-colonial, may inform us about the particular subject matter that attracted the photographer and also provide insights into the way subjects and their culture were represented in the photographs. Drawing upon these literatures, the chapter looks at the visual materials produced on the Naga Hills by Milada Ganguli and its relationship to ideas of identity, culture, and social change.

The variety of images reveals that there are many subjects which the camera recorded. Of these, the collection contains several ethnographic illustrations representing the various Naga communities which are arranged under the classified tribal categories such as the Angami, Ao, Chakhesang, Chang, Lower Konyak, Upper Konyak, Pochuri, Western Rengma, Central Sangtam, Lotha, Sema, Phom, Mao, Maram, Khiamniungam, Yimchunger, Rongmei and Tangkhul. What is interesting here is that in recording these communities, the pictures emphasise the external markers of these diverse identities. Thus, pictures of individuals or groups of people are often photographed in ways, which deliberately stressed differences in dress, hairstyles, tattooing, clothes and body ornaments. A focus on these images, then, draws our attention to the role of pictures in further producing, representing, and entrenching ideas about the various Naga communities and their identities.

An important theme that the photo collection highlights is the patterns and variations in political structures in the Naga Hills. Thus, pictures of Konyak and Sema chiefs are matched by the pictures of village elders among the Angamis. These pictures are put forth to explain the oscillation from the 'autocratic' *anghs* (chiefs) to the more 'democratic' forms of political organisation in the Naga Hills. Closely linked to the political and social life of the Nagas are the practice of headhunting and the performance of feasts of merit. Ganguli's photo collection, thus, includes pictures of individuals and warriors who were 'headhunters' and renowned for their exploits in war or raids. In recording this practi.e. she draws our attention to the nuanced relations that existed between villages in the Naga Hills. What, however, seems to appear from such representation is the tendency to reproduce the often quoted and exoticised image of the Nagas and their 'proclivities' for war, a characteristic which has been associated with the Nagas since colonial times. The photographs are also an account of the manifold art forms which developed in close relation with the headhunting practices and ritual feasts. For instance, body decorations or tattoos, the right to wear particular ornaments as well as architectural designs are remnants or traces of the 'past' when headhunting constituted an important part of the cultural practices of the Nagas.

While headhunting constituted an important marker of individual success and standing as a warrior in the community, there were other practices through which high status was conferred to an individual. She, thus, records how the Nagas displayed wealth and status in the past through the performance of 'Feast of Merit'. She also notes. 'The holding of the Feasts of Merit entitles the giver and the members of his family to wear magnificent dresses and special ornaments. His elevated social status is further reflected in the architectural style and decorations on the house in which he lives' (Ganguli, 1984, p. 130). In other words, it was through this feast of merit that an individual enhanced his social standing or status in the village, which ultimately culminated by way of erecting wooden posts or large stone slabs in the village.

Another important theme that stands out in the collection is the focus on material culture. For instance, ceremonial dress in the photographs shows weaving patterns and strong colours. In fact, photographs of costumes and other clothing adornments show different clothing styles and patterns among the Ao, Angami, Konyak, Mao Nagas, etc. Cloth making, knowledge on dyeing, weaving, etc., were other important everyday practices which Ganguli records through the camera. Apart from these clothing styles, the photographs also draw attention to the decorative elements such as rows of beadwork and embroidery woven into the textiles, in basketry work, weapons, jewellery, etc. These ornamental elements were then associated with the status displays of the wearer. What is also important here is the fact that the use of beads and ornaments suggest the existence of a long history of contact between the hills and the plains through trade. The photographs also indicate the difference in the art and crafts of the Nagas especially between the crafts dominated by men and those that are the speciality of women. Ganguli admired the woodcarving of the Nagas especially in creating utilitarian objects of wood, cane, and bamboo and noted how they incorporated them in their domestic architecture. These various types of photographic evidence provide a unique insight into the material culture and the changes that were being gradually adapted into the everyday practices among the Nagas.

Nagas generally build their villages on hilltops and the architectural pattern or house styles constitute an important focus of Ganguli's photographs. Among the Maram Nagas, for instance, the house of an ordinary villager is roofed with thatched grass, in contrast, to the rough wooden shingles roof of the chief, which distinguishes his high social standing (Ganguli, 1984, p. 62). Ganguli also records the variations in house structure such as the longhouses of the Konyak *anghs*, and the *morungs* or men's club house and the log drum which *morungs* contained. The log drum is usually carved with extraordinary skills from a 'carefully selected huge tree' and could be from 12 metres in length and 3 metres in circumference (Ganguli, 1984, p. 120). The log drum played a vital role in the life of the inhabitants of the village and was beaten to warn of the approach of enemies, fire or death. On the other hand, wood carvings on a house often distinguished and symbolised an individual of high social status in the village. An example here is the remarkable carvings on the house of Senipa, a member of Meluri village from the Eastern Rengma.

Other photographs record and introduce us to aspects of jhum cultivation, which was prevalent especially among the Yimchungers, Changs, Konyaks, etc., and the practice of terraced cultivation among the Angamis. The photographs also suggest gender division in labour, and roles for women such as weaving, fetching water, winding yarns, etc. in the everyday life. The photographs also include details of hunting and the importance of mithun or *Bos frontalis* in the socio-economic life of the Nagas. Photographs in the collection also draw attention to the importance of the customs and beliefs in spirits among the Nagas and the festivals, rituals, dances, and ceremonies associated with them. A variety of customs associated with death such as platform burials or the custom of burying the dead inside the house among the Chang Nagas and the erection of ceremonials in memory of important chiefs tells us about the deep belief of life after death.

While Milada Ganguli recorded these varied facets of the Naga socio-cultural practices, she also observed the rapidly vanishing practices and institutions in the Naga Hills such as tattooing, feast of merit, the *morungs*, etc. For instance, during her visit to Khesa village in the Ao areas, Ganguli notes how 'the morung has fallen into disrepair and has not been replaced by a new one' (Ganguli, 1984, p. 120). This is attributed largely to the impact of Christianity that has increasingly come to permeate the Naga society as well as a result of the government endeavour to stop cultural practices such as headhunting, which was considered abhorrent in a 'modern' society (Ganguli, 1984, pp. 173, 214).

The collections resonate with and extend the idea of colonial representation of the Nagas as the exotic other. Evidently, she was deeply influenced by the pictorial collections of administrators-cum-ethnographers of the Naga Hills such as J.H. Hutton, J.P. Mills and others. The picture she captures were, therefore, not innocent representation, but rather it fit in with the older celebration of the traditional Nagas. While her photo collection highlights the varied political structures, material culture, and belief systems that both link and define the various Naga 'tribes', what also seems to appear is the fact that it also tends to reify the Nagas and, at times, represent their culture as frozen in time. Nevertheless, her photographs also did capture flashes of modernity and changes that were slowly taking place in the hills – improved infrastructures, modern roads, bridges, hospitals, and educational institutions.

Milada Ganguli's collection is housed and secured in resource centres and museums. These are available for use for the Nagas to sustain and preserve a universal collection of knowledge and creativity for future generation. Not only have these lasting images captured some ancestors, these photographs have also become valuable as historical sources and as objects for strengthening identity. Her photographic album is a remarkable record and observation of the cultural heritage of the Nagas which should be of interest to the public, especially to anthropologists, visual practitioners, and historians of the region.

REFERENCES

Barthes, Roland. (1981). *Camera Lucida: Reflections on Photography*. (R. Howard, Trans.). Hill and Wang.

Bateson, Gregory and Margaret Mead. (1942). *Balinese Character: A Photographic Analysis*. New York Academy of the Sciences.

Edwards, Elizabeth. (1992). Introduction. In Elizabeth Edwards (ed.). *Anthropology and Photography, 1860-1920* (pp. 3-17). Yale University Press.

Canete Ma. L, Aloysius. (2008). Exploring Photography: A Prelude Towards Inquiries into Visual Anthropology in the Phillipines. *Phillipines Quarterly of Society and Culture*, 36(1/ 2), 1-14.

Douglas, Nickel R. (2001). History of Photography: The State of Research. *The Art Bulletin*, 83(3), 548-558.

Evans-Pritchard, E.E. (1940). *The Nuer: A Description of the Modes of Livelihood and Political Institutions of a Nilotic People*. Oxford University Press.

Ferrarotti, Franco. (1993). Culture and Photography: Reading Sociology through a Lens. *International Journal of Politics, Culture, and Society*, 7(1), 75-95.

Ganguli, Milada. (1984). *A Pilgrimage to the Nagas*. Oxford & IBH Publishing Co.

Harper, Douglas. (1996). Seeing Sociology. *The American Sociologist*, 27(3), 69-78.

Hight M., Eleanor and Gary D. Sampson. (2002). Introduction: Photography, 'Race' and Post-Colonial Theory. In Hight M., Eleanor and Sampson, Gary D. (eds.). *Colonialist Photography: Imag(in)ing Race and Place* (pp. 1-19). Routledge.

Jacobs, Julian. (1990). *The Nagas: The Hill people of Northeast India: Society, Culture and the Colonial Encounter.* Thames and Hudson.

James R. Ryan. (1997). *Picturing Empire: Photography and the Visualization of the British Empire.* Reaktion Books.

Landau, Paul & Kaspin, Deborah. (eds.). (2002). *Images and Empires: Visuality in Colonial and Postcolonial Africa.* University of California Press.

Macfarlane, Alan & Turin, Mark. (2008). The Digitization of Naga Collections in the West and the Return of Culture. In Opitz, Michael., Kaiser, Thomas., Stockhausen, Alban., & Wettstein, Marion. (eds.). *Naga Identities: Changing Local Cultures in the Northeast of India* (pp. 364-377). Snoeck-Ducaji & Zoon.

Opitz, Michael., Kaiser, Thomas., Stockhausen, Alban., & Wettstein, Marion. (eds.). (2008). *Naga Identities: Changing Local Cultures in the Northeast of India.* Snoeck-Ducaji & Zoon.

Pinney, Christopher. (2008) *The Coming of Photography in India.* The British Library.

Seven Theses on photography. *Thesis Eleven*, 113(1), 141-156.

Ramaswamy, Sumathi, (ed.). (2003). *Beyond Appearances? Visual Practices and Ideologies in Modern India.* Sage Publications.

Rycroft, Daniel J. (2004). Capturing Birsa Munda: The Virtuality of Colonial-Era Photograph. *Indian Folklore Research Journal*, 1(4), 53-68.

Sontag, Susan. (1973). *On Photography.* Penguin.

Valeri, Burri Regul. (2012). Visual Rationalities: Towards a Sociology of Images. *Current Sociology,* 60(1), 45-60.

van Schendel, Willem. (2002). A Politics of Nudity: Photographs of the 'Naked Mru' of Bangladesh. *Modern Asian Studies,* 36(2), 341-37.

Wouters, Jelle & Henei.e. Michael. (2017). Nagas in the 21st Century. In Wouters, Jelle & Henei.e. Michael. (eds.). *Nagas in the 21st Century* (pp. 1-12). Highlander.

CHAPTER 11

Voices from the Margins Ecocritical Reading of Mamang Dai

Sneha Sawai

The roots of the Indian cultural heritage can be traced to the rich oral traditions and cultures of various tribes and ethnic groups of India. However, with the colonial encounter, the written word gained ascendency over the oral form and English language and the western culture became the markers of modernity and development.

Neo-colonialism, further, created a divide among the newly freed Indians where the educated modern class became a part of the mainstream, resulting in the marginalisation of the 'underdeveloped and poor' tribal and ethnic communities. The forces of urbanisation, modernity, commerce and print culture played a pivotal role in the marginalisation of the tribal communities.

Northeast Tribal Literature

Placed within this power discourse of the center and the margin, northeast tribal literature highlights their conflict with and their difference from the ideologies of the mainstream India.

By virtue of being at the periphery due to its geographical distance from the mainland, the north eastern states of India get categorised and often homogenised within the umbrella term of 'Northeast'. The diverse ethnic cultures, traditions, languages, belief systems and the varied experiences of more than three hundred tribes of eight different states get marginalised and subsumed within the dominant ethnic stereotypes created by the center. Facing discrimination at socio-political and economic levels from the mainland and witnessing the political conflict between the armed insurgent groups and the state at home, people from northeast feel displaced and alienated within their own country. Seen as backward and underdeveloped, tribal communities incessantly struggle to adapt to the new waves of modernisation and to assert their ethnic identity in the face of the overarching Indian identity.

While negotiating their identity with the mainstream, northeast tribal literature not only depicts the conflict in the contemporary times, but also attempts to reclaim and preserve their oral tradition and culture in the wake of increasing commercialisation and mass migration of their community members to metropolitan cities.

However, like the geopolitical condition of their states, the literature from these regions is often neglected and excluded from the established literary canon. As Tilottoma Misra states that for mainland India North-East 'has never has the privilege of being the centre of epistemic imagination.' (Basu, 2015, p. 422) This absence of the voices from the northeast reflects the implicit hierarchical division between the mainstream and the periphery and the continual socio-economic and cultural discrimination that they face.

Adi Tribe

Known as the 'land' (*anchal*) of the 'Rising Sun' (*arun*), Arunachal Pradesh is surrounded by Assam, Tibet and Bhutan. With a long history of conflict over ownership between India and China, the region is known for its scenic beauty with snow covered Himalayan mountains and three major rivers of Kmeng, Siang (Tsangpo/ the Brahmaputra) and Dibang.

Historically located at the periphery of two civilisations, Tibetan in the north and Hindu/Ahom (Assam) in the south, Arunachal Pradesh is said to be inhabited by approximately 26 tribes consisting of more than 100 sub-clans with different languages and dialects. Except for a few tribes, like the Khamptis and other Tibetan tribes that have historically used a written script, all tribal cultures in this region were essentially oral in nature. Their myths, traditions, legends, customs, songs and religion were passed down from one generation to another orally and did not have any written record. The earliest mention of the ethnic tribes in Arunachal Pradesh was made in the official reports, books and diaries written by the colonisers. Howevr, under their colonial gaze as Indian 'subjects' and the lack of knowledge about their diversity, the tribes lost their distinct ethnic identities. Based on the various parts of the region they come from, most of these tribes were labelled as 'hill tribes', 'frontier tribe' and 'wild frontier tribes' and were renamed (e.g., Adi to Abor, Nyishi to Dafla) as per the convenience of the colonisers.

Although colonialism reached the Northeast in the 19th century, the impact of the British colonial rule could be seen through the new social and economic arrangements established within the state. The traditional barter system was replaced by monetary currency, English/western education system and church was established, community councils were displaced by new political set ups and the socio-economic relations between the tribes were governed and controlled. Despite India's independence in 1947, Arunachal Pradesh, like other northeastern states, had limited administrative control over their land and was governed by the centre. Although the Indian government had set up NEFA, North East Frontier Agency, for the welfare of the northeastern states, the immediate needs and demands of the people of the North East often went unheard by the centre.

The Adi tribe is one of the largest tribes of Arunachal Pradesh comprising of approximately one third of the entire populace. The term 'Adi' is a generic term that refers to people living in the hills. It refers to all tribes around the Brahmaputra valley in the East and the West Siang districts. The Adis integrally believe in Doyni-Polo faith that is based upon the dualistic figure of Sun (Donyi) and Moon (Polo). With close affinity with nature, Adis believe in a supreme power that governs the universe. Heavily dependent upon nature for agriculture and other needs, the Adis also have a tradition belief in Animism, whereby everything in the surroundings including plants, animals, nature, mountains, weather, water, tress, etc. are believed to have a 'living presence' (Dai). They believe in the idea of 'coexistence' rather than creating a dichotomous hierarchy between humans and nature. Based upon this idea, their rituals and traditional ceremonies become a means of maintaining an equilibrium with nature. The Adis have two major languages, *Adi Agom*, which is used for day-to-day conversation and *Miri Agom*, a highly rhythmic language used by Miris (spiritual shamans) to chant during festivals and rituals.

A member of the Adi Tribe (from the east and west Siang districts of Arunachal Pradesh), Mamang Dai, a celebrated writer from the Northeast, attempts to give voice and capture the spirit to the marginalised tribal community in her writings. A poet and novelist from Pasighat, Arunachal Pradesh, Dai has extensively written about her tribe the socio-political scenario and the cultural conflicts of the region. In an interview with Ananya Guha, Dai declares, 'I am tribal, and the geography, landscape, our myths, stories…have shaped my thoughts.' (Akhtar, 2017, p. 217)

While criticised by critics and other writers for using English language as the medium, Dai projects the politics of language and power in her works. At a time when tribal cultures face the dangers of assimilation within the mainstream modern culture, Dai not only attempts to preserve, but also celebrates the 'spirit' of her tribal culture. Fusing the often-neglected oral culture with the much-acknowledged written English word, Dai reclaims her tribal ancestry that were lost and subsumed within the larger political structures.

Nature

Nature plays a pivotal role in the works of Northeast literature. Due to their close proximity with nature and their belief in Animism, people in the Northeast are said to be much aware of their ecological surroundings. Having worked as a programme officer with World Wide Fund for Nature, Mamang Dai is both aware and influenced by her ecological surroundings. For her, natural landscapes not only have physical presence, but also have 'mystic' or spiritual presence. In her interview with Arundhati Subramaniam, Dai states, '...the physical presence of the land is very tangible. Beyond this, these journeys here have another dimension. They take me into a landscape full of stories. My writing is an exploration into this world… it is still a mysterious landscape to me, even though I was born here… To me it is a living presence.' (Subramaniam, 2015, p. 447). Mamang Dai's poetry, therefore, is rich with imageries and references to the natural beauty of the landscape. Lands, rain, forest, rivers, clouds and mountains are shown to have a spirit of its own. In her poem 'Small Towns and The River,' published in her poetry collection River Poems (2004), Dai juxtaposes the deathly silence and stillness of the town to the living force of the river. While the small towns lie 'calmly amidst the trees', nature, on the other hand, is shown to be an active participant in the funeral rites. In complete contrast to the inertia of the tribal people who are unable to grieve, natural elements express their sadness and grief. The dust flies, the wind howls and the river 'holds its breath'. The river, we are told:

Has a soul
In the summer it cuts through the land
Like a torrent of grief.
Sometimes, I think it hold its breath
Seeking a land of fish and stars. (Dai, 2004)

Similarly, in her poem 'The Voice of the Mountain', Dai presents the mountain as:

An old man sipping the breeze
That is forever young.
In my life I have lived many lives.
My voice is sea waves and mountain peaks,
In the transfer of symbols
I am the chance syllable that orders the world

Instructed with history and miracles. (Dai, 2004)

The majestic presence of the mountain is symbolic of the tribe's belief in Animism. As an old man, the mountain represents rich ancestral knowledge and tradition. The dualities of nature and culture where the latter is considered to be superior and powerful gets deconstructed here as we find both the mountain and the river represent vast knowledge and wisdom bearing a sense of permanence as opposed to the new 'breeze' of modernism that is 'forever young'. For instance, the mountain states,

I know the towns, the estuary mouth…
I can outline the chapters of the world…
For thousands of years -
I know, I know these things
As rocks know, burning in the sun's embrace,
About clouds, and sudden rain. (Dai, 2004)

Further, the transience of human life is juxtaposed to the permanent ancient presence of nature and traditions. While the theme of death is pervasive in 'Small Towns and the River', we find that no individual details of the person who died are mentioned. The subjective experience or individuality of the people is shown to be temporary and have less significance. As pointed out by Chinmaya Lal Thakur, death becomes ordinary and inconsequential as it loses its power to evoke fear. While humans are shown to be caught in the cyclical patterns of life and death, it is only the tribal rituals, customs and nature that are permanent. As Dai writes:

Life and death, life and death,
Only rituals are permanent (Dai, 2004)

Due to its omnipresence across time and space, nature not only witnesses the social transitions but also becomes a cultural reservoir of the tribes. As pointed by Amrita Bhattacharya, the rigid nature-culture divide has ceased to exist. Both, nature and culture are not seen as static entities leading an isolated existence, instead they synthesise and constantly 'reshape' and 'reform' each other. This amalgamation between the tribes and nature highlights how the ecology or the native landscape becomes an integral part of ethnic identity. (Bhattacharya, 2015, p. 491-513)

Celebrating the oral traditions of Adi tribe and connecting nature with their ancestral history, Dai in her poem 'An Obscure Place' writes:

> The History of our race begins with the place of stories
> We do not know if the language we speak
> Belong to a written past
> Nothing is certain
> There are mountains, Oh! There are Mountains
> We climbed every slope, we slept by the river
> But we do not speak of victory yet. (Dai, 2000)

In the age of uncertainty and cultural conflicts, it is the very presence of the mountains that gives a sense of relief and a sense of belonging to the indigenous tribe who feel hopeless and incessantly struggle with the new modern changes. In her essay 'An Ecocritical Approach: A Study of Selected Northeast Indian Poets', Dr. Chingangbam Anupama (2014), also elaborates upon how the spirit of nature becomes an indispensable part of the communal identity. She further argues that it is through nature that Mamang Dai 'seeks the ancestral chord' as a means to resolve the identity crisis that the tribes experience.

The idea of fragmented/fractured self has been an important concern in postcolonial and postmodern discourse. Since nature plays a pivotal role in the lives of the tribal communities, their identity crisis also arises due to their separation from their land. Caught up in the constant tussle with authoritative power regimes that seeks to not only control and exploit the land, but also its inhabitants, the tribal communities view their past, tradition and nature as a means of reclaiming their identity.

Nature, therefore, becomes the reservoir of the cultural past when the humans lived in complete harmony with its ecology. In the poem 'The Missing Link', Dai highlights this beautiful relationship between nature and the tribe where nature fuses and becomes an integral part of their identity:

There are no records,
The river was the green
And white vein of our lives... (Dai, 2000)

Longing for a sense of identity and belonging, in the modern times of globalisation where the tribal communities are constantly discriminated and face the threat of assimilation within the dominant mainstream culture, Dai evokes the pre-colonial memories of her community as a source of stable identity:

Remember
The river's voi.e.
Where else could we
Be born, where else
Could we belong,
If not of memory
Divining life and form
Out of silence. (Dai, 2000)

In 'River Poems' Dai again illustrates how the tribal community lived in close affinity with nature and influenced their culture:

Without speech
We practiced a craft
Leaving imprints
On the sky walls,
Linking the seasons,
Coding the trailing mist
In silent messages
Across the vast landscape. (Dai, 2000)

Nature, thus, not only functions as a picturesque setting in Northeast poetry, but also reflects the tribal culture and their contemporary issues. In the wake of increasing commercialisation, Northeast regions face the massive issue of deforestation and ecological disturbances. These sociological changes disrupt their relationship with nature and leads to a split in their identity. The sense of anxiety, hopelessness and dispossession that the tribal people experience is depicted in the very first line of 'Small Towns and the River' where the poet mentions how small towns always remind her of death. In the Preface to her book *Arunachal Pradesh: The Hidden Land* (2002) Dai states, 'Today change has come like a steam roller. The transition from unknown frontier to modern state has been sharp and rapid and the question of direction and destiny has become of great complexity and soul searching.'

In literary discourse, this study of the representation of the relationship between nature and humans in literature is called Ecocriticism. The term was coined by William Rueckert in his 1978 essay 'Literature and Ecology: An experiment in

Ecocriticism' where he defined ecocriticism as 'the application of ecology and ecological concepts to the study of literature.' Etymologically, the term comes from the word 'ecology' which refers to the branch of biology that deals with the relationship between living organisms and their environment and surrounding. The term 'eco' comes from the Greek word '*oikos*' that means house and 'critic' comes from *krites* which literally means to judge. In his book *Contemporary Literary and Cultural Theory*, Pramod K. Nayar defines Ecocriticism as a 'critical mode that looks at the representation of nature and landscape texts, paying particular attention to attitude towards 'nature' and the rhetoric employed when speaking about it.' (Nayar, 2013, p. 242) This definition implies how the interdisciplinary approach of ecocriticism incorporates both the study of, what Amrita Bhattacharya calls, the physical and the spiritual.

Although varied representation and references to nature have always been present in literature since the ancient times, such as in the epics, pastoral literature and religious texts; the study of this exceptional relationship between humans and nature began only in the 19th century English Romantic period. As opposed to the scientific approach of the Enlightenment period that emphasised upon logic and reasoning as the core for human progress and culture and viewed nature as a mere object in the larger system of production, the Romantic movement celebrated nature and its beauty. The rigid duality of subject/object and culture/nature came into question with the new romantic sentiment that valorized the spirit of the nature. The beautiful healing spirit of the nature was contrasted with the dark, grim, polluted reality of the industrial modern society. Critiquing the excessive use of intellect, William Wordsworth in one of his most influential work, *Lyrical Ballads* (1978) states:

Sweet is the lore which nature brings;
Our meddling intellect
Misshapes the beauteous forms of things
We murder to dissect. (Wordsworth, 1978)

This shift from human logic/reason to nature, feelings and subjectivity ushered a new form of literature that recognised the intrinsic value of nature and delved into the unknown mysteries of the unseen. Amrita Bhattacharya in her essay 'An Ecocritical Reading of Select Northeast Indian English Poetry' talks about deep ecology as an important aspect of northeast literature. The term 'Deep Ecology' was coined by a Norwegian philosopher, Arne Naes in 1973 that rejected the human centered anthropological approach to a more 'biocentric' view centered around life. It views man as only a single component in the larger ecosystem and compels men to realise that they are not entitled to harm nature or animals or other living beings for their own interest. This emphasis on the existence of the unknown larger structure and the urgency of maintaining an equilibrium for coexistence can be seen in northeast literature.

Historically, the environmental damage to the ecology of the northeast began with colonialism when the harmony between the indigenous and its surroundings was disrupted in favor of material/capitalist interest. Massive deforestation, climate change, extinction of various species, toxicity and pollution are major consequences of such colonial enterprise that continues to be a threat in the contemporary times. With the passage of ti.e. nature lost its value and came to be seen only through commercial interests.

Drawing a parallel between the oppression and marginalisation of nature with that of the tribal communities, Paban Chakraborty in his essay 'The Hidden Valley of My Home: Home, Identity, and Environmental Justice in the Select Works of Mamang Dai' (2019) discusses how both nature and the tribal communities have been sidelined by the technology and powerful structures through the interdisciplinary approach of Environmental Justice. Environmental Justice is a social movement that emerged in the United States in the 1980s that aimed at providing fair and equal opportunities and environmental benefits to all people.

The movement aims at creating and providing an environment where all people, irrespective of their class, race and color can engage in the decision-making process of creating and implementing environmental laws and policies to maintain a healthy environment. In the introduction to her book *Environmental Justice in the New Millennium: Global Perspectives on Race, Ethnicity and Human Rights (2009)*, Filomena Steady states that Environmental Justice represents 'the history and continuing struggles of ordinary people for their civil, special and human rights as members of a global ecological community.' Throughout history, humans and nature have been exploited and turned into labour and wealth by the hegemonic groups. Through its emphasis on this hierarchical relationship and social injusti.e. Environmental Justice seeks to protest and challenge 'discrimination and disparities in the allocation of benefits and burdens of economic development.' (Steady, 2009)

Highlighting the ill effects of modernisation, Chakraborty points out how technology tries to encroach and control nature and the lives of the tribal people, which eventually results in their conflicted identity and conflicted relationship with their ecosystem. The historical process of colonisation and the subsequent control established by the state has not only resulted in identity crisis but also overturned and threatened their view of their culture and history. Giving voice to the marginalised, the movement of Environmental Justice seeks to give justice to the displaced tribal people who are considered to be backward and inferior as they have not accepted and are far away from modernisation.

As pointed by Chakraborthy, Mamang Dai's depiction of Adi culture and their belief system is not just an act of preservation, but is also a form of outright protest against hegemonic forces that disregard tribal cultures. By depicting the harmonious relationship between the Adi tribe and nature, Dai exhibits how humans can coexist along with nature without the intention of dominating it. This act of cultural assertion exposes and critiques the futility of the modern sciences and their worldview.

Celebrating the beautiful harmonious relationship between humans and nature, northeast writers reclaim and reestablish their lost cultural history within the dominant mainstream discourses and history. However, through this act of preserving their lost oral culture, northeast writers also delve deeper to understand the ancient mysteries of the human existence and ecology that were completely dismissed by the western culture and are now only limited to the few '*shamans*' (the tribal healers how have access to ancient knowledge and wisdom) in their community.

In her essay, 'On Creation Myths and Oral Narratives', Mamang Dai talks about how folktales and myths that have been passed down to generations orally, represent the tribal community's belief system. She calls these myths and stories 'ancient religion of the world which, over a period of time developed into parables and a set of beliefs.' Referring to their intrinsic value, she further says that these stories 'did not come into the minds of men like a bolt of lightning. They must have seeped in over the centuries, like a gift of understanding generated by life itself.' (Dai, 2005)

Nature plays a pivotal role in the creation of these myths and the rituals that the tribes followed or observed. For Adis, nature is not just a mere surrounding or space that provides sustenance, but also entails a larger system of knowledge and power that are hitherto unknown to humans. The presence of nature in Mamang Dai's poetry, therefore, symbolically represents the amalgamation of the immediate physical reality and the unknown spiritual realm. Dai's writing is both an assertion of her marginalised tribal community and the often-neglected nature. It highlights the imminent threat of destruction and exploitation of both the ecology/ the beautiful landscape and the tribal culture.

In her powerful poem 'Be Careful How You Cut that Tree' Dai addresses the modern men who want to cut the trees and reminds them that these trees:

...are priests, gods of a pre-human age
Carrying a knotted stick
Every posture, angle,
Arrangement of limb and eye
A pathway of time
Unfurling destruction, and returning life
In the inherited tattoo of a green leaf.

Warning these men she cautions them about the immense power of nature:

Be careful how you cut that tree.
It is the same tree that watches the hunter
Alone on the hard earth, laying his traps.
Ancient stairway to heaven,
Send him a fierce bird with a wing span of the sky. (Dai, 2017)

In another poem 'Saturn' Dai depicts the disappointment and despair of both the tribe who did not want to be confined to 'small rooms, full of cigarette smoke and glasses' and nature which is described as 'inaccessible gods' who are pleading:

And all across the land
They were singing
The big trees have fallen
Breaking our dreams,
And all across the land
They are still singing
Blind eyes
Blind space still expanding
Full of hope (Dai, 2000)

Although nature and the tribal people are shown to be in a helpless state where their voices are completely silenced by the commercial demands, Dai instills a sense of protest and hope at the end of her poem:

Do not ask
How remedies are made…
We stand
On the turning road again
Planting green seedlings. (Dai, 2000)

Furthermore, we find that in the new modern age of utter chaos, despair and hopelessness, the tribe is shown to be holding onto their traditions as a means to survive and find some meaning to their existence. In 'The Voice of Mountain,' Dai mentions how:

The other day a young man arrived from the village
Because he could not speak
He brought a gift of fish
From the land of rivers.
It seems such acts are repeated
We live in territories, forever ancient and new
And as we speak in changing languages.
I, also, leave my spear leaning by the tree
And try to make a sign. (Dai, 2004)

Caught within the throes of modern capitalism, the young man visits the mountain and gives 'gift of fish' as traditional offerings. In return, the mountain also tries to make communication with the man. This depicts how relationship between nature and the tribe plays a significant role in the lives of the indigenous.

At the backdrop of the celebration of nature and tribal culture, violence and bloodshed are also the central motifs in Dai's poetry. Known for the internal conflict due to the insurgent groups, much of the northeast writings reflect the contemporary everyday reality of these regions. The sense of urgency, uncertainty, fear and danger that the indigenous people experience can be seen in the poem 'Remembrance' where the danger is also reflected through nature:

This summer it rains more than ever
The footfall of soldiers is drowned and scattered.

In the hidden exchange of news we hear
That weapons are multiplying in the forest. (Basu, 2015, p. 426)

Several repeated references to death can be found in Dai's poetry. Death as a common theme does not only represent the biocentric view of deep ecology that reminds us of the transience of human life, but is also emblematic of the imminent danger that the northeastern people living in these region face.

Ecofeminism

The study of ecofeminism is closely connected to ecocriticism. Drawing upon the hierarchical dichotomies created by capitalist patriarchal society, ecofeminism associates the exploitation and oppression of women with that of nature. Emerged during the 1970's feminist movement, ecofeminism is a significant political movement that connects other social structures such as gender, race and class to nature. For its life-giving properties, nature has always been associated with the feminine gender. Rendered voiceless by patriarchal structures, women's bodies are associated with nature. However, like other marginalised groups, nature is exploited and often objectified by patriarchal capitalism. The study of ecofeminism draws parallel between the two experiences and attempts to deconstruct the discriminatory dualities of nature/culture, masculine/femini.e. human/animal, reason/emotion and subject/object. In her essay 'Mamang Dai: The Postcolonial Paradigm', Nivedita Basu states the major tenets of Ecofeminism. She states that ecofeminist ideology 'deems the worth of woman-nature relationships' and the connection of nature and culture. It not only emphasises upon gender equality, but also ecological sustainable development.

Challenging the larger discourse of gender and nature-man relationship it went on to 'inspire human minds to realise the 'spiritual' element in all living creatures.'

This interconnection between women and nature can be seen in 'The Voice of the Mountain' where the mountain declares itself as:

[I am] the woman lost in translation
Who survives, with happiness to carry on. (Dai, 2004)

Citing Rini Barman, Nivedita Basu states that these lines depict the bodies of men and women who are 'personified with the help of tribal animist associations with nature and partly through the reconceptualisation of nature as a dynamic agent.'

In the poem 'The River' Dai again associates nature with women and highlights the kind of marginalisation that both nature and woman face:

I thought the river is a woman
A country, a name
A note of music trapped in the white current (Bhattacharya, 2015, p.500)

Set against the backdrop of the dominant socio-political scenario the issues of tribal women and nature are often sidelined and negated. Their everyday struggle to survive and adapt to the new social changes and imminent danger and violence is often unheard and neglected by the dominant structures. Voicing the feminist concerns, Mamang Dai depicts the woes of these women through her writings. In her poem 'The Sorrow of Women', Dai presents women's predicament in a conflict-ridden region where they are marginalised and find themselves to be at the receiving end of violence and oppression from the state, militants and their home:

They are talking about displacement...
And they are talking about escape
About liberty, men and guns
Ah! The urgency for survival!
But what will they do
Not knowing the sorrows of women? (Basu, 2015, p.432)

In the face of socio-political and economic hardships and 'the urgency of survival' the voices and the anguish cries of the women from indigenous tribes are suppressed and lost -

To war, and big issues
More important than me. (Basu, 2015, p.432)

However, it is important to note that while Dai depicts the helpless marginal position of women, she also celebrates the perseverant fighting spirit of both women and nature. Though the voices of these women are lost in translation in the larger paradigm of power; they still continue to happily survive and protest ('The Voice of the Mountain'). Similarly, in 'The River' Dai presents both nature and women as 'a sheet of paper carrying a secret map' that people are not aware of:

The skyline is where it begins
Between the darkness and the summit
In the birthplace of thirst. (Ngangom and Nongkinrih, 2009)

Thus, this association of women with nature does not only emphasise the marginalisation that they experience at the hands of the capitalist patriarchal structures, but also celebrates the immense knowledge, mysteries and capacities that both women and nature entail.

Women's protest against the social and gender inequality has been a major concern for all northeast writers. In his poem

'Everywhere I go' Robin S. Ngagom describes the immense strength demonstrated by women as a part of their protest:

Everywhere I go
I carry my homeland with me...
I often hear about its future
In conflict resolution symposiums...
But I can see it returning with women
And water in rural evenings
And I want to tell my poet-friends
Of the twelve mothers who stripped themselves
And asked soldiers to rape them... (Mishra, 2011)

By tapping into these unexplored subaltern experiences, Dai not only interrogates the patriarchal relationship with women and nature, but also posits a larger political question to the state that marginalises the north east:

Life is so hard like this
Nobody knows why...

To conclude, Dai's poetry represents the communal voices of the marginalised tribal groups and becomes an assertion of their sovereign identity.

REFERENCES

Dai, Mamang (2005). On Creation Myths and Oral Narratives. *India International Centre Quarterly, 32* (2/3), 1-6. http://www.jstor.org/stable/23005996.

Tarr, Michael Aram and Stuart Blackburn. (2008). *Through the Eye of Time: Photographs of Arunachal Pradesh 1839-2006*. Brill.

Basu, Nivedita. (2015). Mamang Dai: The Postcolonial Paradigm and Writing from India's Periphery. In Someshwar Sati (Eds.), *A Warble of Postcolonial Voices: An Anthology of Short Stories and Poems, vol. II: Poems* (pp.419-435). Worldview Publication.

Bhattacharya, Amrita. (2015). An Ecocritical Reading of Select Northeast Indian English Poetry. In Someshwar Sati (Eds.), *A Warble of Postcolonial Voices: An Anthology of Short Stories and Poems, vol. II: Poems* (pp.491-513). Worldview Publication.

Thakur, Chinmaya Lal. (2015). Living Matters: Mamang Dai's 'Small Towns and the River' and 'The Voice of the Mountain'. In Someshwar Sati (Eds.), *A Warble of Postcolonial Voices: An Anthology of Short Stories and Poems, vol. II: Poems* (pp.524-532). Worldview Publication.

Anupama, Chingangbam (2014). An Eco-Critical Approach: A Study of Selected North East Indian Poets. The Criterion: An International Journal in English. 5(2), 59-67. https://www.the-criterion.com/V5/n2/Anupama.pdf

Dai, Mamang. (2013) *River Poems*. Writers Workshop.

MEHROTRA, N., & LALGOULIAN. (2008). A Report on 'Towards a New Understanding of North East India.' *Indian Anthropologist, 38*(1), 95–102. http://www.jstor.org/stable/41920060

Dai, M. (2017). Be Careful How You Cut that Tree. *Indian Literature, 61*(1 (297)), 82–83. https://www.jstor.org/stable/26791114

Dai, M. (2000). Saturn. *Indian Literature, 44*(3 (197)), 62–64. http://www.jstor.org/stable/23343168

Dai, M. (2000). River Poems. *Indian Literature, 44*(3 (197)), 66–66. http://www.jstor.org/stable/23343170

Chakraborty, Paban. (2019). The Hidden Valley of My Home: Home, Identity, and Environmental Justice in the Select Works of Mamang Dai. *Sanglap: Journal of Literary and Cultural Inquiry*, 5(2), 53-60.

https://pdfs.semanticscholar.org/fd0c/f716ab0dcf61246eba733bfbdbd6be7e9006.pdf

CHAPTER 12

Goan Tribes & Personal Narratives A Postcolonial Reading

Sneha Umarye

The term colonialism conjures up images of the exploitation that happened for a long period in the history. In the process of colonisation, the colonisers imposed their religion, language, and other cultural and economic practices on the colonised.

Postcolonialism emerged as a response to the aftermath of western colonisation. It is a critique of western representation of culture, ethnicity and human identity after colonisation. It studies the power relationships between previously colonised cultures and people.

According to Bill Ashcroft et al., postcolonialism studied the strained cultural relations between colonisers that attacked the colonies in Africa, Asia, and the Western world. Great Britain emerged as the chief coloniser and became an imperial power by the 19th century. It gained control over one-quarter of the landmass. British believed that Great Britain was bound to rule the world. Such beliefs directly affected how the colonisers treated the colonised. Using its political and economic strength, Great Britain dominated its colonies.

The terms postcolonial or postcolonialism first appeared

in the mid-1980s (Bill Ashcrof, 2000). Both terms became firmly established in academic and popular discourse in the years that followed. Postcolonial theory developed as a part of new and politicised fields of humanistic studies. Postcolonial theory is concerned with the political, economic, historical, and social impact of European colonial rule around the world. It is a set of theoretical strategies used to observe and study the culture, literature, history, and politics of the former colonies. The postcolonial theory has progressed with and responds to colonial texts. It is a theoretical approach that attempts to disrupt the dominant discourse of colonial power. It is about colonialism, emphasising the effects of colonialism on both the colonised and the coloniser. In the contemporary era, the prefix 'post' in 'postcolonial theory' has been highly debated, but it has never implied that colonialism has ended. However, much of postcolonial theory is concerned with the residual forms of colonial authority after the formal end of the Empire. Therefore, postcolonialism is one of those theories that is still relevant and applies to the ongoing struggles.

Postcolonial theory has been found useful in examining a variety of colonial relationships beyond the classic colonisation of the British Empire. The concept of boundaries and margins has been crucial in the domination of indigenous space. Westerners propagated the colonialist ideology that all races other than white were inferior or subhuman. In the postcolonial world, these sub-humans are referred to as the subalterns or the

Others. They were excluded from positions of power and viewed as both different and inferior. The inferior groups varied across different states of India, generally called the subalterns. The study of subalterns includes a wide range of groups such as the Dalits, the tribes, the transgenders, etc.

Keeping this in mind, the contemporary narratives of two Goan tribes through the postcolonial lens are analysed. The personal narratives chosen for this study are published in a blog series, *Hanv Konn? (Who Am I?): Re-searching the Self.* The three narratives are: *A Velip Writes Back* by Priyanka Velip, *Where Have All the Songs and Rituals Gone?* by Monzinha Fernandes, and *To Gawda or Not to Gawda* by Favita Dias. Postcolonialism applies to the ongoing lives of these tribes and allows us to learn, gain insights, and sympathise with these tribes who have been relegated to the margins for the longest time. The chapter attempts to highlight some of the specific aspects of postcolonialism like language, the practice of othering, and the process of writing back. An attempt will be made to understand these concepts through the perspectives of the tribal community, who have always been subjected to discrimination. The chapter will focus on life experiences, culture, pain, and injustice faced by the tribes at the hands of the dominant mainstream groups.

Goa's extensive colonial history makes it similar to Indian history, despite being the smallest state in the country. Goa was under the direct control of ancient and medieval kingdoms. Initially, it was ruled by the Kadamba dynasty, which was then invaded by Muslim rulers of the Deccan. Furthermore, it was also ruled by the Vijayanagar kingdom. The final invasion of Goa occurred in 1510, when seafarers from Portugal reached India. Goa was attacked in March 1510 by the Portuguese under Afonso de Albuquerque. Goa was the first territorial possession of the Portuguese in Asia and soon became the capital of the Portuguese empire. It was during this time that Goa became one of the major trade centres in India. The tribes like Gawda, Kunbi, and the Velip communities were the original settlers of Goa. These tribes were the first settlers, also known as the aboriginals, who inhabited the forest areas. They earned their livelihood from the land, forest, livestock, and wildlife. The fear of the colonisers led the tribal groups to move to the interior of the forests, where they lived according to their customs and created stable settlements in different locations. They created villages with their own administrations and traditions. The colonial rulers took a keen interest in this system and found vast potential for revenue generation. Through intellectual and political power, the colonisers soon gained control over these Goan tribes. These tribes were marginalised and their rights over the land had been nullified after Portuguese rule. The tribal ways of li.e. their cultures, social structures, and economic systems were treated as inferior as compared to the advanced or modernised western societies.

During Portuguese rule, systematisation enabled the transfer of large quantities of land into the hands of the affluent class. The affluent class manipulated the Comunidade for a long ti.e. and as a result, the tribals in Goa eventually lost their land. Ultimately, this resulted in their impoverishment as their significant means of livelihood were taken away from them. The scheduled tribes of Gawda, Kunbi, and Velip hence became marginalised and lost their basic rights on their own land. These tribal communities were not only oppressed by the colonial rulers but also by the dominant upper-caste class of Goan society.

The origin of the word 'tribe' is derived from the Latin word 'Tribus' which means 'one-third'. The word originally referred to one of the three territorial groups that united to make Rome. Today, tribe refers to a socially, politically, and ethnically connected group of people. They are also referred to as *Adivasis,* or the aboriginals. The various tribal communities in India are categorised as Scheduled Tribes (ST) under Article 366 of the Indian Constitution. These diverse tribes are spread across several states and union territories. Goa has the highest percentage of the scheduled tribes. The scheduled tribes constitute 10 percent of the total population of Goa. The four chief tribes of Goa are known as the *Gowdas, Kunbis, Velips,* and *Dhangars.* They belong to the Proto-Australoid group of tribes, living in segregated villages. Poverty, economic and technological backwardness and socio-cultural difficulties like abuse and mistreatment are some of the problems faced by the tribal communities of Goa. Alienation from their own lands has led to the marginalisation of tribal communities till date. These marginalised tribes have recently begun to speak and challenge the dominant culture and its dictates. They try to highlight the emerging voices of the folk, though silent, resonating their tribal identity, their race and pri.e. their ethnicity, their history, culture, and tradition.

The personal narratives chosen discuss issues like discrimination, a sense of low self-esteem, and othering experienced by the Goan tribal groups. The personal narrative authors belong to three different tribal groups. Postcolonialism applies to the ongoing lives of these tribes and allows us to learn, gain insights, and sympathise with these tribes who have been living on the peripheries for the longest time.

Each story in the series *Hanv Konn?* is inspiring and real. The unique aspect of this work is that it is based on the life stories of the writers themselves. It makes their writing autobiographical, and hence the reader is exposed to the voice of the silenced subaltern.

The narrative *To Gawda or Not to Gawda* by the Goan writer Favita Dias (2015), discusses the difficulties of the *Gawda* community, in particular. It is one of the prominent *Adivasi* communities of Goa. In this narrati.e. Dias finds herself in an identity conflict: to identify herself with the *Gawda* community to which she belongs through her ancestry or not. In the last paragraph of her narrati.e. she says that sometimes she regrets having discovered her tribal identity as a *Gawda*, because the recognition has turned her into someone new. She says, 'I wish I had not discovered my tribal identity and faced such a situation.' She suffers from being the marginalised one after discovering her original identity, so she says she would rather not know her original identity. She says that this discovery has shaped her thoughts differently and made her a new person. She has become a person with a new set of questions that requires new answers. Therefore, the persistent conflict of identity in a tribe's life is evident through Dias's writings. Mozinha Fernandes addresses the issue of othering in her narrative titled as *Where, Have All the Songs and Rituals Gone?*. The term 'othering' was coined by Gayatri Spivak for 'the process by which the imperial discourse creates Others.' The process of othering occurs in all types of colonialist narratives. For instance, the Goan tribes have been consistently othered since the colonial period. They are considered to be the communities that have remained loyal to their ancestral traditions and customs. Hence, they have been living in isolated areas, away from mainstream culture. Fernandes says, 'Tribes have been transformed into castes with the policy of reservation in India. While castes that are notified in the Indian Constitution are referred to as 'Scheduled Castes,' my community is a 'Scheduled Tribe'. This, she says, is often referred to as belonging to the *Gawda* caste. Thus, the community is subjected to double marginalisation as a tribe and also as a caste belonging to the lower strata. The tribes that are being othered desire the power and self-esteem that the superior possesses. For instance, the surnames in Goa, particularly the Hindu surnames, have been traditionally associated with places and communities. Due to the colonisation and the massive conversion to Catholicism and change of names, 'the new surnames like Colaço or Fernandes offered no clues to the status of the newly christened individual.' (Cielo G. Festino, 2021) It is in this context that the Konkani question 'Tu Konna-lo' was coined. The question literally translates as 'Who are you?' (in terms of one's cultural or social background). As Hindu surnames are associated with the names of villages and, in turn, villages are associated with different social groups, asking for a person's surname helps place the person's origin within the local social hierarchy and the caste system. Hence, we come across tribes who choose to change their surname in order to fit into society and feel accepted. Individuals from tribal communities are asked for their surname and their origin within the localities to know their social background and identity. This is a method of discrimination based on social class and the caste system. The tribes thus try to follow the process of *Sanskritisation*, i.e., to convert themselves to the standards of the higher castes or classes. Fernandes concludes her narrative by saying, 'The Gawda tribes are trying to get rid of their own traditional customs and imitate the customs of others because they see this as being a part of the process of becoming civilised.' (Cielo G. Festino, 2021) This suggests that tribal communities imitate the so-called civilised, in order to boost their self-esteem or social status.

Tribal communities choose to imitate the ones authorising them in terms of language, atti.e. and lifestyle. Priyanka Velip, in her narrative *A Velip Writes Back,* elaborates more on othering. She writes about the Velip tribe which is a sub-caste of the *Kunbi* or *Gawda* community. Othering has become the norm in society, with the powerful being considered as superior and the powerless being labelled as inferior. The tribal communities are specifically labelled for their cultural and traditional customs. Tribal dances are widely used to entertain tourists as they represent the authentic Goan community. For example, the '*dhentli*', which is a traditional Goan tribal way of tying the saree, is a distinctive feature of Goan tribal identity. It is ironic that tribes wearing the same attire are looked down upon by society. Though it stands as a symbol that represents the identity of a tribe it is used to stigmatise the tribal communities. In her narrati.e. Fernandes mentions that when she interviewed people of her own community to learn about rituals and songs, many of the time they would be hesitant to speak. They would question her about why she is inquiring about the past. She encountered many rejections like '*Tem poilichem tuka kiteak zai*? (Why do you want those old things?). I do not remember anything.' Even the aged *vhoddil* (leader) refused to speak about his past.

Fernandes understood and knew, from experience, the conflict of the people she interviewed. On the one hand, the culture of the *Gawdas* had to be remembered and preserved, while on the other hand, they faced discrimination when they stuck to it. Fernandes concludes by saying, 'The Gawda people are dropping their own traditional customs and imitating the customs of others because they see this as being part of the process of becoming 'civilised.' (Cielo G. Festino, 2021) They imitate the other (dominating) castes in order to be able to compete with them in terms of acquiring land, money, education, and social status.

In the third narrative of Favita Dias, *To Gawda Or Not to Gawda,* she speaks about various issues like language, caste certificates, discrimination, etc. When looking into the aspect of language, we have noted that Konkani is the original Goan language. Historians have successfully proven the contributions of *Kukna* and *Gamit* tribals, the original Konkani-speaking inhabitants of Konkan, as the true speakers of the Konkani language. (Kamat, 2014). There is not much evidence about demographic changes and the specifics of migration from Konkan and Goa during the previous millennia. There is a large debate on the origin of the Konkani language and the actual number of Konkani speakers. However, it is proved that the greatness of the Konkani language lies in the resilience of Goa's original tribal inhabitants. (Kamat, 2014) *Kokna* tribals are also referred to as *Kokni, Kukni*, or *Kukna* were the original inhabitants of the Konkan. They speak Kokni, which is an Indo-Aryan language. The Goan tribes have preserved this language, and yet they are being discriminated against for its use. The tribal communities are humiliated for their use of original Konkani words or dialects and are stigmatised by others. Those who speak in Catholic dialects are made to feel ashamed of this by others. It is ironic that the tribes are the original speakers of the language, yet they are being differentiated based on their language. Although the regional languages are preserved and used by the tribes, they are being ill-treated because of their language. They are treated as different or the 'other' based on their use of language and dialect.

From the concept of othering and inequality in narratives discussed above, we are introduced to one of the prominent concepts of postcolonial studies, i.e., 'writing back'. It is a term applied to literary works that openly reflect and reveal the experiences of the colonised and their problems like othering, marginalisation, etc. Postcolonial authors have retold colonial versions of stories and history wherein the silenced and marginalised are brought to the centre. They write in contrast to the civilised and coloniser and hence it is called 'writing back' or 'de-othering'. For them, it is a kind of self-discovery that gives a sense of self-identification. The authors of *Hanv Konn* have written back not only by collecting and transcribing the songs and rituals of the community to show their cultural and aesthetic value, also by writing in English so that they reach a broader audience. The narratives by Dias, Fernandes, and Velip helped them come to terms with their own cultural identities. Despite being constantly marginalised, they have voiced these narratives of shame and repression.

Thus, they show their resistance and healing through the narratives.

Some of the events may have happened in the past, but their effects continue to impact the current tribal communities. These narratives are shaped by traumatic events and long-lasting oppression that have been passed on to the second generation by their ancestors. It is usually the family members who have survived the ill-treatment that inhabits both their minds and their identities. Today, the current generation still faces discrimination and inequality that is carried out in different ways. It is through such personal narratives that these victims voice themselves and their community. These narratives give us insight into the deep-rooted discrimination and oppression of the tribal communities that is present till date.

The tribal community, like any other community, wishes and deserves equal rights and treatment from other communities. Hence, they chose to write back to fight for their rights. *Gawdas, Kunbi*, and *Velips* were the original settlers of Goa. It is important to note that they have the first right to call themselves 'Goans'. Their culture, rituals, lifestyle,

dialects, etc. are known to signify the identity of the true Goans. The scope of the narratives in *Hanv Konn* is broad and covers different matters like the assertion of identity, the process of being othered, the recovery of the culture's traditions, displacement, and discrimination.

The writers of these narratives are speaking for the oppressed, suppressed, and silenced. Their writings give voice to the silenced communities such as *Gawdas, Kunbis*, and *Velips*, making them heard among the cacophony of the persistent, dominant, and all-encompassing culture. They desire to voice their feelings, their concerns, and their opinions about their lives without being treated as marginal, minor, or insignificant participants. Writers from these communities refuse to be silenced and choose defiance. They emphasise a different perspecti.e. not of the dominant culture, but one from which to view the world and its people. They speak for not just one culture, but many for their community as a whole.

Therefore, we see how postcolonial theory is born out of the colonised peoples' frustrations and their personal and direct clashes with the conquering culture. It speaks of their fears, hopes, and dreams about their own identities. Therefore, the response of the colonised to the changes in language, education, racial differences, economic issues, morals, ethics, and the act of writing becomes the context for the evolving theories and practice of postcolonialism.

REFERENCES

Ashcroft, B., Griffiths, G., & Tiffin, H. (2008). *Post-colonial studies: The key concepts.*

Routledge.

Festino, C. G., & Mattos, A. M. de A. (30 July 2021). *Memory, Postmemory and the role of narratives among women writers from the Adivasi communities of Goa.* Ilha do Desterro. Retrieved 25 January 2022, from https://www.scielo.br/j/ides/a/F96zpVc8dSLGpn57ySWrL9v/

Herald, T. (24 January 2016,). *To Gawda or not to Gawda.* oHeraldo. Retrieved 25 January 2022, from https://www.heraldgoa.in/Review/Voice-Of-Opinion/TO-GAWDA-OR-NOT-TO-GAWDA/98150

Khedekar , V. (24 March 2013). *Goa's rural society - the navhind times.* The Navhind Times. Retrieved 25 January 2022, from https://www.navhindtimes.in/2012/03/24/magazines/panorama/panorama-goa-s-rural-society/

Kamat, N. (1 December 2014). *The tribal origin of Konkani language - researchgate.net.*

Researchgate.net. Retrieved 25 January 2022, from https://www.researchgate.net/profile/Nandkumar-Kamat/publication/267449407_The_Tribal_Origin_of_Konkani_Language/links/544fa7320cf26dda089209a2/The-Tribal-Origin-of-Konkani-Language.pdf

Pinto, A. P. (28 August 2021). *Goan identity crises.* The Navhind Times. Retrieved 25 January 2022.

CHAPTER 13

Tribal Subaltern Narrative
The Adivasi Will Not Dance

Shubhaangi Thakur

Antonio Gramsci coined the term subaltern so as to identify the social groups, which have been systemically excluded from the society in order to subjugate their political voices in socio-economic situations. Subaltern is very commonly used in the post-colonial context to describe the marginalised classes and groups of a society. If we extend this meaning of subaltern to the Indian context, we will see that there are many social groups which have been relegated to the precincts of the society. Among such social groups, tribals are one such marginalised community in India as they do not have access to either education or employment. Their lands on which they depend heavily for food and survival, have been snatched away from them. Additionally, because of their geographical location, the tribals in India are isolated from the mainland India. As a result of these conditions, it would be safe to say that the tribals are a subaltern community in the Indian context. Keeping the subalternity of the tribal community in mind, the present chapter will be analysing the systemic marginalisation of *Santhal* tribe as depicted in Hansda Sowvendra Shekhar's collection of short stories, *The Adivasi Will Not Dance*.

Most of the tribal communities in India have existed since the pre-Aryan era. They survived the Mughal rule and some of them also led rebellions against the brutal practices of the British colonisers. *Adivasis* are one such tribal community of India. Etymologically, *adi* means *beginning/origin* and *vasin* means *dweller*. Thus, *Adivasi* means original dweller and is a collective term for tribes of the Indian subcontinent who are considered native to places within India wherein they reside. They consist of a considerable minority population of India making up 8.6 percent of India's population according to 2011 census. However, according to the Indian constitution, the *Adivasi* have been officially termed as scheduled tribes in India.

Before we look at the current condition of the tribals, it is imperative to trace the trajectory of the marginalisation of tribals through history. In the ancient and the medieval period in India, *Adivasi* commanded a lot of respect. In fact, in some areas, *Adivasi* held so much respect that securing their approval and support was considered critical by local rulers and as a result, larger *Adivasi* groups were able to secure their own territories in central India. However, this collective ownership and relative autonomy of *Adivasi* land by *Adivasis* did not last long and was severely disrupted by the arrival of Mughals in the 16th century who started seizing *Adivasi* land. As a result of confiscation of their lands, the *Adivasi* led a rebellion against the Mughals which, however, was pacified by Mughal soldiers. The advent of the Mughal rule, in many ways, was a premonition for the way *Adivasi* would be treated in the coming time. After the Mughals came the Britishers and the colonial administration who impinged upon the *Adivasi* tribal system. Land, forest areas which belonged to the *Adivasi* were rapidly converted into the legal property of British designated *zamindars.* Here onwards, the *Adivasi* not only lost rights over their own lands, but also were steeped under financial debts as a result of the *zamindari* system. The subjugation of *Adivasi* began with the Mughals, continued with the British rule, and is still ongoing in contemporary India.

The current chapter focusses on one such *Adivasi* tribe called *Santhal,* who are an integral part of the book *The Adivasi Will Not Dance*. *Santhals* constitute an ethnic group which is native to eastern India. In terms of population, *Santhals* are the largest tribe in the Jharkhand state, third largest tribe of India and are also found in the states of Assam, Tripura, Bihar, Odisha and West Bengal. After independence, the *Santhals* were given the status of the Scheduled Tribes in India. The *Santhals* are considered as one of the most progressive tribes of India because their society has much less stratification and is more egalitarian than neighbouring caste Hindu society. However, their history is one of subjugation in the form of heavy taxation from the zamindars, oppression by the moneylenders, the upper caste populace and the bureaucracy in general. Today, the *Santhals* are majorly cereal agriculturalists, with rice as their chief crop which they further supplement with millet, maize and some vegetable crops.

It is important to point out that while Dalit literature in India has gained substantial limelight, *Adivasi* literature has been limited because of the restrictions of regional languages. Although both Dalits and *Adivasis* are subaltern in the Indian context, yet there are crucial differences between them. Although *Adivasis* are considered to be uncivilised and primitive, they were not considered to be inherently impure by their surrounding population, unlike Dalits who are considered impure and untouchable. Unlike Dalits, the *Adivasis* often had sovereignty and a joint control upon their lands. Tribal society tends to be more egalitarian and democratic because its leadership is not based on hereditary status. Tribal religion, unlike caste system recognises no other authority outside the tribe.

Hence, keeping in mind the dormant status of *Adivasi* literature, Hansda Sowvendra Shekar's collection of 10 short stories, *The Adivasi Will Not Dance* becomes a vital testament to the lives of minority community living in the margins of India.

Being a *Santhal*, Hansda Sowvendra Shekhar's background is reflected in his fiction. His stories primarily contain a nuanced understanding into the lives of the *Santhal.* He is a doctor by profession based in the Pakur district in Jharkhand. For his debut novel, *The Mysterious Ailment of Rupi Baskey*, he won the 2015 *Yuva Puraskar*, was shortlisted for the 2014 *Hindu Literary Prize* and the 2014 *Crossword Book Award* among other accolades. Over the years from 2002 to 2015, Shekhar gathered stories his people, the *Santhals* of Jharkhand and published them as *The Adivasi Will Not Dance.* Stories from the short story collection examine the lives of *Santhals* in contemporary India ranging from the urban to the rural setting. His collection of 10 short stories can be seen as a significant testimony to the lives of the *Adivasis* consigned to the precincts of India.

The titular story, *The Adivasi Will Not Dance*, is set in the Pakur district of Jharkhand, where the writer has been posted as a medical officer. Through the protagonist of the story, Mangal Murmu, a *Santhal,* we witness the plight of the tribals as a result of the mindless greed of the corporates. For example, at the very beginning of the story, Mangal Murmu says, 'Only a few of us have farmland; most of it has been acquired by a mining company.' (Shekhar, 2017, p. 171). He further goes on to say how not only the coal merchants but also the stone merchants have snatched away their land. 'They turn our land upside down, inside out, with their heavy machines. They sell stones they mine from our earth in faraway places—Dilli, Noida, Panjab.' (Shekhar, 2017, p. 172). The coal company and the quarry owners mint a lot of money from the land of the *Santhals* and have built mansions for themselves in the city and in this process, they impoverish the tribal lands. While they prosper, wear nice clothes, send their children to good schools, get treatment at the best hospitals, the *Santhals* on the other hand are left in tatters, 'barely enough food' (Shekhar, 2017, p. 172) and are afflicted with 'such diseases that we can't breathe properly.' (Shekhar, 2017, p. 172).

It is pertinent to note that it is not only the lands that have been snatched away from the *Santhals*, their art and culture has also been reduced to mere performatives. *Santhals* take pride in their folk dance and songs and have preserved their art over the years. 'Our music, our dance, our songs are sacred to us *Santhals*. But hunger and poverty has driven us to sell what is sacred to us', claims Murmu (Shekhar, 2017, p. 179). This long preserved art of *Santhals* has been diminished to a sheer form of entertainment for the rich. They are asked to perform at the weddings and the functions of the upper caste but they are only a background noi.e. 'Which Diku pays attention to our music?

Even at the high-profile functions, most Diku just wait for our performance to end.' (Shekhar, 2017, p. 179) Ironically, despite being indifferent to their culture, the Diku makes the *Adivasi* dance in 'an athletic meet, some inauguration or any function organised by the high and the mighty – in the name of Adivasi culture and Jharkhandi culture.' (Shekhar, 2017, p. 179) On the one hand, while the upper caste is ready to call Jharkhand their own in order to amass benefits in job and in education on the other hand, they are conveniently willing to let the *Adivasi* go to hell. 'But when it comes to displaying Jharkhandi culture, the onus of singing and dancing is upon the Adivasi alone.' (Shekhar, 2017, p. 179)

Irony stares us straight in the face in the story *The Adivasi Will Not Dance*. While the *Santhal* inhabitants of one village are forced to vacate their own land to accommodate a thermal power plant, the *Santhals* of some other villages are then asked to sing and dance at the inauguration of the very same thermal plant. One can feel their plight and abject hopelessness when Murmu says in utter exasperation, 'How can all of you be so indifferent? How can you expect us to sing and dance when our families are being uprooted from their villages?...You are making us Santhals dance in Pakur, and you are displacing Santhals from their village in Godda?' (Shekhar, 2017, p. 183). It is in the name of so-called development that the *Santhals* are being displaced. As a result, an ever-prevalent development-displacement debate arises. The question that needs to be asked is that the development is being done at whose cost? 'All were happy with the progress, the development.' (Shekar, 2017, p. 185). However, were the *Santhals*, the people who were being displaced in the name of development, happy?

By the end of the titular story, the protagonist Mangal Murmu is utterly frustrated and dejected at the way *Santhals* have been mistreated and systemically displaced from their own lands. He has been asked along with his troop to give a song and dance performance at the inauguration of the thermal plant. Murmu dejectedly asks, 'We will sing and dance before you but tell us, do we have a reason to sing and dance? Do we have a reason to be happy? You will now start building the power plant, but this plant will be the end of all the Adivasi…We have nowhere to go, nowhere to grow our crops. How can this powerplant be good for us? And how can we Adivasis dance and be happy?' (Shekhar, 2017, p. 187). In these series of rhetorical questions, the plight of *Santhals* is laid bare before us. When someone shouts 'Bharat mahaan' from the stage, Mangal Murmu asks, 'What mahaan?...Which great nation displaces thousands of its people from their homes and livelihoods to produce electricity for cities and factories?' (Shekhar, 2017, p. 185) This rhetorical question of Murmu is a punch in the gut to the mindless glorification of India in the name of development. Murmu calls them 'a bunch of shrewd, greedy, thief leaders, officers and businessmen who ran the state and controlled its land, people and resources.' (Shekhar, 2017, p. 187)

In another story titled *Baso-Jhi*, we see how Sarjomdih, a small village, 'which for about sixty years was another nondescript dot on a map' (Shekhar, 2017, p. 114) suffered the repercussions of development, 'the nationalisation of the mine and the copper factory, the opening up of two or more quarries, and the confiscation of the villagers' properties so roads and living quarters could be built.' (Shekhar, 2017,

p. 115). The men of Sarjomdih who used to be farmers and tended to their crops were given jobs in the factory and the mines as unskilled laborers in return for their land. In this way, Sarjomidh, like many other *Santhal* villages and lands became 'a standing testimony to the collapse of an agrarian Adivasi society and the dilution of Adivasi culture, the twin gifts of industrialisation and progress.' (Shekhar, 2017, p. 115)

The plight of *Santhals* doesnot end with the seizure of their lands. In addition to these atrocious acts of land grabbing and heedless mining and quarrying, the rich upper caste Hindus also intrude into the personal food habits of the *Santhals* and patronise them in the garb of helping them; 'they will say that we Santhals need to stop eating cow-meat and pig-meat...They, too, want to make us forget our Sarna religion...to become more valuable vote banks.' (Shekhar, 2017, p. 173). In the story, *They Eat Meat!* a *Santhal* family moves from Vadodara to Bhubaneshwar and find themselves being interrogated for their eating habits. 'People here don't like to mix with those people who eat meat and eggs. It's like that.' (Shekhar, 2017, p. 4). It is important to note here that the whole discourse of vegetarian food being pure and meat eating being impure is an indication of Brahminical hegemony. It is a way for the upper caste to establish their purity and hence, assert their superiority over the other castes and tribes. 'Vadodara is a strongly Hindu city. People here believe in purity...people don't eat non-veg... Meat, fish, chicken, eggs. Nor do they approve of people who eat non-veg... Tribals, even lower-caste Hindus, they are seen as impure.' (Shekhar, 2017, p. 6). Throughout the story, we see that how even in an urban city like Vadodara, Brahminical hegemony through the lives of everyone via food regardless of their caste, class and social standing. *Santhals* have to alter their food and habits, refrain from meat eating because it is unacceptable and is considered impure. They have to sneak around to eat meat. The *Santhal* family goes to ridiculous extents to eat meat and eggs. When they go out to eat eggs, they 'look around to make sure there were no familiar eyes spying on them, buy two eggs, wrap them up discreetly, put them in their cloth shopping bag, and return home' (Shekhar, 2017, p. 13). The very act of meat eating has to be draped in such secrecy and comes across as a criminal act. The utter desperation to take calculative steps like 'if buying an egg was a difficult task, cooking one was a mission in itself. Cooking more than one egg at the same time was the same as getting caught.' (Shekhar, 2017, p. 13)

This hegemony begins with something as innocent as food and it is not difficult to see how *Santhals* eventually had to conform to the upper caste norms, 'And while it was well-known that the Sorens were of Adivasi origin, they conformed to the norms—they went to mandirs, celebrated Hindu festivals, fasted on certain days, lit dhoop-batti in their house and were accepted.' (Shekhar, 2017, p. 15). They were accepted solely because they conformed to the 'pure' eating habits of the upper caste Hindus. Panmuni-Jhi, the protagonist of *They Eat Meat*, often compares Vadodara with Bhubhaneshwar, where her husband was posted earlier. In one such instance in the story, 'Panmuni-Jhi would regularly cook two-egg omelettes... She would make delicious katla-machh which all the Santhal women of the city would praise.' (Shekhar, 2017, p. 13-14). She further ruminates, 'The aroma of eggs, fish, chicken and mutton dishes would waft out of her kitchen...No one raised an eyebrow, no one came to house to grab her husband's collar and demand of him: 'Soren, didn't I tell you not to cook non-veg'.' (Shekhar, 2017, p. 14) Like any other community, food is an important part of the everyday life of *Santhals* and as a result of forcibly changed food habits, Panmuni-Jhi began to question her identity and grieves over it, 'In Odisha, Panmuni-Jhi could be a Santhal, an Odia, a Bengali. In Gujarat, she had to only be a Gujarati.' (Shekhar, 2017, p. 14)

The plight of *Santhals* doesn't end at the seizure of their lands, labelling their food impure and usurping their identities. As can be seen in the story *November Is the Month of Migrations*, *Santhal* women are reduced to objects of perversion. It recounts the story of a young *Santhal* girl who sells her body for a meagre 50 rupees and two pieces of cold bread pakodas. 20-year-old Talamai Kisku, the protagonist of *November Is the Month of Migrations* is a *Santhal* girl who along with other *Santhals* leave their lands in the month of November to reach West Bengal where they plant rice and other crops in zamindar owned farms. The story recounts in very raw detail how she has to sell her body because she is hungry and needs the money. The humiliation is not only physical, but psychological as well. The man while having intercourse with her at one point says, 'Saali, you Santhal women are made for this only. You are good!' (Shekhar, 2017, p. 41) Through Talamai, the story brings forth the need, desperation, hunger and utter poverty which *Santhals* encounter and cannot escape from.

Another story, *Getting Even,* brings forth the issue of how *Santhal* girls are sold as commodities. Santhal girls are brought, 'from villages on the pretext of giving them education and training and work and sell them away.' (Shekhar, 2017, p.

54). One of the characters in the story recounts a harrowing account of his daughter who was lured, 'these people had told her that they would send her to a place with a lot of money... She went with them. The next thing she saw was that she was in Delhi. These people had sold her!' (Shekhar, 2017, p. 55). While on the one hand there are *Santhal* girls like Talamai who sell their body of their own accord because of the desperate circumstances, on the other hand, there are *Santhal* women who are lied to on the pretext of providing them a better life and are then sold off like commodities. Hence, in the stories like *November Is the Month of Migrations* and *Getting Even*, we see how *Santhal* women are subaltern and doubly marginalised because of their gender and the tribal status.

In an interview, Hansada Sowvendra Shekhar says 'why should the truth be whitewashed?' (Shekhar, 2018) His deliberate use of brutal, raw language and hard-hitting descriptions is intentional because he doesn't intend to sugar-coat the plight of *Santhals*. For example, the scenes of intercourse between a jawan and a *Santhal* girl in the story *November Is the Month of Migrations* are described in explicit, ruthless detail and clearly demonstrate the desperation of the *Santhal* girl who out of desperation and hunger lies there 'passi.e. unthinking, unblinking.' (Shekhar, 2017, p. 41) The writer repeatedly labels the intercourse as 'work' because it is bereft of any emotion and adoration. At one point he says, 'The work does not take much time.' At another point he says, 'In less than ten minutes, the work is done.' (Shekhar, 2017, p. 41) Gujarat riots are at the centre of the story *They Eat Meat*. In the story, as the riots escalate, angry Hindu mob attacks a Muslim home inhabited by four women. Shekar, deliberately uses crass language and abusive phrases like 'Madarch*d' and 'Motherf*cking Mussalman' because he doesn't wish to veil the abject cruelty of riots and the violence that ensues.

Hansada Sowvendra Shekhar through his writings brings forth the voices from the margins. In the postcolonial terms his stories are a great example of writing back to the empire. The empi.e. in this case is the corporate bigwigs of India, the upper caste and the city dwellers. The confiscation of the lands of the tribals at the hands of the rich city dwellers is an example of neo colonisation. Through his stories, Shekhar wakes us up from our stupor and makes us witness the unfolding of colonisation of our own indigenous people at the hands of the powerful. This volume, hence, becomes a tribute to the struggle and marginalisation of the *Santhals* at the hands of their own country. Since Shekhar himself is a *Santhal*, he manages to avoid the self-pitying and exotic tone, which is usually a hallmark of such writings. The tribal aspect of India that the grand narratives in Indian English writing have often ignored is brought to the forefront through this collection of short stories. Arguably, the most interesting part of these stories is the fact that they not only deal with the hardships *Adivasis* face under capitalism and modernity, but also provide a rare glimpse of middle-class *Santhal* li.e. something which most of us have not been acquainted with. The characters in the stories are varied and debunk any kind of stereotype which might be prevalent about the *Adivasis*. Shekar's stories lend voice to the Adivasi community, which has been bereft of any agency or worse have only persisted and have been depicted as stereotype. The stories do not shy away from bringing to light the lives of *Santhals* struggling to live their life with dignity in their own lands which have been systemically and brutally taken away from them. As Mangal Murmu, at one point in the titular story laments, 'We are becoming people from nowhere.' (Shekhar, 2017, p. 173)

REFERENCES

Burman, J J Roy. (2009) *Adivasi: A contentious term to denote tribes as indigenous peoples of India.* Mainstream Vol XLVII, No 32. https://www.mainstreamweekly.net/article1537.html

Adivasis (scheduled tribes) are the largest tribal population in the world – world directory of minorities. Tribal Cultural Heritage in India Foundation. (n.d.). https://indiantribalheritage.org/?p=11056#gsc.tab=0.

Encyclopædia Britannica, inc. (n.d.). *Santhal.* Encyclopædia Britannica. https://www.britannica.com/topic/Santhal

Encyclopædia Britannica, inc. (n.d.). *Scheduled tribe.* Encyclopædia Britannica. https://www.britannica.com/topic/Scheduled-Tribe

Guruswamy, M. (2016). *Adivasis: India's original inhabitants have suffered the most at its hands.* Scroll.in. https://scroll.in/article/773759/adivasis-indias-original-inhabitants-have-suffered-the-most-at-its-hands.

Indian Writers Forum (2016). *Yes, the Adivasi will not dance!* NewsClick. https://www.newsclick.in/yes-adivasi-will-not-dance

Minj, N. (2019). *The Adivasi will not dance: 'Why should the truth be whitewashed?'.* Feminism In India. https://feminisminindia.com/2018/04/17/book-review-the-adivasi-will-not-dance/.

Nag, C. B. (2019). *Adivasis and the Indian state: Stereotyped as 'primitive' and 'savage', Tribal Communities Fight for right to choose social, cultural, land-owning systems-India News.* Firstpost.

https://www.firstpost.com/india/adivasis-and-the-indian-state-stereotyped-as-primitive-savage-tribal-communities-fight-for-right-to-choose-social-cultural-land-owning-systems-7200111.html

Nimmi. (n.d.). *Santhal tribes*. Santhal Tri.e. Art and Culture of Santhal Tri.e. Santhal Tribe in India. https://www.indianmirror.com/tribes/santhaltribes.html

Project, J. (n.d.). *Santal (sawntal) in India*. Joshua Project. https://joshuaproject.net/people_groups/14743/IN

Roy, Kakoli (2018). *Santhal tribes - the santhal tribes are the oldest tribes in India*. youngisthan.in. https://www.youngisthan.in/india/santhal-tribes-oldest-indian-tribe/67520.

Scheduled Tribes in India (n.d.). Vikaspedia. https://vikaspedia.in/social-welfare/scheduled-tribes-welfare/scheduled-tribes-in-india

Scroll Staff. (2017). *Four months after ban, Jharkhand finds nothing objectionable in Hansda Shekhar's book on adivasis*. Scroll.in. https://scroll.in/latest/861308/four-months-after-ban-jharkhand-finds-nothing-objectionable-in-hansda-shekhars-book-on-adivasis.

Sengupta, I. (2018). *'I feel crippled but I am emboldened,' says author of Adivasi Will Not Dance on dissent and the ban on his book*. The Indian Express. https://indianexpress.com/article/lifestyle/books/i-feel-crippled-but-i-am-emboldened-says-author-of-adivasi-will-not-dance-on-dissent-and-the-ban-on-his-book-5042467/.

Shekhar, H. S. (2017). *The Adivasi will not dance: Stories*. Speaking Tiger.

Srivastava, Sanjay. (2017). *What the ban on the Adivasi will not dance tells us about India's political life*. Hindustan Times. https://www.hindustantimes.com/opinion/what-the-ban-on-the-adivasi-will-not-dance-tells-us-about-india-s-political-life/story-gPtXIRpKwDcwl0zTEgEdVN.html.

The Adivasi will not dance and santhal identity. Goi Monitor. (2018). https://www.goimonitor.com/story/adivasi-will-not-dance-and-santhal-identity-0

Tripathi, Priyanka. (2017). *Review Article: The Adivasi Will Not Dance: Stories by Hansda Sowvendra Shekhar*. Rupkatha Journal on Interdisciplinary Studies in Humanities. https://rupkatha.com/v9n4r0

Swati Pal, Professor and Principal, Janki Devi Memorial College, University of Delhi, recipient of several awards, has been a Charles Wallace and John McGrath Theatre Studies Scholar. She has authored several books on theatre, creative and academic writing. She also translates and writes poetry. Prof Pal is the Vice-President of the Indian Association for Commonwealth Literature and Language Studies.

Ruby Bhardwaj, Associate Professor, Department of Sociology, JDMC, has researched and published on medical pluralism, assisted reproductive technologies and other issues of relevance in Medical Sociology.

Charu Kala is an Associate Professor at the Department of Sociology, JDMC. Her areas of interest include Sociology of Religion, Kinship and Social Research.